Advanced Praise for Work Disrupted

"Jeff's fresh work codifies the possibilities—and uncertainties—ahead as organizations everywhere struggle to reshape employment models fueled by the blistering pace of technology advances. Just as importantly, WORK DISRUPTED offers pragmatic, agile solutions for the ever-evolving next normal workforce and workplace."

—Cathy Benko, Member, Board of Directors, NIKE, Inc.;
former Vice Chairman, Deloitte LLP; and best-selling
author of Mass Career Customization and The Corporate Lattice

"As the Future of Work becomes the 'new normal' - finding navigation tools will be crucial. This is exactly what WORK DISRUPTED offers. With a range of case studies and industry insights it brings much needed clarity in these unprecedented times."

—Professor Lynda Gratton, founder of HSM
and author, The New Long Life

"In what seemed like the blink of an eye, the Coronavirus pandemic seemed to challenge everything we know about work. In WORK DISRUPTED, Jeff Schwartz delivers decades of expertise and sheds new light on the topics we're all grappling with — the intersection of humanity and AI, where and what work looks like today and tomorrow, the rising importance of teams and many fresh nuances on the shifts we can make as leaders. This is a timely must read for managers and associates alike."

—Jeffrey J. Jones II, President and CEO of H&R Block

"The far reaching impact of the novel coronavirus, the acceleration of digital transformation in our personal and professional lives, and seminal events concerning racial equality and social justice make the case that we need new mental models to confront with challenges to the future of work, careers, business, sports, and education in the years ahead. WORK DISRUPTED provides a compelling, enjoyable, and thought providing journey through the opportunities we are all facing as individuals, organizational leaders, and citizens. Whether you are relating Jeff's research to a new business model, culture change, civic engagement, diversity and inclusion, or are simply bringing it to a boardroom discussion, this is a timely and important read which will help shift thinking to what's next, what's possible, and what choices we want to, and can, make."

—Cathy Engelbert, retired CEO of Deloitte and
Commissioner of the WNBA

"The future of work does not fit in the containers, or structures or mindsets of the past. This book not only explains why but then shows how work will change and then lays out a map to follow to ensure your company and your career will thrive. It's a book both provocative and practical."

—Rishad Tobaccowala. Author of "Restoring the Soul
of Business: Staying Human in the Age of Data" and former Chief
Strategist and Growth Officer of Publicis Groupe

WORK
DISRUPTED

IWARTZ

NE RISS

FISHBURNE

WORK
DISRUPTED

OPPORTUNITY, RESILIENCE, AND

GROWTH IN THE *ACCELERATED*

FUTURE OF WORK

WILEY

Library of Congress Cataloging-in-Publication Data is Available,
ISBN 9781119762270 (Hardcover)
ISBN 9781119763505 (ePDF)
ISBN 9781119763512 (ePub)

Cover Design: Wiley
Cover Images: Paper Texture:© koosen/Shutterstock
Paper Tear: © rakim-/Getty Images
All others: Wiley

SKY10022880_113020

This book is dedicated to the memory of my parents, Arlene and Ira, who gave me the wings to live a life of adventure and find work I love, including writing this book, and to my daughters, Rachel and Biz, who now get to be the explorers as they navigate the future of work, along with all of you.

Contents

Foreword

Ajourney like the future of work requires more than a roadmap; it requires a trusted guide. A guide who doesn't jump to answers that don't really exist, but rather frames the questions that must be asked. A guide who has the sensibility—the combination of wisdom, humor, and curiosity—to give you confidence that although the mountain is steep, the ascent will be completely worth it. A guide whose love of exploration reminds us at every turn what is possible. For me, and for so many of our clients in the world of Human Capital, that guide is Jeff Schwartz.

As the leader of Deloitte's Global Human Capital practice, the largest human capital consultancy in the world, I'm proud to have Jeff help spearhead our future of work efforts. And as a new mother, I'm comforted to have Jeff help me ask the right questions to prepare my son for the future—a future that elicits hope, fear, and excitement all wrapped into one. I met Jeff about 15 years ago, when we first worked together, launching a forum on the evolving Chief Human Resources Officer agenda. The discussions that emerged were dynamic investigations of the developing role of HR leaders as future-of-work strategists, risk advisors, cultural stewards, and business partners. My first impression of Jeff was that he fully leaned into "what's next." This has continued to be true, whether he was establishing one of the first international management consultancies in Moscow or building a technology adoption practice for global SAP projects in Brussels. Jeff's curiosity and explorer temperament have made him especially well-suited to identify and illuminate promising paths and opportunities. He also enjoys sharing new ideas, as he has done for a decade as founder and global editor of Deloitte's influential *Global Human Trends Report*, a leading longitudinal survey on insights and trends for workforce, organization, talent, and HR issues.

For those of you who have not met Jeff or read his musings on the future of work, this book is the perfect opportunity to gain an introduction to a man who didn't just jump on the future-of-work bandwagon, but rather helped put it in motion. For those of you who know Jeff, sit back and enjoy his famous stories and anecdotes that draw you in and bring to life concepts and theories that may have seemed too academic or conceptual to be put into organizational reality. This is what Jeff knows how to do so incredibly well and what has made him one of my personal guides as I have navigated a long, productive career in the Human Capital space.

Throughout *Work Disrupted*, Jeff becomes a twenty-first-century Sherpa, presenting us with the maps we need to thrive in the future of work. Like any great guide, he not only presents us with a view of the destination, but with the guideposts we need to follow along the way. He keeps us intrigued about the opportunities ahead, and by sharing the history of how we got here, he increases our own understanding of the future, giving us the gift of resilience by using his knowledge and experience to prepare us for what's coming. That's because, at his core, Jeff is a teacher—someone who has an unparalleled thirst for knowledge, and an even a stronger desire to share that knowledge. I'm just honored to have been one of many he encountered and stopped to educate along the way.

As the future of work has turned from an idea discussed amongst futurists to a reality now accepted by even the most change-resistant organizational leaders, we need teachers and guides more than ever. It now feels as though there are more questions than answers, more unknowns than certainties, and more opportunities to shape the future in completely new directions without the constraints that we find so often in the world of work. I feel an urgency to make sense of our fast-changing world and discern the opportunities that lie ahead, especially for my son Robbie, almost two as I write this. I can imagine no one better to guide us through the disruption at our doorsteps than Jeff, teacher, Sherpa, knowledge seeker, and pathfinder. The future is uncertain, but that's no longer something to fear. With Jeff's guidance, it's something to embrace. There is no doubt that the future of work is here, and no better time to let the journey begin than with Jeff as our guide.

Erica Volini
Global Human Capital Leader
Deloitte Consulting

Introduction

The difficulty is not so much in developing new ideas as in escaping from old ones.

—John Maynard Keynes

I've been traveling somewhere in the world for my work every month—often every week—for the past 20 years; that is, until Covid-19 stopped me in my tracks. Suddenly, I had to pause. All at once, the packing, the rushing, and the business travel ended. I had no idea that my trip to Israel in early March, leading a global panel on the future of work, would be the last time I would board an international flight in 2020. A few days after returning home to New York City from Tel Aviv on March 3, my workplace relocated from the Deloitte Consulting offices at Rockefeller Center to my small home office on the Upper West Side of Manhattan. As I sheltered in place, along with the rest of the world, tracking the sobering devastation wrought by the pandemic, I had the chance—perhaps for the first time in my career—to stay in one place for longer than a few weeks and reflect on the changes underfoot and ahead.

My work on this book had been well underway before the global pandemic took hold in early 2020. However, there's no doubt that it brought a new sense of urgency to my exploration of the future of work that had begun seven years earlier. The need to shift to new ways of working, new frames, new expectations, and new possibilities was accelerated by the pandemic. At a time that technologies, including artificial intelligence, are ubiquitous, and, to some, represent a threat to jobs and livelihoods, we have also witnessed our fundamental vulnerability as humans exposed by a virus that has already killed more people in the United States than all wars since World War II. What I have discovered about the future of work, as a global and U.S. pioneer and leader for the Future of Work practice with Deloitte Consulting, in interviews with dozens of leading experts in the field, and in my conversations with business leaders across the globe, is that, above all else, it celebrates our essential human capabilities—innovation, creation, ingenuity, entrepreneurship, empathy, caring, and relationships.

Though the future of work is shorthand for some for "the robots are taking our jobs," what has emerged for many is a growing belief that innovation and creativity will indeed rule the day. We can only automate processes, reduce costs, and increase speed so much—eventually we will need to *create* something new. We will need to *innovate*. And that's what many of us did, in ways small and large, during the Covid-19 outbreak. I continued to work with clients and colleagues around the world, no longer in person but over Zoom, WebEx, and similar platforms, while spending every evening and weekend researching and writing this book. This was a time to take stock, feel the discomfort of uncertainty, adapt, and seek out opportunities to do things in new ways. Very quickly, with my colleagues at Deloitte, we figured out how to continue to do our work, remotely, and *better*. As with the adoption of any new technology, we started by lifting and shifting what we'd done before, to Zoom, Teams, Slack, and other collaborative technologies. Then we saw we could do *more*. Things we thought we could never do remotely, we did, such as launching large technology systems for organizations without having hundreds of consultants onsite. We discovered we could deliver successful, interactive, online workshops with breakout groups; collaborate on virtual whiteboards; and even brainstorm virtually. We also learned more about each other as we worked from our homes. As I would share with my teams, if we don't hear children and dogs in the background, something is missing. Our lives should be evident in the flow of our work. That's something we don't want to lose as we move into our new normal.

Our Collective Pause

The pause, the uncertainty, the need to adapt remind us that our lives are stories of disruption, adaptability, and survival. I was born the year after the first satellite launched from Earth (*Sputnik* by the Soviet Union in 1957), watched the first men walking on the moon when I was 11 (the United States in 1969), and witnessed the first commercial space launches to the International Space Station in 2020. My career has extended across stock market crashes, Y2K, 9/11, the Great Recession, and pandemics (H1NI, Ebola, and Covid-19). And, yes, technology. I wrote my college papers on electric typewriters, before welcoming tablets with the processing power of supercomputers. I've worked as a researcher, teacher, banker, government agency program director, consultant, writer, and professor. I've lived in the United States, Nepal, Sri Lanka, Kenya, Russia, Belgium, India, and Israel. I realize that I've been learning lessons in adaptability throughout my career. I've shifted my expectations and adjusted to what was occurring, not what I'd imagined would come next.

My daughters received similar lessons in adaptability when Covid-19 upended their routines. My daughter Rachel, 28, a graduate MBA student at Emory University in Atlanta, shifted to virtual learning for the second half of the semester, along with 1.6 billion other college students around the world, and then she took a virtual summer internship. My younger daughter, Bizzie, 25, was three weeks into training as a U.S. Peace Corps volunteer in Madagascar, when she, along with 7,000 volunteers and trainees around the world, evacuated back to the United States. This was the first time since its founding in 1961 that the entire U.S. Peace Corps returned home. I watched my daughters accept the shifts and grow more resilient.

Our Long and Winding Careers

I learned lessons in adaptability early in my career. In fact, the start of many of my jobs coincided with major world events. After graduate school, I was in the middle of onboarding training for a position as a corporate finance associate at Chemical's Investment Bank, now part of JPMorgan Chase, in October 1987, when the stock market experienced its largest one-day percentage drop since the Great Depression. A few years later, after the fall of the Berlin Wall in 1989, I took a leave from my "business" life to become one of the first associate directors of the U.S. Peace Corps as it launched in Russia, following the dissolution of the former Soviet Union. I joined Deloitte on September 1, 2001, just days before the 9/11 attacks. Seven years later, we lived through the Great Recession and the global financial crisis.

The challenges were offset by career high points. These include leading the consulting practices for Deloitte in India, both global delivery teams and professionals working with some of India's largest companies. I worked for Reliance Industries from 2011 to 2016, as the company launched Jio (which means "live life" in Hindi), now the largest 4G and mobile company in India. The company introduced its customer operations in September 2016, and by the summer of 2020 had almost 400 million customers, becoming India's largest telecom company with a focus on mobile 4G connectivity. During this time, India was a country in transition—both in its domestic economy and its relationship with the global economy. I was able to contribute in a small way to the creation of the world's second largest 4G telecom company and the rapid introduction to India of smart mobile and app services.

Our Frame

I didn't study the future of work or adaptability in school—nobody does. In retrospect, I see that I've been remarkably prepared to help business leaders understand the future world of work in part because of what I learned as an undergraduate and graduate student studying history, philosophy, and government, and then business and economics, and, perhaps most of all, as a result of experiences exposing and preparing me for the breadth of what has been unfolding during our lifetimes. In 1983 I was completing my service as a Peace Corps teacher in Nepal, one of the world's most beautiful and poorest countries, where I taught math and science in a village with no running water or electricity, a village that was a day's walk to a road. Two years later, in the summer of 1985, I was a summer associate in corporate finance on Park Avenue in New York. Somewhere between Nepal and New York City, I'd been lucky to have been exposed to vastly different faces of the human experience.

What I continue to learn, and what I hope my daughters are learning, is that how we frame the world, what we think is relevant and possible, shapes what we *can* do and what we *actually* do. New times and new conditions create new opportunities. Unless we reshape our views—our time horizons, relationships, speed—we will miss opportunities. For us as individuals, and as organizations and communities, Covid-19 has indeed been an accelerator to the future. But the future was already underway, with opportunities for people and machines to work together, and careers composed of chapters of reinvention. To embrace all that's possible, a new mindset—a growth mindset—is critical.

The concept of a growth mindset, developed by psychologist Carol Dweck, speaks to our capacity for change and growth. She contrasts a growth mindset with a limiting view, what she calls a fixed mindset. Her research demonstrates that much of what we think we understand about ourselves and what we can do comes from our mindset. This can either propel us forward or prevent us from fulfilling our potential. According to Dweck, whether or not we're aware of our mental models, they can have a profound effect on our skill acquisition, personal relationships, professional success, and many other dimensions of life. People with a growth mindset believe that their most fundamental abilities can be developed through dedication and hard work. This view builds a love of learning and a resilience that will serve us well in the future world of work. People with fixed mindsets believe they're good or bad at something based on their inherent nature, closing out the possibility that they can acquire new skills and capabilities. Similarly, editor and anthropologist Gillian Tett teaches us that the way we label and categorize the world indeed influences what we think we can do.

Our Challenge

As Covid-19 proves to be a storm hovering for longer than many of us expected, I remind myself that it has been during times of disruption and stress that we've seen some of the biggest changes in our economy and society. We're living through a period of pivoting and acceleration. Covid-19 has dramatically challenged us to think about the future that we want to create. Reflecting upon the future of work over the last half dozen years, I've been particularly mindful of the fact that, all too often, we've viewed the future of work as a way to produce the same work, using the same work processes, with little bits of new technology thrown in. However, the real opportunities lie not in doing the same things that we're doing today, only a little bit better and a little bit faster. The real opportunities lie in the exploration and journey that allow us to discover how we can do things differently. *How can we produce different results with more impact and more meaning? How can we create new combinations of human–machine teams reinforcing the unique capabilities of each? How can we create more flexible ways of working for ourselves and members of the workforce? How can we create workplaces that combine our ability to work virtually and in person? And, finally, how we can create a future of work that not only creates economic value but reflects our social and communal values as well?* This book is an attempt to explore these possibilities and advance this dialog.

The fundamental question *Work Disrupted* raises, is what lens are we choosing as we look ahead? Are we viewing the future as an extension of a predictable past, or are we viewing the future as a broad set of new opportunities that will reflect whatever we think is possible? In other words, are we viewing the future through a fixed or growth mindset? Are we doing more of the same, only faster and cheaper (fixed), or are we creating and innovating? If I were asking this question in 1910 or 1920, I might be asking if you plan to work for the railroad or for the upstart automotive companies.

Our Opportunity

In these pages I share some of what I've experienced and reflected upon, acting as a twenty-first-century Sherpa, as we navigate the accelerating future of work—or the beginning of what I think of as the Human Era. The era has been labeled the Anthropocene, the current geological age, viewed as a period in which human activity has been the leading influence on our climate and our environment. One of the debates coming to the fore that economists have been having for many decades is the interplay of technological innovation and creative destruction. Increasingly, when I look at the history of economic growth, I see that it has been in the process of entrepreneurship, innovation, and creative disruption that we've actually pushed forward what it means to be human, and to create meaning and impact.

I wrote this book to share my view that the future of work, a source of fear for so many, is actually about the opportunities, the resilience, and the growth that we can leverage to do things differently, to establish new priorities and new patterns, and to create a new order in our own lives, and in our communities. Work disrupted is in no way about things stopping. It reflects the continual movement and evolution of how we work. Disruption is hard. It challenges us to change how we frame and prepare for the future, reminding us that a preferred future requires new mindsets—an openness to new ways of working.

The intersection of the future of work and what we're now experiencing as the Covid-19 era represents a fault line in our lives, a uniquely instructive moment. We're invited to reimagine how we work, our educational institutions, and how we build our careers, our companies, and our communities. Adopting new mindsets and building new capabilities may be one of the critical challenges of our time. My hope as you read this book is that you gain a better sense of the opportunities that await you, the resilience that will serve you, and the growth paths that you can pursue in your own life to create, innovate, and thrive.

Jeff Schwartz
New York
August, 2020

CHAPTER 1

From Fear to Growth

Mindsets and Playbooks for Twenty-first-century Careers and Work

When we least expect it, life sets us a challenge to test our courage and willingness to change; at such a moment, there is no point in pretending that nothing has happened or in saying that we are not yet ready. The challenge will not wait. Life does not look back.

—Paulo Coelho, novelist[1]

When the coronavirus pandemic took root in the United States, we entered a time machine to the future.[2] Practically overnight, people in industries that had restricted telecommuting found themselves crawling out of bed and dialing into Zoom conference calls from their couch. For many teachers, bankers, lawyers, even NASA aerospace engineers, the coronavirus crisis was a trial run for remote work.[3] With most of the country under orders to shelter in place, many business leaders pivoted on a dime to reimagine products, reassign workers, reshape supply chains, and reconfigure operations to join the heated race to save lives. Near the top of the critical list of needs was the demand for ventilators, potentially hundreds of thousands of ventilators. In an unprecedented move, Ford and General Motors shut down car production and went into the ventilator production business.[4]

Overhauling production and ramping up that production beyond anything your company has ever done before are feats of magic that business leaders have known they would be expected to perform in the future world of

work. When Anne-Marie Slaughter, the chief executive of New America, said the coronavirus exposed "an opportunity to make the changes we knew we were going to have to make eventually," and also "deep fissures and failures in our culture," she captured both the sense of inevitability and vulnerability that many business leaders were experiencing.[5] They knew the future world of work would require boosting efficiency, proceeding at warp speed, seeking talent and expertise outside the walls of their organization, and a heavy dose of resourcefulness. However, they did not realize the future would arrive wholesale and so soon. After all, in survey after survey, business leaders consistently reported they did not feel ready for the future of work.[6]

Enter the coronavirus pandemic, an abrupt fast-forward to the future of work. Changes expected to take decades, occurred within weeks. Slaughter, a former director of policy planning for the U.S. Department of State, declared that with the pandemic "the future of work is here."[7] Indeed, the coronavirus has illustrated both the extreme challenges and inspiring possibilities ushered in by a future that swept in sooner than expected.

Panic or Pivot

Around the country, business leaders were among the first to act during the pandemic. Why the need for so many ventilators? The coronavirus often kills through the lungs as patients develop Covid-19 pneumonia.[8] Ventilators help the sickest patients stay alive by providing extra oxygen to keep their lungs pumping once they fill with fluid. General Motors scrambled to train workers and locate the 700 parts needed to create a prototype ventilator, sourced from about 80 global suppliers.[9] Leaders at the car manufacturer were well-suited to the challenge: Assembling a 700-part ventilator sounds daunting but cars are typically assembled from about 2,500 parts. Auto makers have already demonstrated their ability to mass produce technical equipment quickly. However, the usual pace of production had to spring into overdrive. What normally might take months had to be done in weeks. They had to produce more, faster than ever before. At stake were the lives of acute Covid-19 patients.

Many companies relinquished business-as-usual approaches to tackle a variety of coronavirus-related shortages, including not only vital medical equipment but personal protective equipment (PPE) and hand sanitizer. In New York City, many doctors and nurses improvised, using trash bags to replace medical scrubs and protective gowns. The Gap Inc., parent company of Banana Republic and Old Navy, shifted its factories to create protective cloth masks, gowns, and scrubs. Fanatics, an online seller of Major League Baseball gear, also started producing masks and gowns.[10] Meanwhile, Pernod Ricard, the alcohol brand, donated pure alcohol for hand sanitizer. French luxury powerhouse LVMH, which owns Louis Vuitton, Bulgari, and other high-end brands, also entered the hand-sanitizer business, using its perfume and make-up factories to produce hydroalcoholic gels.[11]

To keep their doors open and their employees on the payroll, many companies changed direction, navigated red tape, and devised innovative approaches. The ability to pivot rather than panic allowed some people to apply their capabilities in new ways.[12] Small mom-and-pop shops like Essations, started by Stephanie Luster's parents almost 40 years ago, could not stay in the business of shipping hair products to salons. When salons shut their doors, after city after city ordered businesses to close and social distancing rules to take effect, Luster had an idea. She would sell directly to customers who were sheltering but still wanted their hair to look styled for Zoom video calls for work. What if the stylists created home-hair-care videos that featured Essations hair products and then posted them on Facebook? At the end of the tutorial, the stylist could provide a code customers could use to get a discount on the Essations website. Essations would know from the code which stylist had sent the customer, and the stylist could get a cut of the sale. Many stylists liked the idea and made videos featuring Essations' products, allowing online product sales to increase by 20 percent.[13]

Some businesses soared during the pandemic. Instacart, the grocery pick-up and delivery service, hired more than 300,000 full-time employees in one month to meet the increased demand at the start of the pandemic, with plans to hire 250,000 more.[14] However, a far greater number of businesses and individuals had to change direction to survive. Furloughed hotel call center operators found themselves subcontracted to operate state and city call centers. Uber launched a courier service so that drivers who could no longer transport passengers could continue to work by delivering packages, medicine, and pet supplies.[15] Spiffy, the U.S. on-demand car cleaning company, rolled-out a service to sanitize and disinfect facilities and properties.[16]

Innovation and experimentation will continue to be lifelines as we transition to a very different world. Author William Gibson reminded us more than 15 years ago that, "The future is already here, it's just not evenly distributed."[17] An important corollary is that the future comes at us in accelerated bursts. The coronavirus is one such accelerator to the future. We have witnessed similar accelerators in recent years, with the great financial crisis of 2008–2009 and Y2K. The challenge is how we navigate and take advantage of these sudden shifts.

Racing with the Machines

"Are robots really coming for our jobs?" a longtime client asked me in hushed tones, his brow furrowed, his voice filled with anxiety.

His business partner leaned in, reframing his question with another. "Won't new technologies relieve us of all the boring, repetitive tasks so we can focus on more meaningful work?" she suggested in a hopeful tone that quickly grew impatient. "Well, which is it?"

In conversations over the past decade with friends, colleagues, and business leaders about how automation, advanced technologies, and new employment models are transforming the American workplace, the worry has been palpable: "How can we keep up with machines?" they wonder. "What skills do I need to prepare for jobs in 2030?" they ask. "We're going to have a dozen careers, not just one—how's that even possible?" they demand. "I still haven't paid off my student loans for one career."

The pervasive feeling is that we're standing on the threshold of something powerful, unstoppable, and unknown, much like a giant tidal wave that is going to wash over everything and transform us—how we work, where we work, the work we do, *if* we work at all. These conversations, more often than not, are characterized by fear. The dizzying advances in robotics, artificial intelligence (AI), digital technology, and new ways of working have created haunting images of a dystopic future world where machines and software can perform most jobs, and human workers are largely unnecessary. Even the acronym FANG, coined in 2013 for the four high-performing tech stocks (Facebook, Amazon, Netflix, and Google), contributes to this conflation of technology and monsters.[18]

People are most concerned about whether AI will complement human capabilities or act as a substitute. While some predict nothing short of a job apocalypse, other forecasters focus on the vast potential of new technologies to create greater value for workers and to liberate us so we can leverage our uniquely human capabilities—those enduring human skills that smart machines have not yet mastered, such as problem-solving, creative thinking, complex decision-making, empathy, and managing teams. In this scenario, groups of remote and diverse teams work together, people and machines collaborate, and workers continue to be employed because they explore and master new skills and capabilities throughout their lives.

"In medicine, law, finance, retailing, manufacturing, and even scientific discovery, the key to winning the race is not to compete against the machines, but to compete *with* machines," observed authors Erik Brynjolfsson and Andrew McAfee in 2012.[19] MIT's Thomas Malone calls the remarkable power of people and computers working together "superminds."[20] From finding new cures for diseases to designing new tools and systems that will create new products and new lines of business, the promise of AI and humans working *together* may be the future.

In the midst of these dramatically different depictions of the future of work—a robot apocalypse versus humanity unleashed—many seek to understand what is different from other periods of great technological advances, where do they fit in, and how can they navigate this landscape without signposts so they can continue to work. For all the hype and headlines about the future of work, guidance on how people can find their way is in short supply. My aim is to provide that guidance.

> Innovation and experimentation will continue to be lifelines as we transition to a very different world.

We Have Choices

While portions of many jobs will change, and some jobs will likely be eliminated entirely, many more jobs will evolve. When agricultural processes were mechanized in the nineteenth century, some farmworkers lost their jobs, but they ultimately earned more money working in factories. The automation of industrial production displaced factory workers in the twentieth century but they moved into service jobs. What we tend to forget is that rising productivity creates new jobs. Indeed, technological innovation has historically delivered more jobs, not fewer. And the new jobs often required more skills and paid higher wages.

As an economist and business consultant who has spent the past decade immersed in the issues surrounding the future of work, I have explored the topic with innovative thinkers and business leaders wrestling with the opportunities and challenges presented by this changing landscape. I spent half of the past decade based in New York and half in Delhi and Mumbai, working across India and Asia. I have advised companies and government agencies grappling with the mysteries that lie ahead. And I continue to bear witness each day to the dramatic changes taking place at the forefront of some of the largest and most successful businesses in the United States and around the world.

This book offers guidance to individuals, business leaders, and institutions so they can make smart choices. Organizations are poised to shape what ultimately becomes the future of work, as individual workers face broad options regarding how and where they work, as well as the skills and capabilities they want to gain to secure their livelihood. While we appear to welcome consumer technologies in our personal lives—we have managed to master more than 10 versions of smartphones (Apple and Android) since they were introduced in 2007 and 2008, respectively—we are more uncomfortable with tech innovations that will ultimately transform in profound and meaningful ways our work, who does the work, and where work is done.[21]

Individuals are searching for ways to continue to contribute their skills, procure value, and have an impact in the marketplace. Employers are facing important choices about whether to use advances in technology to drive efficiency and reduce costs or to explore how to harness technology to reshape jobs in ways that yield more value and meaning. Citizens, educators, and policy makers face a call to reconsider how we prepare and train people for the changing workplace and what paths are available to individuals to gain new skills throughout longer lives with multiple chapters of career reinvention.

Perhaps the most important question concerning the future of work is not what might happen in the future, but what do we want to have happen— *the future of work to what end?* When asked what employment relations would look like in 2030, the answer provided by Louis Hyman, a professor of labor history at Cornell, struck a chord. "It's hard to talk about the future," he said, "because we actually have choices."[22] The challenge in this century is to understand and take advantage of the opportunities that technology and new ways of working afford us. In research at the Center for the Edge, Deloitte found that most future-of-work efforts are focused on reducing cost, increasing efficiency, and replacing workers with technology.[23] Daron Acemoglu, a professor of economics at MIT, refers to this as the "wrong kind of AI."[24] The opportunities, as yet largely unrealized, are to expand our focus beyond cost, which is important but not the end in itself, to include value for customers and to provide meaning for the workforce and society. We return to this topic in the last section of the book.

The Future of Work – To What End?

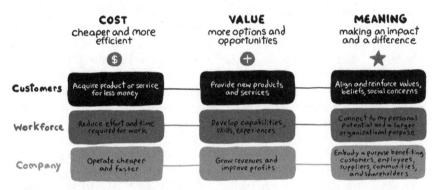

Source: Chart courtesy of MIT Sloan Management Review, ©MIT; "Reframing the Future of Work," by Jeff Schwartz et al, February 2019

From Disruption to Innovation to Creation

When we think of a disruption, we generally think of a disturbance that interrupts. In business theory, a disruptive innovation is one that creates a new market, shaking up the existing market, and displacing it.[25] Disruptive innovation is a powerful way to think about innovation-driven growth. Disruption shifts profitability from one prevailing business model to another. The new model typically provides customers with the same or better value at a much lower cost.[26] The fallout: Companies that relied upon the old business model lose ground or are pushed out of business. Netflix is an example of digital disruption, as are Uber, Amazon, Airbnb, and countless other digital services that changed prior business models.

The word "disruption" was popularized by Clayton Christensen in 1997 in his book *The Innovator's Dilemma: When New Technologies Cause Great Firms to Fail.*[27] However, the economist Joseph Schumpeter had introduced the concept of "creative destruction" and the disruptive power of innovation more than 50 years earlier. Schumpeter's thesis was that innovation is responsible for both the progress and the instabilities of capitalism. He attributed those instabilities to the principle of creative destruction, which recognizes that innovation by entrepreneurs is the disruptive force that drives and sustains economic growth. The earlier products and processes are suddenly obsolete, forcing companies to quickly adapt to a new environment or fail.[28]

Schumpeter's theories powerfully anticipated the future of work. He often used the example of the railroad as a transforming agent in the economy that opened up new opportunities while clearing out old approaches. He pointed to the ability of entrepreneurs, by advancing new products and services, to provide "a perennial gale of creative destruction."[29] Fascinated by the entrepreneurial spirit, he recognized destruction as a mechanism for progress. Schumpeter realized that economic innovation is fueled by entrepreneurs who discover better ways of doing things (the creative part), and their success leads to the collapse of old companies and methods (the destructive part). Automobiles replaced horse-drawn buggies; word processors supplanted typewriters; Internet advertising overpowered print ads.

The rise of the Internet and mobile computing are fundamental disruptors—world-changing events that have altered everything that followed. The 2020 coronavirus pandemic may be a similar event, presenting both an immediate crisis and long-term opportunity. Things may never be the same. New technologies and crises can lead to new modes of collaboration and new institutional relationships; they can be accelerators to the future.

> While portions of many jobs will change, and some jobs will likely be eliminated entirely, many more jobs will evolve.

Defining the Future of Work

Even before the coronavirus pandemic, changes in how and where we work were well underway. The future of work refers to the changes that technology (including automation, robotics, and artificial intelligence) along with new employment models (including freelancers, gig workers, and crowds) will bring about in how we work, where we work, who we work with, and the skills and capabilities we need to work.

Predicting the future is hard, especially when technology is involved. Ken Olsen, the founder of Digital Equipment Corp., likely wishes he had not been so confident in 1977 when he said, "There is no reason for any individual to have a computer in his home."[30] Steve Ballmer, the CEO of Microsoft, had low expectations for the iPhone in 2007, when he announced, "There's no chance that the iPhone is going to get any significant market share."[31] And Robert Metcalfe, founder of 3Com and inventor of Ethernet, surely regrets his 1995 prediction that the Internet "will soon go spectacularly supernova and in 1996 catastrophically collapse."[32] These predictions all underestimated the growth and adoption of new technology.

My interest lies not in attempting to predict the future but in providing signposts to help others navigate the new world of work. By understanding these signposts, individuals can feel more empowered to evolve their current careers or even craft new ones altogether and to develop educational strategies to succeed in the capabilities-based market AI brings. For business leaders seeking to adopt and scale new models of working, these signposts can help explore the opportunities that novel forms of human–machine collaboration bring to the workplace. And for public policy makers, these signposts can spur the reimagination of regulations, laws, and institutional arrangements as new forms of working emerge through alternative workforce arrangements, education and workforce development, work transition programs, and financing to support lifelong learning and reinvention. Though we may not be able to change the impact of AI or future proof against the disruptions ahead, we can change the way we navigate alongside them. We can become smarter in the way we work, think, and live in the world of AI and the open talent economy of multiple forms of employment. And we can change the way we design and think about our work and workplaces of tomorrow.

Maps That Matter

Since the first maps were carved into cave walls in 16,500 BC, we have relied on these pictures and navigational tools to explore new terrain and make our way through the world.[33] Maps tell stories. Maps are knowledge. Maps provide context. As author Reif Larsen noted, "A map does not just chart, it unlocks and formulates meaning; it forms bridges between here and there, between disparate ideas that we did not know were previously connected."[34] A road to the right, a river to the left, a steep drop ahead. As an avid traveler, I am in awe of the power of great maps to help us condense and visualize data so that we can take on complex routes and challenges, whether hiking up a mountain or finding our way to a new restaurant. Maps allow us to make more informed decisions.

Maps have kept me from getting lost countless times in the more than 75 countries I have visited and worked in throughout my life. I remember going on summer road trips with my parents, sister, and brother when I was growing up, flipping through a huge paper atlas map to help my father navigate unknown roads to new destinations. Today, GPS apps on our smartphones, from Google Maps to Waze, offer near-instantaneous options for getting from one place to another. They provide real-time information on traffic flows and accidents, rerouting us to keep us going safely and quickly in the directions we choose. Though we have mapped just about every corner of the physical world, we are just starting to map the future world of work.

This is a story about the value of mapping, the importance of direction setting, and the need to create new maps and mental models when traveling in unchartered terrain. We need to understand not only the path but also the changing conditions along that path. The 1996 Mount Everest climbing disaster illustrates the tragic consequences of misjudging the conditions along a chosen route. Eight people perished while attempting to descend the mountain during a blizzard. After several unexpected delays, many of the climbers had not yet reached the summit by 2 p.m., considered the last safe time to turn around

> Much as Sherpas did for me in traversing mountain paths and basecamps in the Himalayas, I hope to help you make your way through the noise and confusion surrounding the twenty-firstcentury landscape of the future of work, jobs, and careers in a way that clarifies your options.

to reach camp before nightfall. By midafternoon, snow started to fall, and the light was diminishing. Soon, the climbers found themselves in a full-on blizzard. Visibility was reduced and fixed ropes were buried under snow. Some climbers developed frost bite, others fell unconscious.[35]

Lives were lost due to the sudden onset of a severe storm that caught the mountaineers by surprise and, perhaps most importantly, the decision to exceed the normal turnaround time back down the mountain. The climbers failed to realistically view the environment and their ability to change the forces of nature. My goal is to help travelers in the new world of work understand new routes and the changing conditions they are likely to encounter along the way. Your understanding of what's ahead and your choice of partners on your travels are critically important to your future success.

A Twenty-first-century Sherpa

At this critical juncture in our work history and our economy, I am eager to share what I have learned, set realistic expectations, and guide readers so they can craft action plans for themselves. Much like a Sherpa or travel guide, I hope to help others navigate a landscape that can feel intimidating.

I met many highly skilled Sherpas after college when I lived in Nepal for two years as a U.S. Peace Corps volunteer, teaching math and science in a rural village. When I decided to hike part of the challenging Annapurna Circuit, a 128-mile trek winding through some of the world's tallest mountains and most extreme climatic zones, I knew I needed an experienced guide. That's when I learned the difference between a mountain climber (me), a porter, and a Sherpa. A mountain climber generally scales a particular mountain once. A porter carries your belongings and gear in a basket up the mountain (for which we are all very grateful). Sherpas, from an ethnic group in Nepal who live in the Himalaya Mountains, are known for their superior strength and endurance, and for knowing the terrain and environment better than anyone else.

Among the most famous Sherpas was Tenzing Norgay, who in 1953, along with Sir Edmund Hillary, were the first two men to reach the peak of Mount Everest, the world's tallest mountain.[36] The Sherpa on my trip to Annapurna base camp told me what to bring, what to expect, and the best routes to take. He was calm in the face of challenges, including predators, or finding the usual paths obscured. He was able to adapt and make adjustments. He knew when the clouds swirled in a particular way that a storm was approaching and the best places to seek shelter. He also helped me feel confident and encouraged about the journey ahead.

Much as Sherpas did for me in traversing mountain paths and basecamps in the Himalayas, I hope to help you make your way through the noise and confusion surrounding the twenty-first-century landscape of the future of work, jobs, and careers in a way that clarifies your options rather than promotes a sense of anxiety about what's to come. The future of work calls for intentionality. This is not the time to leave matters to chance but to take deliberate action. The questions before us are too consequential; they cannot be relegated to technologists alone or financial pundits with a short-term focus on substitution and cost cutting. Indeed, organizations and business leaders are poised to shape what ultimately becomes the future of work. They have the chance to be thoughtful about how they redesign jobs and teams, redefine work itself, and find new ways to facilitate learning and development. Individuals will face decisions about how to gain new skills and capabilities as their jobs change or are phased out. As a society, we need better ways to help people gain new work skills and transition through multiple careers. We also need new laws to protect workers, especially those in the growing gig economy, who often lack minimum wage protection or health and social benefits.

Jeff, on left, in Nepal, with US Peace Corps 1982

New Technology Has Always Created More Jobs

Whether it's a client at a business meeting or an acquaintance at a cocktail party, the first question I am always asked when the topic of automation comes up is, "*how many* jobs will the robots take away from us?" Understandably, the persistence of this question stems from the accelerating pace of technological change and the specter of a future without work. Such fears are widespread: 82 percent of the United States thinks robots will take over much of the work currently done by humans, according to a recent Pew Research Center survey.[37] Relatively few adults surveyed saw an upside for workers as a result of automation and new workplace technologies.

One of the aims of this book is to persuade you that this is not the most important question or where we should direct our energy and focus. First, no one knows just how many jobs will be threatened by robots and other forms of automation. Second, it is not *how many* that matters. What matters is *how* we will navigate the new job and business opportunities created by technology and new ways of working.

"Clearly, a world in which five percent of jobs are eliminated by automation is very different from a world in which 50 percent of jobs are eliminated," noted Gideon Lichfield, the editor-in-chief of *MIT Technology Review*. "But regardless of the numbers, we're going to face a lot of the same kinds of issues, just in differing degrees."[38] Of greater interest than any number or percent is *how* automation, and not only robotics but also cognitive technology and AI, natural language processing, and machine learning will change our jobs and how we work.

Though we have been creating machines to do our work for us for centuries—including tractors, assembly lines, and computers—the proportion of adults in the United States with a formal full-time job has consistently risen during this time. Technology has not made human labor redundant and our skills obsolete. A 2018 report by the World Economic Forum projected that although nearly 1 million jobs may be lost to automation, another 1.75 million will be gained.[39]

Economists are quick to point out that although new technology may displace certain types of work, history has shown us that technology has created more jobs than it has taken.[40] The challenge has often been the transition paths for workers to have access to the skills required for new jobs. Over the past 200 years, technology has *changed* human work but has not eliminated it. Department of Labor data shows that over the past two decades, many of the tasks that make up a job have changed. Though some tasks have disappeared, job growth has continued. This scenario includes groups of remote and diverse teams working together, productive collaboration between people and machines, and workers continuing to be employed by learning new capabilities throughout their lives.

> Economists are quick to point out that while new technology may displace certain types of work, history has shown us that technology has created more jobs than it has taken.

What is new is the accelerated rate of the changes, which makes thinking about the future more important than it has ever been. The transformation from an agricultural economy to an industrial economy was linear, happening at a steady rate, where you *add* the same amount again and again over time. The current acceleration is exponential, which means you *multiply* the same amount again and again.[41] Though technological advances are moving quickly, they can be more complicated to implement than we realize. Take autonomous cars. Who can forget the relentless hype around self-driving cars? Predicted to be the greatest disruptors to transportation since Henry Ford's Model T, autonomous-driving cars were said to be only months away from being tried out by the general public.[42] It turns out that few understood what was required to complete one of these cars. Navigating unpredictable traffic and weather patterns, as well as knowing how to react to distracted pedestrians in danger of being hit, added to the complexity of bringing self-driving cars to a street near you. When a few test vehicles crashed, it became clear that deploying robot cars was far more complex than many envisioned just a few years earlier. In addition to technology challenges, liability issues had to be addressed. Some now say it may be many years before self-driving cars replace human drivers on our highways. But they are coming.

Why ATMs Did Not Replace Bank Tellers

The surprising story of automated teller machines (ATMs) and bank tellers offers a fascinating illustration of how new technology, if properly harnessed, can change individual jobs—or the tasks that make up the job—without eliminating the worker. The transformation of bank tellers provides a useful counterpoint to arguments by automation alarmists. When ATMs were first introduced in the 1970s, many predicted that bank tellers would lose their jobs. After all, ATMs took over their basic job functions, making it possible to deposit a check or withdraw cash from a machine.[43] This new "automatic" teller seemed to be able to do everything the human teller did. So what happened to bank tellers? Since ATMs appeared on the scene, the number of human bank tellers in the United States has roughly doubled, according to Boston University economist James Bessen. He has noted that the adoption of ATMs did not, in fact, reduce the number of teller jobs—it *changed* their jobs.[44] Indeed, their jobs evolved. New skills were needed. Bank tellers took on different roles, learning to assist customers with loans, open new accounts, market financial products, troubleshoot, and more—jobs that machines were unable to do.

Bessen reports that between the mid-1990s, when about 400,000 ATMs were introduced, and the year 2000, the number of teller jobs grew faster than the labor force as a whole. And while that may eventually change, the near-term impact of ATM technology actually created *more* jobs.[45] The ATM created more full-time teller jobs at banks because it allowed banks to open more branches, since each branch could operate with fewer tellers, which also meant banks could hire more tellers overall. It should be noted that the jobs of bank tellers are not forever secure, however, due to continued industry consolidation and technological changes. And let's not forget about mobile banking, which also involves automation of work previously handled by humans. However, it is interesting to note that the evolution of bank tellers' jobs is similar to what happened in the nineteenth century with the textile industry. Though most of the work suddenly was automated, the number of weavers continued to grow for decades.[46] More automation meant the price of cotton cloth fell, and people used more of it.

Projections that the future of work will usher in mass unemployment rest upon several flawed assumptions. The first is that a job consists of a single task. Most jobs consist of many tasks, not all of which can be automated. The second is that technology is a substitute rather than a complement to human labor. In most cases to date, technology augments but does not wholly eliminate human workers. What we tend to forget is that technological innovation could create jobs that we have not yet imagined. Changes in how we work have been underway for decades, as the activities in most occupations have shifted from basic and repetitive tasks to more advanced tasks. This means we spend less time collecting data and more time solving problems.

Elevator operators have the distinction of being one of the very few occupations in the past 60 years that has been eliminated from the Census Bureau logs due to automation.[47] Add to this list the switchboard operator and the bowling alley pinsetter. Meanwhile, new job titles like app developer, social media director, and data scientist have emerged. A rule of thumb today is that if your job is repetitive, routine, and predictable, and you can easily describe it, chances are large portions of it can be automated. If someone can write a script that describes the job, or create a set of algorithms or rules, then a machine will be able follow those rules and do the work.

Our cultural idea of work has undergone dramatic shifts before. In the preindustrial economy, work was synonymous with craftsmanship, with someone creating a product from start to finish. For example, a cobbler would do everything from measure the customer's feet to make any adjustments in the finished pair of shoes. The Industrial Revolution changed this conception of work, as it became clear that products could be manufactured more quickly and cheaply if work was divided into smaller, repeatable tasks in which workers could specialize. For many, the notion of a "job" became a collection of distinct tasks. Today, we appear to be redefining work again, with the shift moving in the opposite direction: As computers can complete more tasks, people may increasingly move from completing tasks to the more human capabilities, such as problem-solving, communicating, interpreting, addressing unexpected challenges, asking questions, and managing human (and human and machine) relationships.

There's a lot of debate over whether things will be different this time around in the so-called Fourth Industrial Revolution. In the past, industrial revolutions centering on mechanization, electrification, and computerization dramatically reshaped jobs, especially for low-skill workers in agriculture and manufacturing. A key difference today is that advances in digital technologies are poised to have an impact on every sector of the economy. Another difference is that we are building machines that can do more than mechanize routine tasks that people already do. Machine learning means machines are able to move beyond the script of an algorithm to actually learn to do something on their own by discovering patterns. Machines can therefore propose new solutions to problems. This type of autonomy is what makes people feel uneasy.

Employees Are More Adaptable Than We Think

A 2019 global survey by Harvard Business School researchers looked at whether employees would be willing to do whatever it takes to survive the twists and turns of a rapidly evolving economy. The survey found that employees are more adaptable than they are often given credit for. The survey focused on business leaders as well as the people most vulnerable to changing dynamics: lower-income and middle-skills workers. The majority of the workers had no more than two years of postsecondary education.[48]

Not surprisingly, business leaders surveyed were worried about finding employees with the skills their companies needed when operating in a climate of perpetual disruption. The workers surveyed, however, focused more on the opportunities and benefits that the future holds for them. They were much more eager to embrace change and learn new skills than their employers expected. According to the survey, a majority of the workers felt that advances such as automation and artificial intelligence would have a positive impact on their future. What concerned them most was that other workers—temporary, freelance, outsourced—would take their jobs. When asked why they had a positive outlook, workers cited two reasons: the prospect of better wages and the prospect of more interesting and meaningful jobs.[49] Both automation and technology, they felt, offered opportunity on those fronts—by contributing to the emergence of more-flexible and self-directed forms of work, by creating alternative ways to earn income, and by making it possible to avoid tasks that were "dirty, dangerous, or dull."

Growth and Innovation

We can learn a lot from past technological transitions. In the absence of dynamic and responsive policies, as well as resources to manage the transitions, displaced workers often faced more uncertainty and pain than was necessary. We can all play a role in shaping the future of work. If AI, robotics, and new employment models do indeed transform most jobs, requiring new skill sets for workers, our challenge is to create paths forward and opportunities that everyone can access. At stake is not only economic survival but psychological well-being as well.

Joblessness brings with it social and psychological challenges, including individual crises of identity, according to Amy Wrzesniewski, professor of organizational behavior at the Yale School of Management. "Our identities have been closely linked to our jobs," she noted in our interview. "Our institutional relationships are central to mental health because of the role that organizational work has played sociologically over the past 100 years."[50]

Writing about the future of work in 1930, economist John Maynard Keynes, in "Economic Possibilities for our Grandchildren," envisioned that within a century, the average person would be working 15 hours a week, and we would face an excessive leisure problem.[51] Keynes's view of the future was "frozen" in the sense that he did not consider the possibility of entirely new fields emerging in economies that have been infused with new technologies. What Keynes did not envision were all the new fields and human endeavors that were yet to be invented, from modern health care and education to the amazing creativity of the technology, media, and service industries. Those are largely what have driven employment and progress, and those are also the reasons that make many of us who are investigating the future of work feel optimistic. The future can offer much more than mechanized work, optimizing workflows, and grinding out efficiency; it can be about creation, and new levels of growth and innovation.

Signposts for the Future

Though the future is unpredictable, there is a lot that we do know about the developments that will change how and where we work. This is because many are already underway. The way we frame what lies ahead is a critical navigational tool. Our traditional mental models and approaches to challenges will not serve as reliable guides. The signposts that follow can serve as practical guides for individuals who have families to support, mortgages to pay, and want to stay gainfully employed no matter what the future holds. These navigational tools can help empower the reader's own journey into the future of work.

The journey ahead begins with recognizing the rapidly evolving opportunities in front of us: The opportunities presented as work, workforces, and workplaces are being redesigned, redefined, and reimagined. The journey continues with the realization of the effort required to build resilience—in our careers, organizations, and leaders—for what lies ahead. And the journey culminates in planning and equipping ourselves for the growth and potential in the future—our growth as individuals, business leaders, citizens, and as a society. The path of this journey is the structure of this book.

Part I: Opportunity (Chapters 2, 3, 4)

- **Opportunity and Work**. Recognize that the future is people and teams *with* machines, not against them. Rather than a substitution play in which robots and advanced technology replace human workers, we redefine the terms of competition, avoiding the trap that people and machines are in opposition to one another. There is the opportunity to create newfound value. As MIT professor, Erik Brynjolfsson, and Andrew McAfee advise, the answer is not to attempt to race against the machine or to try to slow down technology but to race with the machine.[52]

- **Opportunity and the Workforce**. Leverage the multiple forms that employment and work will take. In recent decades, the structure of employment models has been changing dramatically and quickly. Whereas the most common conception of employment is a full-time job, the diversity of work arrangements is growing to include part time, contractors, freelancers, gig workers, and crowd workers. How we integrate these talent models into our careers, our businesses, and our communities and societies will be a major challenge in the coming years.

- **Opportunity and Workplace**. Expect to work anywhere, anytime, with anyone . . . or thing. We are learning from the Covid-19 pandemic how our work and personal lives could intersect. We witnessed the virtualization and shift to remote work and education. In the future many organizations may have as many people working offsite (at home, in coffee shops, and everywhere else) as in the office. As collaborative technologies along with digital reality, both virtual and augmented, become more pervasive and powerful, how we work may become more important than where we work.

Part II: Resilience (Chapters 5, 6, 7)

- **Resilience and Careers**. Plan for longer lives with multiple phases. Resilience involves ongoing reinvention—being able to adapt, reskill, and upskill throughout our lifetimes. Enduring human capabilities that will be important in the future will include curiosity, creativity, problem-solving, empathy, communication, and leadership. We will need to develop and nurture our critical capabilities, including the ability to acquire new context-specific knowledge and routines, and to be comfortable with technology and data as our companions, along with our human colleagues and team members.[53]

- **Resilience and Organizations**. Prepare for the shift to teams and eco-systems as organizations transition from twentiethcentury approaches to twenty-first-century models. We are moving from hierarchies to networks of teams, from work being done in common locations to multiple locations—physical and digital. Work will increasingly evolve beyond a focus on process to a focus on projects, assignments, and initiatives. Teams and networks will strengthen organizational resilience and become the critical units of organizational performance and professional development.

- **Resilience and Leadership**. Embrace new capabilities to lead teams and manage new forms of work; move from controlling to coaching; shift from an almost singular focus on costs and efficiency to an expanded view of growth, innovation, value, and meaning; accept dynamic ongoing change; and gain a new level of comfort with technology and data, ambiguity and risk, and people and machines. Leadership resilience will be empowered as leaders continue to experience the shift from managing through control and direct supervision to managing with increased coaching, design, influence, and inspiration.

Part III: Growth (Chapters 8, 9, 10)

- **Growth and Individuals**. Embrace adaptation and a growth mindset. Develop and curate a portfolio of experiences and the range of human skills and capabilities that will be essential in 100-year, multistage lives.[54] Build the skills to thrive in teams; drive your own development;

and integrate combinations of education, work, and personal pursuits throughout your life.

- **Growth and Business**. Focus on creating new value and augmentation—not on replacement and automation. Redesign jobs and redefine work for cost, value, and meaning for customers, the workforce, and the enterprise. Partner with the workforce to build career marketplaces and opportunity pathways for growth and development; and design ways of working and workplaces integrating our personal and professional lives and accessing talent and capabilities from anywhere.

- **Growth and Society**. Rethink and reset education, labor regulations, job transitions, and ethics to empower the future of work in communities and regions. Question whether our social and public institutions and programs reflect our values as citizens, communities, and societies, especially as we face technological, social, and political changes, including recent movements in the United States concerning racial equity and inclusion. Recognize the impact of work, workforce, and workplace design and regulation on our lives and on the future of local communities and our shared global environment.

What Lies Ahead

To help make sense of the rapidly changing world of work around us, this book is organized in these three parts: opportunity, resilience, and growth.

- **Part I** is dedicated to discovering opportunity in the midst of turbulent change. The chapters explore the shifting dynamics in how machines and people work together; who will do the work; and where will work be done.

- **Part II** explores how to build long-term resilience as we plan for many careers, organizations promote teams and networks, and leaders extend their roles as coaches and designers.

- **Part III** offers playbooks—integrating the insights we have explored—to guide individuals, businesses, and societies preparing for the changes ahead.

By exploring new mental models—such as people *and* machines working in tandem, 100-year lives with multichapter careers, the need to redesign jobs and redefine work, and the importance of resetting our institutions to help accelerate the path forward—we can gain a deeper understanding of how our complex landscape of work is evolving. Individuals can decide how to protect their livelihood while businesses and public institutions can consider how they can lead and support workforces to thrive in twenty-first-century careers and work.

Find Opportunity in a Time of Accelerated Change

Redesigning Work, Workforces, and Workplaces

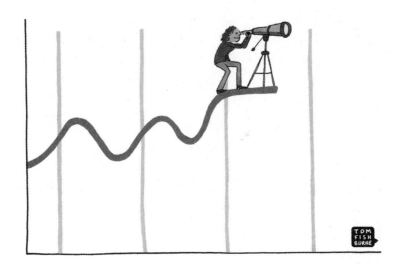

CHAPTER 2

People and Machines Working Together

Integrating AI and Workers on Every Team, in Every Job

AI systems will need to be smart and to be good teammates.

—Barbara Grosz, computer scientist[1]

"Tell me a joke," is the first request I usually make to see if one of my voice-based assistants is listening.

I also ask, "What's your favorite movie?" "What should I eat for lunch?" and even, "How are you feeling today?" Though I bought these AI-powered devices to help with practical tasks, like scheduling appointments, looking up information, and setting daily reminders, I can't resist trying to detect a glimmer of humanity. The manufacturers of these machines know this, and have started to re-engineer them to demonstrate more of a personality, even a sense of humor. Now if you ask some devices, "Who's on first?" the answer will be, "Yes, he is."

AI has become part of our daily lives, as AI-powered virtual assistants like Siri, Alexa, and Google Home have placed smart machines at our fingertips. AI, or Artificial Intelligence, refers to machines capable of performing tasks that typically involves some aspect of human intelligence—the ability of a computer program or a machine to identify patterns, make predictions, and

increasingly, to learn on its own. Every time Amazon recommends a product or Netflix prompts the next TV show or movie, the recommendation is driven by AI. Algorithms suggest what may interest us based on our buying history and other products we have viewed. Sometimes robots and smart systems toil in the background, vacuuming our carpets or powering our e-commerce purchases. Increasingly, AI is also joining us at work, as super-powered colleagues who help us do our jobs in new ways. For years, airplanes have operated with two co-pilots—a human co-pilot and a second co-pilot powered by machine learning along with other AI technologies. Airplanes are now on autopilot for most of each flight. Human pilots generally actively steer the aircraft only during takeoff and landing, monitoring the computer that takes the helm for the duration of the flight. AI powers everything from gameplay to medical diagnosis.[2]

One of the paradoxes of robots, AI, and machine learning is that we want them to make our lives easier—*what was life like before Google Maps, spam filters, and mobile check deposits?*—but we are terrified they will one day replace us. This adversarial relationship between humans and technology taps into fears that date back to the steam engine and are fueled today by pop culture. Robots that cannot be trusted have appeared in movies like *The Terminator, The Matrix*, and *Blade Runner*. It's not a stretch to wonder how soon AI will do parts of our job far better than we can and how many jobs AI will replace. Though we cannot know the number of jobs that will be lost to AI due to unpredictable variables that will be at play, such as cost, regulatory issues, political pressure, and social resistance, this mythic number has been chased relentlessly.

For six years, the media seized upon one alarming statistic that sensationalized the impact of the future of work by striking terror in the masses.

Headlines warned that 47 percent of the workforce would lose their jobs to automation in the next one or two decades. Almost every story about the future of work included a mention that 47 percent of jobs would be lost to robots. The figure was cited by academic researchers more than 5,600 times.[3] Government agencies, think tanks, and news organizations all quoted this figure, creating widespread panic that almost half the population would soon be unemployed.

This single most frequently quoted statistic about the future of work has the distinction of also being among the most widely misinterpreted. The source of this notorious 47 percent is a 2013 academic paper, "The Future of Employment," written by Oxford University researchers Carl Benedikt Frey and Michael Osborne.[4] They analyzed the U.S. labor market, job code by job code, using a machine-learning algorithm to determine how easily tasks within 702 jobs could be automated. Their theoretical calculation was mistakenly reported as a firm forecast that 47 percent of jobs would disappear by 2023. The term *future of work*, which first appeared in Google searches in 2004, started its steady increase in popularity around this time.[5] This coincidence was not lost on Chris Kutarna, a noted author and scholar. "[Future of work's] recent climb into popular lingo began only in late 2013," Kutarna noted. "Why *then*? I have a hunch," he added, citing the Frey and Osborne research paper.[6]

Frey and Osborne have since explained that the ubiquitous 47 percent was misinterpreted: Their research looked at jobs with tasks *most vulnerable* to automation but made no prediction about how many jobs would be automated. They clarified that machines could perform *some tasks and functions* within 47 percent of jobs in the United States over the next decade or two.[7] Their correction barely received a nod from the press.

With dire, often misleading, forecasts about automation making news, it's no wonder that we tend to think of machines in an adversarial or mutually exclusive way—people *versus* machines; people *or* machines. More likely, however, we will race *with* machines, not against them.[8] We will collaborate with machines more often than we will be replaced by them. A critical distinction highlighted by the "47 percent" misunderstanding is that the Oxford researchers were looking at which jobs had *parts* that were vulnerable to automation. Though jobs that consist primarily of repetitive, predictable tasks are more likely to be replaced by machines—and go the way of telephone switchboard operators, film projectionists, and lamppost lighters—many more jobs will see only *portions* of work

> This adversarial relationship between humans and technology taps into fears that date back to the steam engine and are fueled today by pop culture.

performed by machines alongside humans. According to some estimates, automation will likely replace 30 percent or more of tasks in 60 percent of occupations but only 5 percent of jobs in their entirety.[9]

Where Robots Come From

Robots have been a part of the workforce for decades, though granted, not sitting at the desk next to ours. The word *robot* was used for the first time to describe an artificial person in the play *R.U.R.*, written by Karel Capek, which premiered in 1921 at the National Theater in Prague. Capek invented the term *robot* from the Czech word for "forced labor." Two years later, *robot* entered the English language.[10]

By definition, a robot is a machine that can perform tasks autonomously and excel at tasks that are routine, repetitive, or dangerous. One of the first industrial robots, Unimate, invented by George Devol, was put to work by General Motors in 1961.[11] The robot reported for duty on the assembly line at the Inland Fisher Guide Plant in Ewing Township in New Jersey. Unimate's robotic arm could transfer objects from one point to another up to a distance of 12 feet.[12] Automated, programmable, and able to move around, the robot could assemble and weld more quickly and with greater precision than humans. Devol's invention accelerated the speed of production lines at manufacturing plants around the world for more than 50 years.[13]

We have long benefited from tools that make our work easier. We have seen tools as varied as the hammer and the printing press lead to efficiency and optimization of work. Most forms of robots and AI can amplify human potential. This amplification offers the opportunity for people to create newfound value. What is different today is that robots, AI, and machine learning are not only making us more efficient but can operate with autonomy. AI can suggest a spelling change or switch off a credit card because of a high probability of fraud.

AI technologies are piloting cars, guiding weapons, and performing tedious or dangerous work. AI is engaging in conversations, making appointments, translating documents, and even matching romantic partners. AI is also making consequential recommendations in areas such as jurisprudence, lending, medicine, university admissions, and hiring.[14] The prominent computer scientist Andrew Ng has conveyed the scope and depth of changes that AI is likely to engender: "Just as electricity transformed almost everything 100 years ago, today I actually have a hard time thinking of an industry that I don't think AI will transform in the next several years."[15]

With great change, there is often great progress, and also, great anxiety. When machines started to perform human jobs, what followed is what MIT economist David Autor calls "automation anxiety."[16] This fear raises a survival question: As robots and AI become better and better at performing human jobs—*our* jobs—will technology remain our co-worker or eventually replace us? Historically, technological changes have indeed eliminated some jobs but also created new ones to replace them, according to Autor. As he and other economists have noted, despite the past two centuries of automation and technological progress, human labor has not become obsolete. Though jobs have changed, work continues to exist. AI will likely cause net positive job growth. According to a report from the World Economic Forum, machines and algorithms in the workplace are expected to cause 75 million jobs to be displaced but create 133 million new roles.[17]

Ultimately, I share the view of many economists that more jobs will be augmented rather than automated or replaced. The challenge we face when working with technology is to use it to augment workers, not replace them. While replacement can create greater efficiency and cost savings, it does not create new value. Eric Topol, director of the Scripps Research Translational Institute in La Jolla, California, and a leading cardiologist who writes about AI and medicine, explores AI's impact on the way doctors work in his book *Deep Medicine*. Topol warns of the danger of creating negative value if the quest for ever-greater efficiency ends up squeezing doctors to work even harder.[18] This could also be the case in other areas, such as call centers, human resources departments, and more. "This gift of time is all ruined if the only objective is more productivity and not about human interaction and the essence of medicine, the care part," said Topol. "But I'm encouraged that medicine will be better than it has been in a long time."[19] Rather than approach AI only as a technology to reduce *costs*, we can also consider its potential for achieving the mutually reinforcing goals of creating more *value* for customers and more meaningful work for employees.

> Often overlooked in discussions about machines and humans working together is the complex emotional and psychological roles work plays in our lives.

Meaningful Work

We face the opportunity to make work more human by expanding the role that humans play on teams with machines and focusing on creativity and context. Often overlooked in discussions about machines and humans working together is the complex emotional and psychological roles work plays in our lives. The work of Amy Wrzesniewski offers perspective on how our work fuels our identity and provides deep meaning to us. Wrzesniewski, a professor of organizational behavior at the Yale School of Management, has researched how people create meaning in their work in difficult contexts. She has been fascinated by the potential of new technology to augment human skills and status or to have the opposite effect. In her study of subway drivers in Paris, she learned that personal meaning derived from a job can be more important than pay or status.

Paris metro drivers were charged with ensuring the safety of passengers and checking that the tracks were clear. "When the system was automated, they didn't fire those people—I mean, it's France, right?" Wrzesniewski said. "Instead, they made them station managers, which was a promotion into managerial work. And the people who went through this transition were absolutely miserable." The reason, she explains, is that the meaning they derived from their work changed. "Their whole connection to the work was feeling this awesome responsibility for the lives of everybody on that train," she said in our interview. "They were no longer in a clutch position that really mattered."[20] The increased prevalence of automation that the future of work will bring causes Wrzesniewski to question whether new technology will liberate us from the repetitive tasks so that we can focus on what we feel makes our work worthwhile, or "take away the very thing that gives our work meaning."[21]

> The challenge we face when working with technology is to use it to augment workers, not replace them. Although replacement can create greater efficiency and cost savings, it does not create new value.

Superminds: Humans Working With and Next to AI

Human and machine intelligence can complement one another's strengths and counterbalance each other's limitations. Thomas Malone, a pioneer in the study of collective intelligence, calls such hybrid human–machine systems "Superminds."[22] Malone, the founding director of the MIT Center for Collective Intelligence, explores how groups of humans and machines can work together to achieve new levels of intelligence in his book, *Superminds: The Surprising Power of People and Computers Thinking Together.*[23] The change in perspective from AI as a substitute for human beings to AI as an enabler of human–machine Superminds has fundamental implications for how organizations can harness AI technologies. Rather than focus primarily on the ability of computer technologies to *automate* tasks, we have the opportunity to consider their ability to *augment* human capabilities. We can explore the vast possibilities of human–computer collaboration.[24]

To appreciate the potential for humans and computers as collaborators, it is helpful to start by considering humans and computers as competitors. The first human versus machine battle in chess in the United States in 1997 was televised.[25] Reigning world chess champion Garry Kasparov went head-to-head with IBM's Deep Blue, a chess computer, and stunned the world by losing.[26] With the world watching, Deep Blue became the first machine to beat a grandmaster in chess.[27] For decades, computer scientists have been obsessed with chess, viewing it as a benchmark for progress in AI. Because chess requires certain qualities that make up human intelligence, such as strategy, foresight, and logic, computer scientists saw the game as the ultimate measuring stick for the development of AI.[28]

The aftermath of Deep Blue's victory over Kasparov illustrates the potential of the human–machine Superminds approach.[29] After his defeat, Kasparov helped create a new game called Advanced Chess, in which teams of humans using computer chess programs competed against one another.[30] In 2005, a global Advanced Chess tournament attracted grandmaster players using some of the most powerful computers of the time. The competition ended in an upset victory: Two amateur chess players using three ordinary laptops, each running a different chess program, beat their grandmaster opponents and supercomputers.[31]

Writing in 2010, Kasparov commented that the winners' skill at manipulating and "coaching" their computers to look very deeply into positions effectively counteracted the superior chess understanding of their grandmaster opponents and the greater computational power of other participants.[32] In Thomas Malone's vernacular, the system of two human players and three computer chess programs formed a *human–computer collective intelligence*—a Supermind—that proved more powerful than competing Superminds composed of superior players and more powerful computers.[33]

Malone has provided a taxonomy for designing human–machine partnerships. He has categorized the roles that computers can serve as[34]:

1. **Tools**. Computers serve as our tools when they function as a word processor or a spreadsheet, performing exactly what they are instructed to do.
2. **Assistants**. Computers act as our assistants when they help us achieve our goals more effectively. The assistant often has autonomy, takes initiative, and may know things we do not know to help us achieve our goals more effectively. An example would be when we access an online banking account and AI performs a first level authentication by using fingerprint recognition, voice recognition, or facial identification. Autocorrect in text messaging is another example of AI functioning as our assistant. Malone explains that when acting as an assistant, a computer

can do some of the tasks cheaper, faster, and often better than the person, just as an electric saw can cut faster than a person can.

3. **Peers/Colleagues**. A machine acts as a peer when an insurance company uses AI to evaluate a claim based on certain parameters and then sends it out for payment. In this instance, the computer is working next to a human claims adjuster and performing a similar task.

4. **Managers**. Alarm bells tend to go off when we think of machines as our manager. However, we experience this every day, such as when a traffic light directs when we cross the street. AI can allocate workload to employees who need to act on the tasks. Kronos Inc., an AI engine, acts as a human resources manager to more than five million shift workers. Kronos can process time-off requests, address shift swaps, and handle other functions that had previously been handled by human managers.

These four modes of collaboration illustrate how computers can augment our human work. In the United States, we have already been working with machines across manufacturing, cybersecurity, construction, senior care, retail, and more. Among the industries likely to see the greatest transformation from a human–machine collaboration are those facing critical staff shortages, such as the healthcare industry, where robots are starting to assist as support staff and AI is powering the detection of diseases.

Humans + Machines in Healthcare

Though it appears perpetually short staffed as an increasing number of practitioners suffer from burnout, the healthcare industry has surpassed manufacturing and retail as the largest source of jobs in the United States. Healthcare spending in the United States[35] is expected to reach nearly 20 percent of the United States Gross Domestic Product by 2025.[36] The three examples that follow illustrate different machine-human collaborations in healthcare that have been successful:

- Moxi, a robot, assists nurses with non-patient-facing tasks, such as picking up and delivering medical supplies. Moxi functions as an assistant and peer/colleague, so that nurses can focus on patient care.
- AI is starting to transform how some doctors work with patients, supporting radiologists, helping to read medical scans, preventing mistakes, and personalizing medicine. In this way, AI functions as a peer/assistant.
- The last example offers a surprising application of AI in an area of the medical profession that one might not expect—mental health—with a successful text-chatbot therapist functioning as a peer/colleague.

Meet Moxi

Diligent Robotics, an Austin, Texas-based AI company that creates robot assistants, is part of the assistive robot market that is estimated to surpass $1 billion by 2024.[37] Diligent developed Moxi to support nurses, decrease nurse "burnout," and address the nursing shortage.[38] In 2018, Texas Health Presbyterian Hospital in Dallas became the first U.S. hospital to use Moxi as part of a pilot program.[39] The need for help was clear. The Bureau of Labor Statistics projects that while the number of nurses will increase 19 percent by 2020,[40] the demand will grow faster than the supply, leaving one million unfilled nursing jobs.[41] At the same time, the need for nursing care will continue to grow in step with the graying of America. By 2030, 21 percent of the U.S. population, about 69 million people, will be senior citizens.[42] What's more, the bedside nurse turnover rate is 16 percent, and close to a quarter of new hires leave within a year.[43]

Diligent took such factors into consideration when it introduced Moxi. The robot works with nurses, taking on nonmedical tasks, or what Diligent calls the grunt work. The company's tagline is: "People should do work they care about most. Robots can do the rest."[44] Moxi can set up a room, restock the supply room, pick up medical supplies, remove soiled linen bags, and deliver patient specimens to a lab. Such logistical tasks can take up 30 percent of a nurse's day. In this way, Diligent believes Moxi can help nurses run around less, experience less burnout, and spend more time caring for patients.[45]

To date, robots have been most successful performing simple, repetitive tasks on automobile assembly lines and moving objects in warehouses with few, if any, human beings in sight. A recent focus is on developing service co-bots (a contraction of "collaborative robot"), which are computer-controlled robotic devices designed to assist people and can work side by side with human colleagues.[46] Co-bots that aim to augment people in the workplace are moving beyond manufacturing plants and warehouses to toil alongside us. The goal is for these co-bots to make us better at our jobs by relieving us of tasks we would rather not perform.

> If AI helps with the diagnosis, doctors will have more time to spend providing context and empathy to patients, rather than wading through the data. This is a new application of deep learning.

Renaissance Radiologists

AI has shown remarkable progress in recognizing patterns in scans, such as X-rays, CTs, and MRIs that can reveal serious health conditions, including cancer. Though applications of the technology are still being tested and are far from wide-spread use, they offer an indication of what may lie ahead. Eric Topol, the leading cardiologist who wrote about AI's impact on the way doctors work in his book *Deep Medicine*,[47] sees the potential of AI not only to help treat patients but to provide much-needed support for the well-being of doctors. Topol notes that physician burnout, depression, and suicide in the United States have reached peak levels. The relationship of doctors and their patients has deteriorated due to time constraints. He welcomes relief in the form of deep learning that trains machines to see things far better than a human ever could. For example, a radiologist can review 20,000 films a year, Topol says, while algorithms could allow the review of millions, or even billions, of images. Studies have suggested that "clinicians who were 'completely certain' of the diagnosis antemortem were wrong 40 percent of the time."[48] According to some estimates, more than 12 million serious diagnostic errors occur each year.[49]

If AI helps with the diagnosis, Topol believes doctors will have more time to spend providing context and empathy to patients, rather than wading through the data. This is a new application of deep learning, which is a powerful form of machine learning. Machine learning uses patterns detected in huge databases to train algorithms capable of making classifications or predictions. Researchers feed computers medical imaging into a system called an artificial neural network. The system follows an algorithm, which is a set of instructions, and is able to learn by following these instructions. Using deep learning in 2017, a Stanford computer science group led by Andrew Ng was able to diagnose pneumonia from chest X-rays better than radiologists using an algorithm it had developed.[50] In a recent study, researchers used AI to read CT scans of people being screened for lung cancer. The deep learning model either beat the doctors or performed as well as they did. It also had fewer false positives and false negatives.[51]

Much of radiology involves interpreting medical images, a task in which deep-learning algorithms excel. Will radiologists be displaced by machines? In *Deep Medicine*, Topol quotes a number of experts who discuss radiology algorithms as assistants to expert radiologists. The Penn Medicine radiology professor Nick Bryan predicted that "just 10 years from now, no medical imaging study will be reviewed by a radiologist until it has been pre-analyzed by a machine."[52] Writing with Michael Recht, Bryan stated, "We believe that machine learning and AI will enhance both the value and the professional satisfaction of radiologists by allowing us to spend more time performing functions that add value and influence patient care and less time doing rote tasks that we neither enjoy nor perform as well as machines."[53]

Using AI to automate voluminous and error-prone tasks so that doctors can spend more time providing personalized, high-value care to patients is the central theme of Topol's book. In the specific case of radiologists, Topol anticipates that these value-adding tasks will include explaining probabilistic outputs of algorithms both to patients and to other medical professionals. For Topol, the "renaissance radiologists" of the future will act less as technicians and more as "real doctors." He believes they will also serve as "master explainers" who display the knowledge of data science and statistical thinking needed to effectively communicate risks and results to patients.[54]

> The top three skills needed to survive in the future of work are complex problem solving, critical thinking, and creativity, according to the World Economic Forum.

AI as Therapist

Robots are proving to be effective in the most unexpected places—such as providing therapy. Alison Darcy saw both the need to assist people suffering from depression and anxiety, and the reality that many are unable to afford therapy or avoid it due to the stigma. As a clinical research psychologist at Stanford University and a former computer programmer, Darcy addressed this problem by creating Woebot, a text-chatbot therapist that can offer cognitive behavioral therapy (CBT). This approach helps patients break negative patterns of thinking. Darcy worked with psychologists and Andrew Ng, the computer scientist and pioneer in artificial intelligence, to develop conversational prompts to help users practice CBT. When Darcy put Woebot online, for free, more than 50,000 people used the chatbot. Today Woebot exchanges between one and two million messages a week with users. Part of the appeal for users, according to Darcy, is that they are not being judged by another human being.[55]

How to Keep a Job While Racing with Machines

Despite the advances of technology, humans continue to excel in areas that technology has not yet mastered, such as intuition, creativity, and persuasion.[56] The top three skills needed to survive in the future of work are complex problem solving, critical thinking, and creativity, according to the World Economic Forum.[57] The other top skills include people management, coordinating with others, emotional intelligence, judgment, decisionmaking, and negotiation.

The jobs most vulnerable to automation consist of routine tasks. A report by the Brookings Institute predicts that many food preparation, office administration, and transportation jobs will be taken over by machines. Workers in jobs that are vulnerable to automation will need to develop new skills. Highly creative or technical positions are most likely to thrive, along with personal care and domestic service jobs that require interpersonal skills and emotional intelligence, the researchers found.[58] The World Economic Forum report identified the fastest growing job opportunities to include data analysts and scientists, software and application developers, and social media specialists. Jobs that require distinctively "human skills," such as sales and marketing professionals, innovation managers, organizational development specialists and customer service workers are also expected to be in demand. The World Economic Forum cited data entry, payroll, secretaries, and certain accounting functions as jobs that would likely go away.[59]

More than half of employees at large companies (54 percent) will need to up-skill, according to the World Economic Forum report.[60] Despite such predictions, many workers feel more adaptive and optimistic about the future than their managers realize. Despite the anxiety expressed in many future-of-work discussions, middle-skills workers see opportunity in change and are optimistic about their future job prospects, according to a recent survey by Harvard Business School's Project on Managing the Future of Work, and the Boston Consulting Group's Henderson Institute. Rather than point to technology as the villain, middle-skill workers surveyed look to the future with confidence and believe that technology can be part of the solution, according to the researchers.[61]

Yet it can feel challenging to prepare for future work and partnering with machines when we do not know what the jobs will be or what steps to take to get ready. What can help prepare for whatever the future brings is to embrace what Carol Dweck calls a "growth mindset." Dweck, the Lewis and Virginia Eaton Professor of psychology at Stanford University and author of the book *Mindset: The New Psychology of Success*, has studied students' different attitudes about failure—namely, why some rebound from challenges while others are devasted by setbacks. She uses the term growth mindset to describe the beliefs people have about their ability to learn and their intelligence. When students believe they can get smarter, they put in extra time and effort, and that leads to higher achievement.[62]

Studies have shown that we can change a person's mindset from fixed to growth, and when we do, it leads to increased motivation and achievement. For example, seventh graders who were taught that intelligence is malleable and shown how the brain grows with effort showed a clear increase in math grades.[63] Studies on different kinds of praise have shown that telling children they are smart encourages a fixed mindset, whereas praising hard work and effort cultivates a growth mindset.[64] These findings have important implications for adults in the workplace. Adapting to change, and putting in time and effort, will be critical to workplace success in the future.

Future success can also be bolstered by developing what John Hagel, formerly of Deloitte's Center for Edge, calls "the capabilities that are uniquely human."[65] He notes that skills are context specific. "If you're operating a certain machine in a certain environment or processing a certain kind of paperwork in a certain environment, you need a set of skills to do that but it's very specific to that machine or that paperwork," Hagel says. He is interested in capabilities that are helpful in any environment and that are context independent. Hagel suggests that the core capabilities that will be essential to thriving in the workplace of the future include curiosity, imagination, creativity, empathy or emotional intelligence, and social intelligence.[66]

Putting AI on Teams

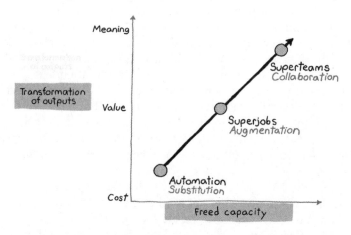

Source: Deloitte Global Human Capital Trends 2020—Superteams.

From Superminds to Superjobs and Superteams

Through research at Deloitte, building on Thomas Malone's idea of Superminds, we have introduced the concepts of "superjobs" and "superteams" to explore the shift to AI-enhanced jobs. Many of us will increasingly have superjobs that reflect the complexity of integrating robots and AI into our work. Superjobs combine what humans and machines each do best to improve business outcomes in our jobs. This involves a mix of automating parts of jobs, augmenting other parts, and freeing up time to do new and different activities. It's the *blend* of automation, augmentation, and time for new activities that transform jobs to superjobs.[67] For example, at one company that employs both humans and robots at its warehouse-distribution centers, the center manager's role has evolved from simply scheduling and overseeing shifts to determining how and when people and robots should hand off work to each other and what human capabilities and coaching is required for these new combinations of people and technology. The evolution of a warehouse supervisor to the manager of human–machines warehouse teams requires different kinds of technical and business expertise.

Superjobs present new challenges for managers because of the dynamic and evolving nature of the new roles. In traditional job design, organizations created fixed, stable roles with written job descriptions and then added supervisory and management positions on top. When parts of jobs are automated by machines, the work that remains for humans is generally more interpretive and service oriented, involving problem-solving, data interpretation, communication, listening, empathy, and collaboration. Since these higher-level skills are not fixed tasks, they are forcing organizations to create more flexible and evolving, less rigidly defined, positions and roles. Superjobs recognize that integrating technology—robotics, robotic process automation (accelerating routine knowledge work), and AI—helps us redesign jobs so people can more efficiently get work done and spend more time on activities that are both engaging and more valuable, such as solving new problems. Think of the renaissance radiologist, whose work is aided by AI, and whose freed-up time can be used to deliver deep care. Consider the teacher using remote learning and flipped classrooms together, and then spending freed-up time tutoring smaller groups or individual students.

Superteams leverage the complementary capabilities of groups of people and machines to solve problems, gain insights, and create value.[68] In superteams, we are challenged to put AI *on* the team. Superteams challenge us to think of the different ways we can put technology—whether robots or AI—*into* workgroups. Although in some cases this involves substitution, in many more cases it involves augmenting human capabilities—reinforcing the value of enduring human capabilities, such creativity and empathy that will be discussed in Chapter 5.

Superjobs and superteams illustrate how the relationship between technology and people is evolving from a focus on *automating* work to replace workers, to *augmenting* workers with technology to create superjobs, to *collaborating* with technology to form superteams. As organizations progress further along this spectrum, the degree to which technology can transform organizational outputs increases. At the first stage, substitution, the new outputs allow for reduced costs and improved efficiency. At the second stage, augmentation, greater transformation drives greater value and expanded opportunities, reduces costs, and improves efficiency. And at the third stage, collaboration, a still greater degree of transformation enables the work and the outputs to take on more meaning for workers and customers, as well as drive greater gains in productivity and value.[69]

Human–machine partnerships, in jobs and teams, can make the most of new technologies in ways that simultaneously create more value for customers and more meaningful work for employees. The future of these partnerships will involve mindset shifts. This is perhaps the greatest opportunity in the next decades. How can we reframe the relationship between people and technology to move beyond a competition to collaboration? It's fundamentally a question of imagination. Perhaps the biggest challenges relative to the future of work and automation and AI will lie in how proactively we design these human–machine partnerships in our jobs, careers, and organizations, preparing, developing and rewarding the human capabilities that are augmented but not replaced by machines.

Note: This chapter is substantially drawn from an article co-authored by James Guszcza and Jeff Schwartz, "Superminds, Not Substitutes: Designing Human–machine Collaboration for a Better Future of Work," published by Deloitte Review, Issue 27, July 2020.

CHAPTER 3

Making Alternative Work a Meaningful Opportunity

The Workforce Will Include More Part-time, Contract, Freelance, Gig, and Crowd Workers

Organizations have traditionally been sites of belonging, Now, in the world of gig work, we have to think about what it means for individuals when they have no membership at all.[1]

—Amy Wrzesniewski, professor, author

When two leading labor market scholars set out to study a decade of job growth, they shed light on changes in how we work that had been underway, though largely under the radar, for decades. Examining the nine million new jobs created in the prior decade, Lawrence Katz at

Harvard University and Alan Krueger at Princeton University discovered that most of these jobs were part-time, lacked consistent paychecks, and did not offer benefits. In fact, 94 percent of the new jobs created in the United States between 2005 and 2015 were "alternative" work.[2] Originally conceived of as contract work, "alternative" work today includes a range of work performed by outsourced teams; temporary and on-call workers; contractors; freelancers; gig workers, who are paid for tasks; and the crowd or outsourced networks.[3]

Katz and Krueger lifted a veil, revealing that what had been perceived as solid job growth was actually dominated by impermanent positions that generally paid less, were not secure, and lacked health insurance and other benefits. Their findings sparked widespread debate in economic journals and the general press. Katz, a former chief economist at the U.S. Department of Labor, and Krueger, a former chairman of the White House Council of Economic Advisers, eventually modified and re-weighted their data, publishing

> The question we now face is a moral one: Can American capitalism create a work world that offers both flexibility and economic security? This is a critical question in a country in which most of our regulations and many of our social safety net programs are predicated on people having full-time jobs.

a new paper in 2019 revising down their original numbers. According to their new calculations, gig work had increased by only one or two percentage points since 2005, rather than the 5-point increase they had reported earlier.[4] The gig economy was smaller than we thought. However, whether it dipped or increased a few percentage points was not the real story. The big news was that the alternative workforce turned out to be not so alternative after all. It had become mainstream. Like a snowball rolling down a mountain after a blizzard, the alternative workforce had steadily been growing in size, and picking up momentum for more than 75 years. Today, more than one-third of U.S. workers (36 percent) participate in the gig economy, either through their primary or secondary jobs. Most notably, for 29 percent of all workers, the alternative work arrangement is their primary job rather than a side hustle. By 2023, the percentage of the workers that participate in the gig economy or have worked independently at some point during their careers, is expected to grow to half of the workforce in the United States (52 percent).[5]

The Rise of Alternative Work

When people talk about the gig economy today, they are often thinking about new technology-enabled work and apps, like Uber, Fiverr, Experfy, and Task-Rabbit. However, gig work as an employment model dates back to World War II. Companies have been splitting up tasks and outsourcing many of them to temporary workers for more than half a century. In his book *Temp: How American Work, American Business, and the American Dream Became Temporary*, economic historian Louis Hyman, a professor at the Cornell University's School of Industrial and Labor Relations, traces the evolution of temporary work as well as the full-time, steady job. Hyman points out that our economy has long been characterized by employment instability. Job insecurity did not begin with ride-sharing companies.[6] "It's actually the traditional work that has failed people," Hyman said in our interview. "Ride sharing companies are a symptom, not a cause, of this insecurity. And it's not about the app, it's about the kinds of businesses and jobs that people have access to. Folding sweaters and selling coffee just doesn't provide the kind of stability that a working-class job did in the 1950s and '60s."[7]

After the Great Depression, Americans yearned for job security and stability. Corporations needed reliable assembly line workers who would show up every day so that expensive machines they had invested in would be in operation. At the time, corporations were more interested in minimizing risks and taking care of employees than maximizing profits, Hyman notes. The rise of the temporary placement service company Manpower would change that. Manpower pitched temporary, emergency support for corporations to fill gaps when an employee was sick or on vacation. However, companies quickly realized that temp workers offered huge cost savings since they were not paid benefits or overtime. Rather than protect workers, Manpower and similar temporary services companies made it possible for companies to more easily hire and fire them. Hyman dates this shift to the late 1960s, when corporate profits were stagnating.[8] One way for companies to cut costs was to outsource some work to temporary or contract workers. The hiring of temp workers continued to grow steadily. By 1988, most businesses in the United States (90 percent) employed some temporary workers.[9]

The Bureau of Labor Statistics categorizes part-time workers based on whether they choose to work fewer than 35 hours per week, or whether they work part time by default because they are unable to secure full-time employment. In 2016, almost 28 million people worked part time. Reasons people choose to work part time include school, childcare, eldercare, and health or medical limitations.[10] As many as 40 percent of younger full-time workers also work part time. These so-called "side-hustles" are very common among Millennials and Generation Z as they enter the workforce.[11]

If current trends march on, work for many people will increasingly be more temporary and less regulated, offering fewer benefits and less predictability. Hyman argues that the gig economy was created by choice, not by accident. The question he believes we now face is a moral one: *Can American capitalism create a work world that offers both flexibility and economic security?*[12] This

---

Alternative Work Comes in Many Shapes and Sizes[13]

- **Alternative workforce:** This group includes outsourcing and managed services contractors, freelance and independent workers, and gig and crowd workers—effectively any worker who is not a traditional full time or part-time employee.
- **Outsourcing and managed services contractors:** Workers who are employed by other firms who provide services, typically at a service level agreement, to other companies. These services can range from cleaning services to data science expertise.
- **Freelance and independent workers:** They extend the core employee workforce and are typically paid by the hour, day, or other unit of time.
- **Gig workers:** They are paid by the task (or microtask) to complete a specified piece of work.
- **Crowd workers:** They compete to participate in a project and are often only paid if they are among the top participants in a competition.
- **Ghost workers:** Coined by anthropologist Mary Gray, the term refers to an underclass of invisible labor that powers our digital economy. The work is often based on micro-projects—effectively high-tech piecework—such as moderating content, editing web pages, flagging controversial content, and similar sorting activities.[14]

is a critical question in a country in which most of our regulations and many of our social safety net programs are predicated on people having full-time jobs. As large companies continue to contract out a portion of their work, most of us will experience a mix of full-time and alternative work arrangements.

The High Price of Flexibility

In the pursuit of greater efficiency for companies and under the guise of offering more flexibility to the workforce, we have been fueling the growth of the alternative workforce for more than half a century. Alternative work offers a clear upside to people seeking a little extra cash. However, it presents significant drawbacks to those who seek a consistent or predictable income with benefits. The flexibility that alternative work arrangements offer has been widely cited as a key advantage. This flexibility comes at a steep price. On average, gig workers earn about 58 percent less than full-time employees and more than half do not have access to employer provided benefits.[15]

"For some, the rise of the gig economy is liberation from the stifled world of corporate America," Hyman wrote in his book *Temp*. "It is a return to the autonomy and independence of an economy before wage labor. No desk. No boss. Every consultant is her own master. Yet for the vast majority of workers the freedom from a paycheck is just the freedom to be afraid. It is the severing of obligations between firms and employees. It is the collapse of the protections that we, in our laws and customs, fought hard to enshrine."[16]

Though alternative work can offer flexible schedules that can improve work–life balance and well-being, they are not necessarily worker-friendly. Alternative work jobs often have irregular schedules that do not allow workers to anticipate when they will work from one week to the next. Many workers are on-call or work evenings and weekends.

Alexandre Mas of Princeton University and Amanda Pallais of Harvard University in their research paper on alternative work arrangements noted that gig economy has put the trade-offs into focus.[17] "Workplace flexibility has been touted as both one of the benefits and costs of the fragmentation (or 'Uberization') of the workplace," they wrote. The authors challenged the widely held views on the importance of workplace flexibility. "The majority of workers do not value flexible

> On average, gig workers earn about 58 percent less than full-time employees and more than half do not have access to employer-provided benefits.

scheduling . . . or the ability to choose the number of hours they work," they wrote. "Workers do value the option to work from home and strongly dislike employers setting their schedules on short notice, mainly because they don't want to work evenings and weekends. Overall, the traditional Monday to Friday, 9 am–5 pm, schedule works well for most people, perhaps because this schedule allows them to coordinate their leisure time."[18]

A Tale of Two Janitors

An increasing number of people are spending significant portions of their careers working for third-party business services companies. The farther away alternative workers are from the company buying their services, the worse their opportunities, prospects, and benefits. *The New York Times* offered a snapshot of the strikingly different opportunities available to two employees over time as some companies have moved to a focus on core competence while outsourcing the rest.[19]

A janitor working at Apple headquarters in the last decade and a janitor working at Kodak in the 1980s both cleaned offices for innovative and highly profitable companies. Their wages are about the same when adjusted for inflation. However, that is where the similarities end. The janitor at Kodak was a full-time employee of Kodak who enjoyed four weeks of paid vacation per year, reimbursement of some tuition costs to attend college part time, and a bonus payment every March. When the facility she cleaned was shut down, Kodak found another job for her. The janitor cleaning the facilities at Apple had a very different experience. She is an employee of a contractor. She has not taken a vacation in years because she cannot afford the lost wages. Tuition reimbursement, bonuses, or transferring to another role at Apple are not options.

The dramatic difference in the work lives of these two women is not their benefits or bonuses but the stark contrast in opportunities available when working for your employer versus working for a third party hired by your employer. The janitor at Kodak took a computer class and was soon teaching other employees how to use spreadsheet software to track inventory. She finished her college degree, was promoted to a professional-track job in information technology, and about a decade later, was the chief technology officer of the whole company. By contrast, the janitor at Apple had little opportunity to advance beyond becoming a team leader who oversaw a few other janitors, which paid 50 cents more an hour. The investment that Kodak made in an employee 35 years ago is one that fewer companies are choosing to make today.

We are seeing a hollowing out of employment models in the United States with the full-time traditional model waning. This trend can be seen in many fields, including academia. Though the number of PhDs has been on the rise, the number of tenure-track positions has been on the decline. As a result, competition has grown fierce for tenured positions. With fewer tenure-track jobs to go around, the number of contingent positions has soared, including part-time adjunct and untenured full-time.[20] More than half of all university positions are part-time, including adjuncts, lecturers, and graduate assistants, with no job security or benefits.[21]

Workers in the Platform Economy

Though the gig economy is not new, the rise of the gig economy through digital platforms is. Today, the terms "gig economy" and "platform economy" are often used interchangeably. Platforms in today's marketplace provide everything from services (Airbnb, TaskRabbit) and products (Amazon and eBay), to payments (Square, PayPal), software development (Apple, Salesforce), and more.[22] In the context of workforce options, platforms are online talent marketplaces for a wide variety of work and skill levels, from driving and performing handyman chores to designing websites and sophisticated marketing programs. More specialized platforms include markets for data scientists and medical professionals.

A trend highlighted in research by Deloitte Consulting LLP is the need to improve opportunities for employees within their companies so they can try out new roles, projects, and geographies without quitting their job. Recognizing the success of talent marketplaces, companies have started to replicate them internally, encouraging employees to look inside their current workplace, rather than outside, for new opportunities. As a result, companies that historically turned to external recruiting to find people for new roles are now tapping their own workforce. At a growing number of corporations in the United States, the traditional job and work assignment is giving way to these marketplaces where workers can select from a portfolio of projects as well as opportunities for professional development, training, mentorship, and networking.[23]

Schneider Electric, the global energy management company, discovered the power of its own internal marketplace when analytics revealed that nearly half the employees who left the organization did so because they felt they lacked visibility of growth opportunities. In 2018, the company launched an open talent market, which used AI to match employees with short-term projects, stretch assignments, side gigs, full-time roles, and mentors. The goal was to encourage employees try out the internal talent market rather than go out into the external market. Schneider's opportunity market was able to guide employees to projects aligned with their own sense of purpose and goals. Schneider found that attrition decreased in areas where the opportunity market had been launched.[24]

External marketplaces continue to be a ready source of jobs. Talent networks focused not only on tasks but also on specific segments of the workforce are starting to emerge, from working parents to active military and veterans (The Mom Project, The Second Shift, WeGoLook, and more). Talent networks now manage more than $2 billion in outsourced activity, employing hundreds of millions of people globally.[25] Hyman sees a chance "to empower people through these new platforms and enable them to find new opportunities, hopefully at higher wages and outside of cities."[26]

On digital work platforms like Fiverr, Upwork, and Freelancer.com, you can buy nearly any service—often from someone halfway around the world, sometimes for only a few dollars. Fiverr, a digital talent marketplace that advertises itself as the largest, offers more than 120 different areas of expertise, from tech to translators.[27] Founded in 2010 and based in Tel Aviv, Israel, the company provides a platform for freelancers to offer services to customers worldwide. The founders came up with the concept of a marketplace that would provide a two-sided platform for people to both buy and sell a variety of digital services typically offered by freelance contractors.[28] "Freelancing has been

---

Popular Freelance Marketplaces[29]

GrabCAD An engineering marketplace[30]
Experfy A data science marketplace[31]
Upwork An independent talent network[32]
TaskRabbit A freelance labor marketplace for odd jobs and errands[33]
Freelancer.com A freelancer marketplace[34]
Fiverr Freelance services marketplace for businesses[35]
Toptal Freelance marketplace from top 3 percent of talent[36]

around for many decades, and it's a very large market," Micha Kaufman, founder and CEO of Fiverr, said in our interview. "It's only now moving online. What Fiverr has done is to both capitalize on that movement from offline to online, [and] also facilitate that movement."[37] Indeed, the platform economy has made it easier to bring people into these marketplaces and attract global talent.

> Ghost workers are an underclass of invisible workers worldwide performing micro-tasks online, such as captioning photos and flagging inappropriate content.

The Ghost Worker Underclass

"Ghost work" is anthropologist Mary L. Gray's term for the invisible labor that powers our technology platforms. When she was curious about the people who pick up the tasks necessary for these platforms to run, she discovered an underclass of invisible workers worldwide performing micro-tasks online, often for large technology companies. They caption photos and flag inappropriate content. They work behind the scenes, labeling images, moderating, cleaning up databases, and categorizing Internet content.[38]

Gray collaborated with Siddharth Suri, a fellow senior researcher at Microsoft Research, to write *Ghost Work, How to Stop Silicon Valley from Building a New Global Underclass*. Their haunting book exposes a dark side of the gig economy, with online marketplaces driving down the price that professionals can charge for work. Gray and Suri found that those requesting a service have the majority of the power, while workers either accept the rate of pay offered or lose the work. There is often no way for workers to bargain. Economists call this monopsony—a labor market with a dominant purchaser of labor.

The authors were also surprised to discover that workers collaborated and communicated in online forums, offering support and sharing stories, as one might around the water cooler.[39] The authors estimate that more than 20 million freelancers worldwide make up the on-demand gig workforce in the micro-task economy.[40]

> If there is no organization or structure that holds people, it creates pressures that can be very difficult for an individual to face alone.

Identity and Work Routines

The psychological impact of the rise in alternative work arrangements on the individual worker is another aspect of the gig economy that is often hidden or overlooked. Amy Wrzesniewski, a professor at the Yale School of Management, has been exploring what occurs when the relationship between organizations and employees is renegotiated. One of the biggest challenges of the gig economy is the loss of a sense of belonging. "Organizations have traditionally been sites of belonging," Wrzesniewski said in our interview.[41] Her research has found that when contract work became more common, workers would get anxious when they felt they were on the periphery of membership. "Now, in the world of gig work, we have to think about what it means for individuals when they have no membership at all," she noted.

Most people set up their work lives in similar ways and choose to re-create on their own the support an organization can provide when that stability is missing. We rely on four patterns to get our work done, Wrzesniewski said: having a place to work, routines, people, and a purpose.[42] "There was almost an inability to work unless there was a specific place where it could happen," she said. "Right along with that were routines: the set of behaviors that led to arriving at work, focusing, calming, and getting into the mindset of the workday. Workers also need a connection to people who know you and can calm, soothe, challenge, or excite you. They helped people manage the highs and lows of independent work."[43]

Wrzesniewski wondered how much business leaders appreciate the psychological and community function that organizations hold for their employees. The organizational structure can "tamp down anxieties so that you can concentrate on and be free to do the kind of work that you most want to do," she said. If there is no organization or

> As the Covid-19 stay-at-home restrictions kept many people indoors, delivery and other contract workers received unprecedented attention. Cities on lockdown even classified their work as "essential," bringing into relief the fact that most of these workers have been denied basic protections like health care, sick leave, workers' compensation, and stable pay.

structure that holds people, Wrzesniewski noted, it creates pressures that can be very difficult for an individual to face alone.[44]

In a study of remote work and employee well-being that appeared in the *European Journal of Work and Organizational Psychology*, the authors noted a striking lack of research into the well-being of remote e-workers, especially their psychosomatic health. The study recognized benefits offered by remote work, including increased job satisfaction, and a sense of greater autonomy and organizational commitment. At the same time, individuals reported that they missed office interactions and felt isolated because they could not share concerns they had with colleagues. "This may then lead to limited access to social support that is crucial in increasing employee engagement," the report noted.[45]

Making Alternative Work
a Meaningful Opportunity

The desire to know our work schedule in advance, to be independent, and feel that we are in control of our time are aspirations held by many. The insecurity of alternative work arrangements and lack of benefits present us with opportunities to improve the support available to these workers as we create our future world of work. The protections gig workers receive is starting to shift. California is the first state to pass landmark legislation requiring that companies like Uber treat contract workers as employees, granting gig employees in America's largest state access to basic protections like a minimum wage and unemployment insurance.[46] The 2019 bill is an acknowledgment that labor laws developed during the Industrial Revolution in the 1930s no longer fit today's gig economy. New York City passed a proposal setting the country's first-ever app-based drivers minimum wage, which went into effect in 2019. The $27.86 per hour minimum wage for ride-sharing app-based drivers like Uber was an increase from about $11.90 per hour, according to the Taxi and Limousine Commission.[47]

The issue of equitable treatment for alternative workers came to a head during the Covid-19 pandemic. In the months prior to the pandemic outbreak in the United States, California passed the Gig-Worker Bill, requiring companies that hire independent contractors and freelancers to reclassify them as employees if their jobs and duties meet certain conditions.[48] When the economy ground to a halt in 2008, most people without W-2 (full-time) jobs did not qualify for unemployment benefits because they could not claim an employer who had paid unemployment taxes. This changed with the outbreak of Covid-19. For the first time, people classified as independent workers, including freelancers and the self-employed, received unemployment benefits under the CARES Act, signed into law in March 2020. The law grants states the option of extending unemployment compensation to independent contractors and other workers who are ordinarily ineligible for unemployment benefits.[49] As the Covid-19 stay-at-home restrictions kept many people indoors, delivery and other contract workers received unprecedented attention. Cities on lockdown even classified their work as "essential," bringing into relief the fact that most of these workers have been denied basic protections like health care, sick leave, workers' compensation, and stable pay.[50] It is unclear whether these temporary fixes will become permanent.

At a Crossroads

Benefits like unemployment insurance arose in the 1930s in response to the Great Depression. Employer-sponsored health insurance came later and in the United States during the World War II; we are still waiting for benefits for all workers for time off for family and medical leave. These earlier systems were designed to provide a safety net at a time that most people worked for one employer for most of their career but did not take into account people with alternative work arrangements.[51]

"Some people say, no, no, no, all this talk of flexibility, empowerment, are just a corporate dodge," Hyman, the economic historian, said in our interview. "I don't think so. I think that it's actually a deep American value to desire to have autonomy. It's a very human value to want control of your time. I think that we're at a crossroads and we can choose to make it work for us or just to have it work us over."[52]

CHAPTER 4

Working from Almost Anywhere

Redesign Workplaces from Where We Work to How We Work: Onsite, Online, and Everything in Between

We like to give people the freedom to work where they want, safe in the knowledge that they have the drive and expertise to perform excellently, whether they [are] at their desk or in their kitchen. Yours truly has never worked out of an office, and never will.

—Richard Branson, founder, Virgin Group[1]

Rachel was in the middle of her MBA at Emory University when the bustling campus in Atlanta, Georgia, shut down. Social distancing mandates to slow the spread of the coronavirus meant that she and her classmates headed home. When Rachel had a business economics class three days later, it was over Zoom. Emory's prestigious Goizueta Business School, known for encouraging students to work in teams to solve complex business problems, abruptly became a remote-learning institution. Lecture halls, labs, and classrooms were replaced by virtual meetings that offered different ways to learn. Some professors broadcast their lectures live to encourage student

questions, others recorded their lectures for students to watch anytime. A professor who teaches advanced spreadsheets presented students with technical problems they could solve together over live-streaming video, or work on alone, giving students the choice of how they preferred to practice applying and assimilating the concepts.

In the spring of 2020, many of the world's schools and offices emptied. Running for shelter from the novel coronavirus, students like my daughter Rachel headed back home, joining more than 1.6 billion students around the world.[2] I joined the group of remote workers, millions strong, when I relocated from a towering office building in Rockefeller Center in New York City to my home office in my apartment on the upper west side of Manhattan, a small, welcoming study with my books and plenty of light, that I had barely used in the past couple of years. School and office life as we knew it took a pause.

The sudden work-from-home requirement as we sheltered at home turned many long-held assumptions about work on their head and fostered opportunities for transformation. The coronavirus showed us that professors can teach effectively outside of campus classrooms, many employees can perform their work and collaborate online, and even doctors can deliver a portion of their work remotely through telemedicine. Our mental models of where work has to be performed to be optimized were disrupted. For centuries we have improved the physical spaces and the physical experiences that work provides to workers, customers, patients, and students. The powerful linkage was blown up so quickly that many were left disoriented. The technology is ready but humans, social creatures that we are, may not be.

Many were able to work remotely, barely missing a beat, thanks to highly collaborative platforms like Slack and Microsoft Teams; real-time video offered by Zoom, GoToMeeting, Google Hangouts, Skype, Facetime and WhatsApp; and augmented reality (AR) and virtual reality (VR) options. Technology has allowed us to explode the limits of space and workplaces. We discovered that the goal was not to replicate the way we worked before but to improve prior work models.

The connection between the work we do and where we do it has been fraying for years. As the coronavirus wore on, *"When will we go back to work?"* was replaced with, *"Will we ever work the same way again?"* More than half of the American workforce had already been working remotely, including telecommuting and telework, at least some of the time, prior to the coronavirus. Across the world, working from home had been rising steadily for more than a decade.[3]

Platforms that make it easier for teams to collaborate remotely, like Slack and Microsoft Teams, saw rapid user growth during the coronavirus pandemic as demand for remote work skyrocketed.[4] Slack, a collaboration hub that can replace email, boasts the ability to help teams collaborate online as efficiently as you do face-to-face.[5] Kristen Swanson, chief of staff at Slack, said that despite spending less time together physically due to social distancing, technology was making it possible for the level of interaction and collaboration to increase. She described a more even playing field as work moved online during the coronavirus pandemic, since every participant had the same tools and the same type of access to work.[6]

"Hopefully this is a moment where we're able to really diversify our teams in lots of new and interesting ways because the access to jobs is going to be a lot broader than perhaps it's ever been," Swanson said in an interview. "What makes me the most optimistic about this moment is that it really allows us to expand the access of different jobs to the entire world. That truly we can say hey, the most talented individuals, wherever they may be, can participate on global teams."[7]

Wearing Our Work

We are discovering that work is not necessarily a place we go. It's what we do. And soon, it may even be what we wear. Even before tools like Slack and Zoom, we saw examples of new possibilities for the kind of work that can be done remotely, starting with HoloLens. If you have the opportunity to try on a HoloLens, you will feel as though you are slipping on a pair of very special ski goggles. These goggles won't protect your eyes from glare and ice but they will alter reality. They are not for gamers; Microsoft designed them to help people work more efficiently.[8]

Called "holo" lenses because they project holograms, or three-dimensional images, onto your workspace, these mixed-reality headsets allow you to experience your office as overlaid with helpful messages, such as how to fix a broken light switch or a faulty car engine. They can project images of blueprints, manuals, or other helpful instructions on top of real world objects so that workers in the field, in auto shops, on factory floors, even in doctors' offices, can refer to them while working on complex challenges.[9] The HoloLens2 is the latest iteration of the headsets that Microsoft first introduced in 2015, in its race with Google Glass and Facebook's Oculus to perfect a head-mounted computer.

An often-heard prediction about the offices of the future is that workers will be wearing their technology.[10] Indeed, Oculus's chief scientist Michael Abrash predicts that augmented reality (AR) glasses will be the great transformational technology of the next 50 years. He believes that in the future, "instead of *carrying* stylish smartphones everywhere, we'll be *wearing* stylish glasses." If the technology keeps progressing, and why would it not, we may soon wear our offices wherever we go, the same way we now tote our smartphones, tablets, and laptops everywhere.[11]

As this technology continues to be perfected, organizations will need to orchestrate a wide range of options as they reimagine workplaces, from the traditional co-located offices to those that rely on virtual interactions, to a hybrid combination of both. Indeed as more work is handled remotely, the physical workplace has been evolving, from the cubicle farm and open workspace, to the corporate campus, coffee shop, home office, co-working space, and virtually anywhere on the go. We can work everywhere—on collaborative, real-time video platforms, augmented- and virtual-reality platforms. Organizations will need to be able to design work, workforce, and workplace experiences that are highly productive, innovative, and meet the social needs of workers.

> As work becomes more borderless, with more collaboration happening virtually, where work gets done will continue to change, too.

The Evolution of Virtual Offices

The first Picturephone made a splash when it was introduced at the World's Fair in Flushing, New York, in 1964.[12] I remember traveling with my family when I was seven years old to see one of the first demonstrations of Bell Telephone's Picturephone in action. The pre-Skype, pre-FaceTime, pre-Zoom, pre-WhatsApp device made it possible for two friends in New York City and

Chicago to see one another on a small black-and-white video screen and have a conversation. Advances in technology have continued and opened the doors for connecting via remote work. Today, people who spend about 70 percent of their working hours remote for at least three to four days a week report the highest engagement rates compared with those who never work off-site.

Virtual offices date back to the 1970s when the first personal computer was introduced. Employees were able to work outside of the office and eventually take their work on the go with a laptop or tablet. In the early 1990s, the World Wide Web was born, connecting remote workers with email and virtual office tools. About a decade later, remote employees were able to work without being tied to a physical location with the arrival of wireless Internet and broadband.[13]

In 2003, a surge of remote workers inspired Skype to make a better video conferencing software for virtual employees. The next year, virtual meeting software GoToMeeting enabled employees to "meet" in a virtual conference room to share presentations, files, and brainstorm together. Within a few years, Slack helped teams and managers to communicate from anywhere.[14] The future of remote work continues to grow as the technology to support these needs keeps getting better. Advances in virtual reality technologies continue to change how we work.[15]

Most industries have embraced the idea of working remotely, including the finance, insurance, and real estate industries. The share of workers in those fields who report working remotely at least sometimes rose eight percentage points, to 47 percent, from 2012 to 2016. In the transportation, computer, information systems, and mathematics industries, more than half of employees work remotely some of the time.[16]

So, where is the office heading if fewer staff are actually going to be there? As work becomes more borderless, with more collaboration happening virtually, where work gets done will continue to change, too. How we divide our time among different workplace options will be determined by two factors: the kind of work we are doing, and how we balance our lives and our work. Work that is highly interactive, such as brainstorming sessions, may continue to take place in common workspaces and creative spaces that have been specifically built for people to share and create ideas. Tech allows the person working from home to participate in these sessions remotely using tools like Zoom, Skype, and Webex.

The changing relationship between work and location is on display at Mercy Hospital's Virtual Care Center, a hospital without patients. Located in Chesterfield, Missouri, off a superhighway, Mercy has doctors, nurses, and a cafeteria just like any other hospital but there are no beds. The staff looks at monitors, checks vital signs, responds to alarms, performs examinations, and talks with patients virtually rather than in person. The first virtual hospital in the United States, Mercy opened in 2015. Mercy offers what Dr. Eric Topol, author of *Deep Medicine*, calls "a glimpse of the future." Patients in intensive care units at other hospitals or at home are monitored remotely. AI surveillance algorithms can pick up a warning and alert a physician. Topol believes that we will see more hospitals without patients by 2030.[17] "If you look at the hospital of the future, it's only going to have intensive care units, operating rooms, an emergency room, and special imaging equipment," Dr. Topol said in our interview. "The rest of it will be in the patient's home."[18]

The Evolution of Physical Offices

The cubicle farm is being put out to pasture. Workspaces are evolving to better accommodate the types of tasks that require people to be together in the same place, at the same time. Physical office sites are now designed to look more like studios, brainstorming venues, theaters, or airy locations for sales pitches.

Offices are no longer where employees need to be. In fact, 70 percent of full-time employees globally work remotely at least once a week. Studies show that telecommuting boosts productivity and job satisfaction, while digital advances have made telecommuting possible for a greater number of workers than ever before.[19] Collaborative platforms allow groups of people around the globe to talk with each other at the same time in ways that were not possible 10 years ago. Working remotely offers greater flexibility to employees, while lowering real estate costs for employers.[20] "The office has changed into a place that you had to go to for the paper supplies or typewriters or other materials you needed to do the work, to a gathering point for collaboration, disseminating culture, and exploring ideas," says Mark Holm-strom, a principal at Deloitte Consulting. "Workspaces today often provide a sense of wellness and peace. They have a very Zen-like open environment. They're a comfortable, warm place to go."[21]

Zen-like is not what the "modern efficiency desk" would have been called. Introduced back in 1915 by the Equitable Life Insurance Company, the aim of these desks was to enable managers to easily see their workers at all times.[22] The command-and-control management style of the time tasked managers with making sure workers were not wasting a minute on company time. This approach to work is still the norm at many organizations that continue to measure productivity in terms of face time. Internet connectivity, laptops, and smartphones have made it possible to work anywhere, and often out of the sight of a manager. Still, many of the conventions of the workplace have not changed much since 1915, including the persistence of time-bound schedules and office-bound work locations. Of course, some employees cannot work remotely due to the nature of their work. Retail employees need to be on-site to assist customers, and industrial workers may work on an assembly line or at a particular site.

The office as we know it has evolved from endless rows of desks to the cubicle farms of the 1980s to the more informal, open-plan workspaces of today that encourage collaboration. In recent years, we have seen more breakout areas for employees to ideate. At the same time, many companies have responded to the increase in the number of remote workers by reducing their real estate investment. As a result, we see more "hot desking," where companies make desks and workstations available on a first-come, first-served basis with many employees having no assigned places.[23] We have also seen the growth of the corporate campus and co-working spaces.

Though we often credit today's high-tech firms with giving life to the corporate campus, they date back to Xerox's PARC (Palo Alto Research Center), established in 1970. The highly customized campuses were created later by Apple and Google, designed like a university, with buildings located close to one another on a large piece of land. This common location, similar to college life, encourages a shared culture, collaboration, and a sense of belonging.[24]

Highly curated physical spaces, known as makerspaces, provide collaborative work spaces inside schools, libraries, and other locations to encourage "making," learning, and exploring. These spaces, open to children, adults, and entrepreneurs, are equipped with a variety of maker equipment, including 3D printers, laser cutters, soldering irons, and sewing machines. Even simple creative spaces including cardboard, Legos, and art supplies can be makerspaces. The goal of these spaces is to explore the maker mindset of creating something out of nothing. Makerspaces help us develop the critical twenty-first-century skills in the fields of science, technology, engineering, and math (STEM). They provide both handson learning and critical thinking. Skills that can be developed in makerspaces include 3D modeling, coding, and robotics.

Makerspaces are also being used as incubators and accelerators for business startups.[25]

An increasing consideration in workplaces of the future is expected to be sustainability as a top business priority. Sustainability as it applies to the workplace means constructing efficient buildings that are well insulated so they retain heat in the winter, and well ventilated so they cool the office in summer without much need for air-conditioning, reducing the organization's carbon footprint.

> As teams find themselves spending less time under the same roof with their colleagues, organizations will face the challenge of rethinking how they build a strong culture and meaningful team connections.

Collaborating Across Platforms Inside Organizations and Ecosystems

Three technological advances have dramatically influenced our ability to collaborate across space and time zones. Highly collaborative platforms like Slack and Teams have made it possible for teams across the globe to work together in real time. The increasing availability of real-time video offered by Facetime and WhatsApp, among others, allows us to call any colleague, anywhere in the world, at almost no cost, something that was not possible five years ago. And finally, we are only starting to discover how the advances in AR and VR options will allow us to connect and work in new ways.

About every 15 years or so, a new game-changing platform is introduced. Some predict artificial reality will become the next big platform. AR technology essentially tricks the senses into seeing, hearing, and interacting with digital objects and scenarios as if they were as real as the people sitting across from us. In the early 1980s, we saw the arrival of personal computing, with Apple and Microsoft leading the way. In the mid 1990s, we saw the explosion of the Internet, led by Google and Amazon. In 2007, the iPhone changed our lives forever.[26]

The biggest shift technology has introduced is that physical proximity is no longer required to get work done. Digital communication, collaboration platforms, and digital reality technologies have made it possible for teams scattered around the world to work together. The cautionary reminder for organizations is that changing the physical workplace—in many cases reducing the size of the workplace—should not be viewed as an opportunity to increase efficiency or to reduce real estate costs without considering what enables employees to be innovative and effective. Workplace culture is highly connected to both innovation and business results.[27]

As teams find themselves spending less time under the same roof with their colleagues, organizations will face the challenge of rethinking how they build a strong culture and meaningful team connections. What will take the place of the informal spaces like the office kitchen or cafeteria where spontaneous conversations happen, new connections are forged, and department silos are broken down. Because teamwork will be a critical part of our work in the future, finding new ways to encourage interaction and provide more opportunities to engage with colleagues who are not in the same location will become increasingly important.

Collaborative platforms like Github and InnoCentive allow people to work together as they never have before. GitHub enables software developers to share code,[28] while companies are using InnoCentive, a crowd competition platform, to solve problems by submitting them to crowdsourcing.[29] Companies are increasingly realizing that they do not need to limit themselves to their own talent to solve problems. When General Electric wanted to figure out how to save fuel by reducing the weight of a fastener that connects an airplane engine to the wing of an airplane, the company went to the engineering website, GrabCAD. GE created a contest to see who could reduce the fastener's weight by the greatest amount, and offered $20,000 in prize money. The winner was a 21-year-old from Indonesia who was not an aeronautical engineer; he reduced the weight of the fastener by more than 80 percent.[30]

Finding Human Connection

The changing shape of offices could have a profound impact on workers' psyches, their connections to one another, and their sense of well-being. Employers will increasingly face the challenge of ensuring that workers feel connected to their colleagues and to a common goal. The importance of these connections should not be understated, says Amy Wrzesniewski, the Michael H. Jordan Professor of Management at the Yale School of Management. She believes people will always want to have a place to gather and feel that they belong. "In previous generations, people would spend decades and even their entire careers embedded in the same organization," Wrzesniewski says. "In those cases, the sense of membership buoyed both individuals' identities and their psychological health."[31]

Wrzesniewski notes that organizations have typically served as "identity workspaces," providing employees with an emotional holding environment that bolsters their sense of security and confidence. What happens when we no longer go to a common workspace? When Wrzesniewski studied gig workers who have more tenuous ties to organizations and do not have a typical office to go to, she found an increased sense of anxiety and isolation. For employers, this suggests a need to prioritize creating connections and community as traditional workplaces become more virtual and include more contingent workers.[32]

The rise in the number of contingent workers, including contractors, freelancers, and gig workers, has created a longing for many for greater security, socializing, and daily routines that full-time employees working together in the same location have enjoyed, Wrzesniewski says. Her research has shown that organizations play a large role in helping shape an employee's identity. She has explored what happens when the organization is no longer present. "Without institutional employment," she says, "you never get to enjoy the benefits of real membership in an organization. You get a little of it from the reliability of the platform or network and the ability to engage with it whenever you want. But you never fully belong. And my research shows that a sense of belonging is a key driver to experiencing meaningful work."[33]

As workplaces evolve, social and psychological well-being must be considered. In Wrzesniewski's research with Gianpiero Petriglieri and Sue Ashford, she found that independent workers, regardless of the type of work they did, had strong patterns in terms of how they organized their work lives. Having a particular place to work and a routine helped independent workers to connect and focus on the work that needs to be done that day.[34] "We were fascinated by just how much attention and care was taken to create or identify a place where the work could happen," Wrzesniewski says. "This element was critical—there was almost an inability to work unless there was a specific place where it could happen. And right along with that were routines: the set of behaviors that led to arriving, focusing, calming, and getting into the mindset of the work day."[35] When the relationship between workers and organizations becomes more distant, the question arises of whose responsibility it will be to provide the support that organizational employment used to supply that will help independent workers thrive—employers, society, or individual workers themselves.

From Office Wars to "Forever" Remote Work

When we move into new ways of working, the challenge is no longer whether the technology is available but whether we are ready to make social, psychological, and emotional shifts. We saw an example of how challenging it can be to work in new ways with the so-called "office wars," one of the last gasps of scientific management. It was a reminder of the perception not so long ago that your coat must be hanging on the back of your chair at the office or you are not truly "at work."

Marissa Mayer, as Yahoo's CEO, created a stir in 2013 when she revoked the company's telecommuting policy, seeking to bring workers back to the office. In a memo to Yahoo staff, employees were told that "to become the absolute best place to work, communication and collaboration will be important, so we need to be working side-by-side. That is why it is critical that we are all present in our offices." The memo went on to tout the "decisions and insights [that] come from hallway and cafeteria discussions, meeting new people, and impromptu team meetings." Mayer was widely criticized for taking a step backward at a time when remote work was proving to be easier and more effective than ever. Yet she was not alone in wanting to see employees return to the office.[36] Aetna CEO Mark Bertolini revoked the insurance company's remote work policy in 2016, believing it was harming collaboration.[37]

The debate that followed both of these announcements raised issues surrounding how the workplace has been evolving. Historically, working long hours—and being visible while doing so—has been rewarded. Arriving before your boss was just what dedicated employees did. Failing to arrive early and stay late was viewed as a lack of commitment to the organization. However, the idea that collaboration can only occur if people are in the same physical space has since been disproven by technology, including Slack, Zoom, and the HoloLens. Though we have been taught that the best way to get a message across is to sit face-to-face in a room with people and receive those verbal and nonverbal cues that provide the feedback we need to do our best work, it turns out this may not be true.

"We've started to see meetings drop off the calendar because it's no longer the most effective way for us to get our work done," said Kristen Swanson from Slack. "People are participating in digital spaces, whether it's Slack channels or Google docs, where they can build on each other's ideas. We call it working in layers. Somebody puts a layer out, and then somebody takes another pass." Swanson has found that this type of collaboration produces something that's "much stronger than if we would have actually sat in a room together and talked about it and then one person would have gone away and done it."[38]

We can collaborate on platforms and in online communities in ways we could not imagine before. As people thrive in virtual brainstorming sessions, including participants from all over the world, we are blowing up past notions that brainstorming could only be effective "working side by side." Twitter CEO Jack Dorsey was one of the first leaders to recognize the advantages of remote work when he dramatically announced to staff that had been working from home for two months due to the coronavirus pandemic that they could do so permanently.[39] "If our employees are in a role and situation that enables them to work from home and they want to continue to do so forever, we will make that happen," the Twitter memo stated.[40]

Collaborate and Innovate Anywhere

The opportunity before us is to redesign remote work so that it can offer new ways to collaborate that are even more effective than before, integrated in our lives as we work anywhere, anytime. We can discover the productivity, collaboration, and innovation that are possible from any mix of work locations. A significant challenge that remains is addressing our psychological safety. Concerns are growing about potential isolation and burnout, as well as the social and emotional price of working across virtual spaces when we may miss the companionship and experience of sitting across from a colleague and feeling their presence. However, the opportunity available to us and the shift are clear: Work for most of us will not be a place; it will be part of *how* we work. Productivity and innovation are more than a function of a physical place.

PART II

Build Long-Term Resilience for Uncertain Futures

Reimagining Careers, Organizations, and Leadership

CHAPTER 5

Plan for Many Careers, Not One

Realistic and Energizing
Transition Strategies
for Multichapter Lives

*Today's workers need to approach the workplace . . . like someone
who is training for the Olympics but doesn't know what sport they
are going to enter.*

—Thomas Friedman,[1] political commentator, author

I magine holding the same job for life. This may sound like a quaint
notion but it was the norm for many of our parents and grandparents.
Loyalty to a single employer was rewarded. Back in the 1940s, PepsiCo
started a tradition of giving an 18-karat gold watch to long-term employees
upon retirement, along with a generous pension, to encourage employees to
spend their career with the company.[2] The gold watch tradition continued
for decades in corporate America. The retirement phase of a career, created
thanks largely to labor unions, has shaped everything from work legislation
and taxation to financial planning. In that linear career model, the longer

employees worked and gained experience, the more they earned. That's the model I heard about growing up, when the advice everyone gave me was to pick a career, then go long and deep. That advice didn't prepare me for the world I am seeing today.

Enter the long and winding career. Today, the average length of employment with a company or organization is just over four years.[3] As employees move around more, they are working for an average of 12 employers over a lifetime.[4] And as we live longer lives, the number of careers we will have is likely to continue to increase too, says Lynda Gratton, a leading psychologist and organizational theorist who has been studying the future of work for more than a decade. She has been fascinated by the impact that our longer lifespans will have on our careers.[5]

"Most of us will live significantly longer than our parents, with many babies born today expected to live for at least 100 years," says Gratton, a professor of management practice at London Business School of Economics, and the co-author, with Andrew Scott, of *The 100-year Life: Living and Working in an Age of Longevity*.[6] With the half-life of a learned skill just five years— meaning much of what we learned 10 years ago is obsolete and half of what we learned five years ago is irrelevant— we all need to become lifelong learners, Gratton says, prepared to transform throughout our lives.[7]

Our Changing Career Model

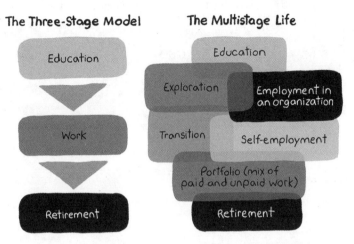

Source: Chart courtesy of MIT *Sloan Management Review*, © MIT; "The Corporate Implications of Longer Lives," by Lynda Gratton and Andrew Scott, Spring 2017.

More Sliding and STEMpathy

In today's tech-driven employment landscape, we cannot apply the rules our parents and grandparents lived by to secure a steady job. What are the new rules to help us thrive? The once-and-done model of learning a trade or going to college and graduate school, and then settling into a career for the rest of a working life will not be the model of the future. The school-work-retirement triad will be replaced by learning and work occurring simultaneously in the flow of our lives. People will dial up or dial down their focus on learning, work, as well as personal and social pursuits, throughout a 50- or 60-year career.

A few years ago, I was invited to speak at a graduate student led conference at the Sloan School of Management, the graduate MBA program at MIT. The theme was the future of people in business. My topic was the future of careers. The challenge was to deliver an eight-minute presentation on what careers would look like in 2050 and then highlight what students today should consider to be on track for future careers. The heart of my discussion was the graphic on twenty-first-century careers shown in the following figure: longer, integrated, and more varied.

Twenty-first-century Careers

The ebb and flow of a portfolio of learning, work, and personal pursuits

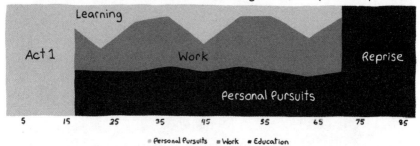

50–60 year careers "mass customized" with personalized levels of family/personal pursuits, work, and education – levers we "dial up and down" throughout our "working" lives

Source: Chart courtesy of Jeff Schwartz; presentation to the MIT Future of People Conference, 2016.

I ended my presentation with a perspective on fulsome careers in 2050. This was a view of careers in an age of abundance, not scarcity. Descriptors of careers in 2050 might include:

1. Long (60 to 70 years)
2. Out of lockstep
3. Nonlinear
4. Dynamic
5. Accelerating
6. Technology augmented
7. Partnerships/teams
8. Portfolio
9. Projects/assignments
10. Mass customized

I also offered a list of books on twenty-first-century careers, starting with Gratton and Scott's book on 100-year lives. Like Gratton, I see us moving away from the three-stage model of education, career, and retirement—the model that is still dominant today—instead embracing a multistage model in which people will continue to learn over the many decades they work.

As our economy continues to be transformed, new jobs will be created, many companies will die, sectors will change, new technologies will require new skills, and the way we work will undergo further changes. How can we plan for a 60-year career in a fast-changing environment? Gratton predicts that more career transitions will be necessary both to gain new skills when the old ones become obsolete and to avoid boredom. "My advice to people is really focus on learning," Gratton says, "life-long learning."[21]

Jeff's Bookshelf to Prepare for Careers in 2050[8]

1. *The 100Year Life: Living and Working in an Age of Longevity* by Lynda Gratton and Andrew Scott[9]

2. *A New Culture of Learning: Cultivating the Imagination for a World of Constant Change* by Douglas Thomas and John Seely Brown[10]

3. *The Second Machine Age: Work, Progress, and Prosperity in a Time of Brilliant Technologies* by Erik Brynjolfsson and Andrew McAfee[11]

4. *Rise of the Robots: Technology and the Threat of a Jobless Future,* Architects of Intelligence, The Lights in the Tunnel–Automation, Accelerating Technology, and the Economy of the Future [12,13,14]

5. *Thank You for Being Late: An Optimist's Guide to Thriving in the Age of Accelerations* by Thomas L. Friedman[15]

6. *The Corporate Lattice: Achieving High Performance in the Changing World of Work* by Cathleen Benko and Molly Anderson[16]

7. *Mass Career Customization: Aligning the Workplace With Today's Nontraditional Workforce* by Cathleen Benko and Anne Weisberg[17]

8. *The Alliance: Managing Talent in the Networked Age* by Reid Hoffman, Ben Casnocha, and Chris Yeh[18]

9. *A Whole New Mind: Why Right-Brainers Will Rule the Future* by Daniel H. Pink[19]

10. *Designing Your Life: Build the Perfect Career, Step by Step* by Bill Burnett and Dave Evans[20]

Gratton believes we will engage in continuing education approaches, such as upskilling and reskilling, as well as career progression, including what she calls "sliding" and "morphing." Sliding is the chance to explore career adjacencies. For example, a print reporter could leverage writing skills to segue into the role of content creator online. Morphing involves a more dramatic transformation, such as adding a fresh skillset that opens up new opportunities so that you can move into a completely different career.[22]

Among the new skills that will be useful to develop for the future of work is what Thomas Friedman calls STEMpathy. Friedman, a Pulitzer Prize–winning weekly columnist for *The New York Times*, describes STEMpathy as a combination of skills in science, technology, engineering, and math with human empathy, which is the ability to connect with another human being. "When you put those two things together in a manager or in an employee, I think you have the sweet spot of where work has to go," Friedman says.[23]

In Friedman's view, no machine can match the accountant's wisdom when handling the planning and values portions of the job, or the empathy and experience of the doctor who can extract the best cancer diagnosis from an AI application and then relate it to a patient.[24] The most critical skills for employees to develop are a *combination* of technical core capabilities for STEM, and basic computer and software application skills, along with behavioral skills—namely, a willingness to be flexible, agile, and adaptable to change—as well as time-management skills and the ability to prioritize.[25]

From Flat Water to Whitewater

To navigate the many twists and turns our careers will take, we can take a page from agile and adaptable whitewater kayakers, says John Seely Brown, known as JSB, the former co-chairman of Deloitte's Center for the Edge and lifelong researcher who specializes in studies at the intersection of technology and organizational change.[26] As the former chief scientist at Xerox Corp. and director of its Palo Alto Research Center (PARC) for nearly two decades, JSB knows about navigating change. PARC helped pioneer several of computing's most important inventions and technological advancements, from the first personal computer to the graphical user interface (GUI) and the computer mouse.[27]

JSB illustrates the change in how we must now approach our work as moving from flat water to whitewater. As an experienced kayaker would explain, flat water moves but is relatively calm and predictable. In contrast, white water is adrenaline-fueled, constantly changing, and never the same. White water brings challenges as well as the chance to surf a wave, play in a roll, or drop into waterfall.[28] "What has helped us historically structure jobs, work, and learning is . . . [that] we have a sense of predictability and stability," says JSB. "We can train people for that." It's far more challenging to train for work in a world that is both dynamic and uneven.[29]

JSB traces the evolution of the education and work life that our grandparents had, which resembled a steamboat, to the sailboat of our parents' generation, to today's model of kayaking in white water. In a steamboat, the water is calm. You set a course and your speed, and you're off. "Not much happening there," JSB says. But in a sailboat, "you're reading the wind. You're working with the wind. And you know how to do that. And, sometimes you get blown off course. And what do you do? You tack."[30]

In contrast, whitewater is far more dynamic. "In the whitewater world, you're [constantly] being hit by something—you have to know how to read *context* in a much deeper way," JBS says. "In the whitewater world . . . you have to get a feeling for what those currents are really doing. You have to be able to work with those currents."[31] The result is that more and more, employees at every stage of their careers will need always to be learning with and from others. It will become more critical than ever, he believes, to develop skills to connect with others "both inside and outside of your own silos, work groups, tribes, and organizations." Cultivating a disposition that's outgoing and well connected will prepare us to productively encounter radically novel and unknown situations, JSB says.[32]

Bulletproof Your Career

How we work, and the very nature of the work we do, are both changing. And as jobs change—remote call center operator, UX designer, app developer, machine learning specialist, telemedicine practitioners, are all jobs that did not exist 20 years ago—so will the skills needed to keep working. Indeed, the technological revolution is forcing us to consider the value and capabilities we as humans bring to the workplace in the age of intelligent machines. To meet the demands of a future world of work with multiple careers, new and more dynamic education models are emerging to help us continue to learn throughout our working lives.

To secure employment in the future, pursue a creative career or a relationship-based career, says Martin Ford, a leading futurist and author who focuses on artificial intelligence and robotics, and the impact of these technologies on the job market. "For now, humans are still best at creativity, but there's a caveat there," says Ford. "I can't guarantee you that in 20 years a computer won't be the most creative entity on the planet."[33]

Ford notes that jobs that require creativity, such as an artist, a chef, a scientist, or a business strategist, are good bets because computers cannot replicate human inspiration. Similar to Freidman's view, Ford sees future demand for relationship-based jobs that require the building and nurturing of complex bonds with other people, such as doctors and other medical professionals, or business professionals who might need to cultivate close relationships with clients, such as a financial planner. Another category in which Ford sees future job opportunities is what he calls unpredictable jobs. These are jobs that are likely to throw up unpredictable scenarios, such as those faced by the emergency services, or trades that could be called out to emergencies in random locations such as plumbers or gas engineers.[34]

Innovative Approaches to Learning

In the race for better jobs and better pay, conventional wisdom might lead us to conclude that the engineering major would swiftly trounce the English major. As with so many quick assumptions involving the future of work, this one bears investigating. The winner of this race for top career and compensation is not a shoo-in, says David Deming, Harvard professor who studies labor and education economics. In fact, his research shows that while the humanities major may lag at first, this will not be the case over the long haul.[35]

Engineering majors will earn more in their first jobs but the advantage fades over time, according to Deming. By age 40, for example, liberal arts majors see their earnings catch up to their peers in STEM (science, technology, engineering and mathematics) fields. This happens because tech skills tend to quickly become out of date. This is not true of the skills a liberal arts degree develops, such as communication, critical thinking, and problem solving, which have long-term value in a wide variety of careers, according to Deming at the Graduate School of Education at Harvard.[36] Remember the tortoise and the hare in that Aesop's fable? Think of the economics or history major as the slow but steady tortoise that can beat or at least keep pace with the quick-to-start hare, played in this scenario by the engineering major. This is not to say that STEM graduates do not have high earnings throughout their careers; they do. However, Deming's research challenges the notion that a liberal arts degree will not have a place in the future of work.

We tend to talk about education and skills relative to a *first* job, rather than in terms of living a productive, evolving, and engaging life. It is easy to lose sight of the trajectory of a work life if we focus on the first job a person lands. After all, Steve Jobs famously bummed around after he dropped out of Reed College, learning about eastern religions, eating nuts and berries, studying calligraphy, and following his interests before becoming one of the leading inventors of the twentieth century. We need to prepare for the long-distance race of our careers rather than the quick sprint of our first jobs.

We cannot support twenty-first-century careers with nineteenth- and twentiethcentury educational models. New models are needed—and quickly. By 2022, as many as 120 million workers in the world's 12 largest economies may need to be retrained or reskilled as a result of AI and intelligent automation, according to a 2019 IBM study.[37] Some companies and businesses are providing upskilling opportunities, including training sessions, at the workplace. AT&T, for example, is reskilling its workforce via online learning opportunities, anticipating and recognizing that its workers need to change roles every four years. While employees expect their employers to help them gain the new skills they need to do their jobs, many organizations worldwide are scrambling to keep up. Software engineers must now redevelop skills every 12 to 18 months. Professionals in marketing, sales, manufacturing, law, accounting, and finance report similar demands.[38]

From Vertical Learning to Integrative Learning

A growing gap exists between the preparation provided by institutions of higher education and the rapidly changing job market. Some pioneers are trying to change that. Erica Muhl believes that to future-proof your career, start by embracing post-disciplinary thinking. She is dean of the University of Southern California Jimmy Iovine and Andre Young Academy for the Arts, Technology, and the Business of Innovation, which, in just five years since its launch, has put integrative and team learning at the core of its curriculum. "Rarely [in history has anything truly complex ever] been solved by a single discipline," says Wanda Austin, the recent interim president at USC. The Academy's goal is to educate makers, not just doers.[39]

Rather than focus on multiple disciplines—technology, design, communications, business—the program has synthesized core disciplines into a wholly new discipline. "What we have endeavored to do is to find where these disciplines intersect, where they not just assist each other but where they augment each other and where they in fact make each other more powerful, more effective," Muhl says. "So you can only look at that as a new disciplinary area. Why have we done that? Because we feel that the world is frankly getting more complex. The problems that the world is dealing with, that society is dealing with, are more complex."[40] As a result, we need to understand problems from multiple perspectives, including multiple human perspectives, Muhl says. "This is a central component for succeeding in the 21st century business environment."[41]

The program also recognizes that twenty-first-century students, as digital and AI natives, learn differently. As Muhl points out, they are autodidacts. We need to design and support learning that allows students to fill in the blanks, she says. The integrative model teaches students to systematize the problem-solving process and nurtures skills that facilitate ongoing education. "Lifelong learning is definitely something that we think about all the time," Muhl says. "The rate at which our students have to shift gears across the curriculum actually makes them very flexible. That is definitely something we have worked very hard to build into the curriculum."[42]

Established with a gift from the founders of Beats Electronics, the school aims to teach the skills necessary to thrive in a business world that is increasingly collaborative, complex, and hybridized. Its Master of Science degree in integrated design, business, and technology, for example, helps students learn to solve complex problems, adapt to uncertainty, and understand the key issues that sit at the intersection of engineering, business management, and the arts. It's a departure from the "vertical" learning that has dominated academia for decades. Muhl says the emphasis is on teaching cross-functional thinking because that is increasingly necessary to thrive in the modern economy.[43]

The program recognizes both the changes in the twenty-first-century learner and the need for new, integrated approaches. One of my favorite stories about this program is one Muhl tells about its original design. When she assembled experts from across the various disciplines—from technology to the arts—they came back with a proposed curriculum of 260 credits. That's more than 60 courses or about twice the number in a typical four-year undergraduate degree. She sent them, as a team, back to the drawing board. The resulting curriculum of 128 credits offered a new approach: more integrated, focused on both team teaching and on team learning. The curriculum offers many opportunities to make, prototype, iterate, and incorporate varied perspectives. Students are treated as motivated learners, members of teams, and creators.[44]

> What liberal arts actually gives you is a way of thinking, And what computing, because it's its own discipline, gives you is also a way of thinking. . . . To get people to think abstractly. To think about models and languages and machines as being all the same thing.

Computer Learning for the Masses

One of the more innovative examples of scaling technical training is Charles Isbell's story of bringing affordable advanced computer learning to the masses, both on campus and online. Isbell, a professor at Georgia Tech and dean of the College of Computing, has spent his academic career increasing access to computing. Isbell took Georgia Tech's Master of Science degree program in computer science, which is a top 10 ranked program, and made the degree available online for less than $7,000.[45]

"We decided to admit every single student we thought could succeed," Isbell says. "We are admitting somewhere between 65 and 70 percent of all our applicants. They're in their 30s. They're working jobs. They're all over the country. And we went from zero [students] five years ago to almost 9,000 students today. And of those 9,000 students, about 97 percent of them would not have pursued a graduate degree if this particular pathway did not exist."[46]

Isbell believes the degree has value even if you do not intend to work as a computer scientist. "What liberal arts actually gives you is a way of thinking," Isbell says. "And what computing, because it's its own discipline, gives you is [also] a way of thinking . . . To get people to think abstractly. To think about models and languages and machines as being all the same thing. And be able to describe tasks that they want to accomplish in a way that you can actually specify them to a machine."[47]

Learning Precampus and Beyond: The University of Everywhere

The opportunities for twenty-first-century education extend well beyond the campus. High-quality, free, or low-cost skills development opportunities are also available outside of formal academia thanks to innovators such as Khan Academy, available to young children through high school students; MOOCs (massive open online courses) like Udacity, Udemy, Coursera, and EdX,[48] and new corporate learning platforms like NovoEd.

Khan Academy teaches millions of students a month—at no charge—flipping the traditional classroom model on its head by offering 5-to-20-minute digestible lessons that are driven by the learner. Sal Khan, a Harvard and MIT-educated hedge fund analyst, breaks down lessons into self-paced learning modules. His mission is "free, world class education for anyone, anywhere." Grants from Google and the Bill and Melinda Gates Foundation have supported Khan Academy, which now has more than 42 million registered users, with tutorials on subjects including basic math, economics, art history, computer science, and medicine.[49]

Though the technology that enables online education is new, the concept of distance learning dates back 170 years to a correspondence course in Great Britain where the instructor sent lessons though the postal system and received students' assignments by mail.[50] Today, universities are under pressure as they navigate, by necessity, varying stages of digital transformation. Faculty members that have never designed or delivered a course online are being asked to reimagine how they teach due to the coronavirus crisis.[51]

As universities scrambled to provide academic continuity to students, many emergency remote teaching practices were put into place. In some cases, this meant relying on existing online courses from other trusted sources, such as Coursera, an online learning platform founded in 2012 by Stanford professors Andrew Ng and Daphne Koller that offers open online courses, specializations, and degrees.[52] As universities strategize for an intermediate period of transition, they also need to begin future-proofing their institutions for the long term.

What lies ahead was imagined by Kevin Carey in his book, *The End of College*, where he introduces the idea of the University of Everywhere, the place where students of the future will go to college. The University of Everywhere will be powered by open, online courses: "Anything that can be digitized—books, lecture videos, images, sounds, and increasingly powerful digital learning environments—will be available to anyone in the world with an Internet connection." Carey's vision is that *anyone, anywhere, at any time* will be able to use these free digital resources to learn and earn a credential. He sees advances in artificial intelligence as a way to "diagnose the strengths and weaknesses of each individual learner and customize his or her education accordingly." He profiles innovations in teaching, learning, and credentialing, including computerized cognitive tutors, open badges, coding boot camps, and more. In the University of Everywhere, resources that have been scarce and expensive for centuries would be free, available to anyone with an Internet connection.[53]

From Replication to Reinvention

Understanding the concept of general purpose technology (GPT) can shed light on the changes underway in how we will learn and upskill in the future. GPTs are technologies and innovations that have a significant impact on our economy on a national or global level. Electricity and information technology probably are the two most important GPTs so far.[54]

Economists talk about how long it takes for the GPTs to be widely adopted and create new levels of productivity. For example, consider the shifts involved in the evolution of the steam engine. Steam power developed slowly over a couple of hundred years, progressing through the early seventeenth century to designs introduced just when the need for mechanical power was growing due to the Industrial Revolution.[55] Then it took decades to take advantage of GPTs and to use them in new ways. Often, new technologies are applied in the same way earlier technologies were applied. This is why the first steam engines in factories were in the same locations as the earlier factories—on rivers, which was essential when factories were powered by watermills. It took decades to change our mental models and recognize that the new technology—in this case, steam—could be moved to factories and locations far beyond rivers and waterways. Our initial instincts are often to apply new technologies in familiar ways.

A similar challenge exists today because discovering new ways to apply new technologies takes time. Educators who had to go digital overnight during the coronavirus at first took a "lift and shift" emergency mode approach.

They delivered in the virtual classroom the same class they had delivered in a physical classroom. The first step is to replicate what we had before, applying new technologies in *old* ways. The second step is to reinvent, applying new technologies in *new* ways. We now face the opportunity to redesign the practices of work and how we do it, as well as how we learn to take advantage of today's GPTs, including computers, digital technology, and AI.

> The Flipped Classroom model changes the traditional relationship between time spent in class and doing homework [and says] goodbye to the "sage on a stage" model that has existed for centuries . . .

The Flipped Classroom Reimagines Teaching and Learning

Khan Academy changed teaching for faculty and students by flipping the classroom—and offering the instruction at no charge. The Flipped Classroom model changes the traditional relationship between time spent in class and doing homework. Saying goodbye to the "sage on a stage" model that has existed for centuries, the new model uses class time as a joint exploration session. Students learn from online courses and lectures that they watch on their own time, not during class time. Teachers use class time not to deliver lectures, as in the past, but to guide practice or projects and answer questions.[56]

This model allows Khan Academy educators to spend class time interacting with students rather than lecturing. Students may be assigned an instructional video to watch online on their own time, so that when they join their instructor and classmates, they focus on solving problems together or other collaborative or hands-on work. Proponents of the Flipped Classroom say students receive more one-on-one attention from their teachers. Students can also personalize their learning experience by referencing prior learning modules to brush up on subjects they find challenging. Students often feel they have greater agency, as they can move faster or slower.[57]

Another popular, free video-instruction site, TED, offers a wide range of information and recently launched a TED Ed section for educators. TED's goal, unlike Khan Academy's, is not to build entire curricula. Rather, the site seeks video content that sparks "curiosity, wonder, and mind-shifting insight."[58]

Preparing for a Portfolio of Careers: Valuing "Human Capabilities"

Employees of all ages wonder how they can prepare for jobs that may not even exist yet. There is also the challenge for an older worker who may need to learn something new after a lifetime in one career. Having access to more ways to gain valuable skills at no cost or at a low cost is a significant development, but what about the seasoned workers who believe they can only do one thing and have not been back at school for 30 years? Can workers of different ages develop the disposition of a learner and be adaptable? John Hagel, a co-director of Deloitte's Center for the Edge, a leading management consultant and author, says employees at every age can learn something new. "We use the metaphor of the muscle, that for many of us the muscles have atrophied because we've been in environments that tell you not to exercise them," Hagel says. "The key we believe is to create environments now that will not only encourage you but make it easier to exercise those muscles."[59]

To Hagel, a key to preparing for the future of work is to focus on developing capabilities, not skills. Hagel defines skills as context specific. For example, you need specific skills to operate a machine or process paperwork in a certain environment. Capabilities are helpful in any environment, and are context independent, such as curiosity, imagination, creativity, critical thinking, writing and argument, the scientific method and statistical thinking, and empathy or emotional and social intelligence "It's really identifying what are those elements that again are essential to addressing unseen problems and opportunities and that are innate within us," Hagel says. "If we just [focus on] reskilling employees, that's just buying time until the machine takes those other routine tasks and you have to reskill again for a different set of routine tasks and it's a race against time." Capabilities, on the other hand, are uniquely human, *can* take a very long time for machines to master, and can create significant value for a company. "That's a pretty winning combination," Hagel says.[60]

Thriving in the future will require a mindset that is curious and open to learning, one that values communication, collaboration, and critical thinking. Millennials in particular generally recognize the importance of continuous learning: 42 percent said they are likely to leave a company if they are not learning quickly enough, according to Glassdoor data.[61] And they recognize the value of learning new skills quickly. A recent future of jobs report by the World Economic Forum found that by 2022, more than half of all employees will require significant reskilling and upskilling. Of these, about 35 percent are expected to require additional training of up to six months, 9 percent will require reskilling lasting six to 12 months, while 10 percent will require additional skills training of more than a year.[62]

Skills that will continue to grow in prominence by 2022 include analytical thinking, technology design, programming, and innovation. In addition to proficiency in new technologies, so called "human skills" will also grow in importance, including creativity, originality and initiative, critical thinking, persuasion, and negotiation. Other skills that are expected to retain or increase their value, according to the report, include attention to detail, resilience, flexibility, and complex problem solving. Emotional intelligence, leadership, and social influence as well as service orientation also see a significant increase in demand.[63]

Each year, LinkedIn provides a look at the soft and hard skills most in demand and how to acquire them. For 2020, LinkedIn highlighted "human skills" as key. LinkedIn listed the top "soft" skills companies need most as creativity, persuasion, collaboration, adaptability and emotional intelligence. The top five most in-demand hard skills LinkedIn listed are blockchain, cloud computing, analytical reasoning, artificial intelligence, and UX design.[64]

Certainly, the skills needed to perform some jobs have changed. Not surprisingly, this is especially true in tech, where job ads for software developers and engineers now ask for skills that did not exist a decade earlier. Some jobs of a decade ago required skills that have since become obsolete. In contrast, some skills developed by liberal arts majors have stayed relevant.[65] The three attributes of college graduates that employers considered most important are written communication, problem solving, and the ability to work in a team, according to a recent survey by the National Association of Colleges and Employers. Quantitative and technical skills both made the top 10, alongside "soft" skills, such as initiative, verbal communication, and leadership.[66] "Jobs that require both socializing and thinking, especially mathematically, have fared best in employment and pay," Deming says. They include those held by doctors and engineers. The jobs that require social skills but not math skills have also grown, such as lawyers and child-care workers. The jobs that have been rapidly disappearing are those that require neither social nor math skills, like manual labor.[67]

A theme we keep returning to is the importance of lifelong learning, and the integration of learning and work as core and complementary capabilities. Louis Hyman told us that when talking to students and alumni from the labor program he teaches at Cornell, he has observed an interesting pattern in the questions he is asked. Students who are in their last year or two at Cornell ask him what programming courses like Python or R (for data analysis) they should be taking. Alumni who have been the in workforce for 10 years ask him where they can learn more about managing teams. Alumni who have been out in the market 20 years or more ask him how they can study history and philosophy to understand patterns and gain insights around leading in complex and dynamic times. The topics change but learning continues.[68]

Transitions: Learning in the Flow of Life

As we live longer, healthier lives, we will face more moments of liminality, whether we are transitioning to our first job or our sixth job or poised for retirement. Our lives will include more transitions, more twists, and more rites of passage. This presents a challenge as many of us are resistant to transitions because they involve change and facing the unknown. A need for continuous reinvention can be daunting for adults. "It's hard to be an adult learner," says Gratton of the London Business School. "Whether you want to take a year off to do a program at a university or you want to just do something in the evening [online] on Coursera, it takes a lot of personal motivation to do that." Adults also find making mistakes and taking risks much more difficult than children. However, in a longer life with consistent technological disruption, Gratton believes that knowing how to make transitions is going to be an important human capability.[69]

In a broad sense, our careers used to involve an initial onboarding and then a final offboarding with retirement, Gratton says. "Each of those [phases] was in lockstep with people in your own peer group," she says, adding that what is interesting about the transitions people are facing now is that they are more likely to occur solo, rather than as "a massive peer group making the same transition."[70] How we navigate these transitions, whether to gain new capabilities on the job, online, or at an institution of higher learning will become an increasingly essential part of our work lives.

Just as the flow of careers will evolve to become portfolios of work and tours of duty, so too will the flow of learning and work itself evolve. One way to think about this new relationship is to take inspiration from the evolution of information technology development in recent years. As the pace of technological change has increased, IT teams have evolved from sequential, "waterfall" design-develop-test-operate models to new, agile models. Sometimes known as DevOps, these models integrate system design, development, security, testing, and operations into a team-based process. Similarly, we can anticipate that new approaches to integrating learning and work will arise, perhaps combining development and work into DevWork—"building on the realization that learning and work are two constantly connected sides of every job."[71]

To create a DevWork environment will involve changes to the way we integrate learning and work. Be on the lookout for the following:[72]

- **Opportunities to integrate real-time learning and knowledge management into the workflow**. With cloud-connected mobile and wearable devices becoming almost omnipresent, and the introduction of augmented reality devices, organizations will be able to explore new approaches to virtual learning in which learning occurs in small doses, almost invisibly, throughout the workday.

- **Making learning more personal** so that it is targeted to the individual and delivered at convenient times and modes so that people can learn on their own time. Here, technology can play an important role. With growing numbers of learning providers now offering video, text, and program-based curricula in smaller, more digestible formats, organizations have an opportunity to craft approaches that allow their workers to learn as and when they see fit.

- **Integrating learning with the work of teams as well as individuals**. As teams become more important in the delivery of more types of work, organizations will offer learning opportunities that support individuals as members of teams, providing content and experiences specific to the context of a worker's team."

Paths to Resilience

We will all need to take responsibility for discovering ways to integrate learning throughout our lives, reinventing ourselves, and transitioning across multiple careers. Our careers will look more like portfolios than stepladders. Reinvention will be the rule, not the exception. How we learn, work, and live will be more integrated—learning in the flow of work, and working in the flow of longer, more varied lives. And finally, we will need to increase our expectations for how our educational institutions, government, and businesses will support these ongoing career reinventions and transitions. Current institutional models will need to adapt and expand to meet the growth and transition needs of lifelong learners and workers. To thrive in our future world of work will require resilience. We will need to recover from challenges, adapt to changes, and keep moving forward. Much like the determined plant that broke through a concrete sidewalk in front of my office building in New York City, we will need to find our way through obstacles in our path to keep growing.

CHAPTER 6

The Rise of Teams

Reinvent Organizations, from Individuals and Hierarchies to Teams and Networks

If your company has an excessively rigid internal structure and employees have a rigid mindset, they don't just miss dangers and miss risks, they also miss big opportunities.[1]

—Gillian Tett, editor and author, United States, *The Financial Times*; author, *The Silo Effect*

The last Apple org chart Steve Wozniak has seen shows that he still reports to Apple co-founder Steve Jobs. Not one to shy away from dark humor at the expense of Jobs, who passed away in 2011, Wozniak noted, "Since Steve died, I can't be fired."[2] Of course, Wozniak stepped down from Apple in 1985, and remains an employee in a ceremonial capacity only, something the org chart failed to capture. Organizational charts have long been the butt of jokes, in part, because they are rarely up to date, and even when they are, they generally fail to reflect reality. More significantly, they no longer represent the more dynamic organizational models that are evolving at many companies, based not on individuals jockeying to edge their way up to the top spot, but, rather, on teams, networks, and platforms working together.

It is easy to picture the traditional org chart, with its branches, sticks, and boxes cascading down from the CEO, who sits at the crown. At their best, org charts offer a visual representation of who is below us, who is above us, and how employees and leaders fit into the hierarchy of the entire company.

At their worst, they reinforce the drive to the top, even if it means working solo to get ahead and forgoing teamwork. Org charts reflect a time when companies were built around silos and scale efficiencies, and designed solely for steadiness, predictability, and efficiency. Organizations were also structured around accountability, with clearly defined jobs that fit within a hierarchical structure. *Who do I report to? Who does my boss report to?* These questions could easily be answered. Traditional organizations performed well in a world of stability but that is not our world today.

Static org charts are becoming artifacts of the past. We are now using advanced analytics to visually represent the team dynamics of how people actually work. New designs are emerging that embrace natural connections and configure multidisciplinary teams to deliver value more effectively.[3] Today, most work is not done in functional silos but in teams or ecosystems, which are networked teams connecting organizations. Newer organization models are flatter and are ordered around projects, relationships, and information flows.

One of the fathers of the org chart and the person responsible for shaping the way we think about the traditional corporation is Alfred Chandler, the influential Harvard Business School professor and business historian who wrote extensively about the scale and management structure of large business enterprises. Chandler believed in the role of hierarchies and the importance of managers in the rise of corporations. He famously wrote in the 1970s that "structure follows strategy," emphasizing that all aspects of an organization's structure, from the creation of departments to the reporting relationships, should be designed with the company's strategic execution in mind.[4]

Organizing work around hierarchies and bureaucracy dates back to the early nineteenth century when offices were introduced in the East India Company, the first joint stock company. The structure reflected predictable workflows in which clerks and accountants moved paper to process transactions and generate managerial and financial reports.[5] As work has shifted from processing transactions, which increasingly can be handled by machines, to solving problems and relationship-based work, we no longer need massive transactional bureaucracies as our default organizational model.

Organizations no longer need to be structured around control, with senior people at top of the hierarchy telling people below what to do. Increasingly decentralized models are moving away from primarily functional structures and embracing networks of teams inside and outside the organization. Networks of teams allow people to move from team to team—and project to project—rather than remain within a rigid or static configuration. Teams are assembled around a product, market, or integrated customer need and not necessarily a business function. Organizational strategies are moving beyond direction, control, and execution to building culture, common purpose, and ways of working to share information, to work within and across teams, and to promote collaboration in multiple directions.

The coronavirus pandemic taught us that advances in technology can facilitate collaboration across and within teams despite operating from disparate physical locations. Changes already underway have sped up, making some question the future role and location of offices. Though it is too soon to know the fate of office spaces, it is clear that the shift to collaborating virtually, across teams, across ecosystems, across functions, and across the globe, is gaining momentum.[6]

> The silo effect occurs when different departments or teams within an organization fail to communicate, and undermine productivity as a result. Two departments could be working on the same initiative, or at cross purposes, without knowing it.

Silo Busting

The opposite of working collaboratively is working in silos. The silo effect occurs when different departments or teams within an organization fail to communicate, and undermine productivity as a result. Two departments could be working on the same initiative, or at cross purposes, without knowing it. Financial journalist and author Gillian Tett has studied silos within companies, finding that their internal structures, the complexity of their businesses, and regulation often reinforced siloed approaches and the associated turf battles. Her research explored the aftermath of the financial crisis, when many financial institutions realized that one of the factors that caused the crisis was their siloed nature.

"The right hand didn't know what the left hand was doing," Tett said in our interview. She noted that both the Bank of England and many major financial institutions had silos that blinded them to the impending collapse of major parts of global financial markets—or at the very least made it harder to see and act on. In the aftermath of the financial crisis, there has been a drive across the financial sector to operate in more holistic and integrated ways. Tett has dubbed the effort for departments in a company to shift away from behaving as isolated islands "silo busting."[7]

Some siloes arise as a result of the way organizations are structured and regulated. They can also arise when we put on blinders or lose perspective, Tett said. In her book *The Silo Effect*, she explores the consequences of companies operating with excessively rigid internal structures and rigid mindsets "where tribes end up killing each other and competing." Tett explains, "siloes can exist on several levels. You can get *structural siloes* where companies are identified into nutty divisions or departments that try and kill each other. You can get *cognitive siloes* where different people are essentially trapped into tunnel vision by having very rigid ways that they divide up the world. And then you get *social siloes*, people basically only ever talking to people like themselves (tribalism). In some ways the social siloes are an increasing problem."[8]

She notes that as the result of these different types of silos, companies miss not only dangers and risks, but also big opportunities. "The world moves on outside their company and they end up essentially not seeing how different categories are collapsing [outside the company], like, say, hardware, software, and content at the time of the death of the Sony Walkman and the move into digital music," Tett said. "That's why Sony lost out in positioning their Walkman. [To win] you need to . . . think about how the world's moving outside but look at your own structures and mental taxonomies as well."[9]

Tett trained as a social anthropologist She is a proponent of finding new ways for us to look at ourselves and to consider how our organizations operate—as though we were outsiders instead of insiders. She notes that a fundamental principle of anthropology is that it's very hard for us to truly see our environment until we step outside of it.[10]

"Learning to look at yourself afresh through someone else's eyes is one of the most powerful tools that you can use to see your taxonomy," she notes. "It's what we live every day. It's how our minds are shaped. It's like asking a fish to think about water. Because you know, they're just in it. They can't see it. So we all think it's entirely natural to put sales in one department, marketing in another, IT in a third department, but is it?" A key feature of the new structure is to move beyond the silos and tunnel vision that have existed in large corporations and toward improved information sharing and greater connections between teams.[11]

Tett challenges us to think about three questions. First, *what is the taxonomy that we hold in our heads to sort out the world and the work structure?* How we classify the world, and the boundaries we envision, matter enormously—although we tend not to think about them because we take them for granted. Second, *what are the structures and classification systems we need to get work done?* These include our functions, divisions, and silos. Third, *are we constantly challenging ourselves to be aware that the organizational constructs we create to get work done are exactly that—constructs?* We need to make sure that we do not become victims of our silos but, instead, that we are able to master them. As Tett summed up, "today's teams need to be porous and cross boundaries."[12]

In the 1800s and early 1900s, the CEO delegated responsibility to functional managers. This model was later extended to include specialists, each with their own domains, such as the chief financial officers, chief information officers, chief human resources officers, each working independently. However, our complex and dynamic world often presents challenges that no single function can address, calling upon organizations to work across functions. These challenges have led to a redesigning of organizational structures to integrate robotics and artificial intelligence technologies, as well as to capitalize on new employment models, such as gig workers and crowds, across industries and functions.

The Rise of Networks of Teams

A key building block of the new market-oriented ecosystem is the role of teams. As teams work together on specific projects and challenges, they form networks. These networks of teams can join forces to tackle larger projects, then disband and move on to new assignments once the project has been completed. Increasingly, companies are using internal talent marketplaces that allow employees to self-select and sign up for projects and teams that they would like to join. For example, at NASA, a talent marketplace allows employees to access a range of internal projects and career development opportunities. As work moved into teams, we can identify three archetypes of organization teams: configurable teams (grouped around a project); production lines, assembly lines, distribution centers, and warehouses; and teams from across ecosystems, in which the project may be the entire company, as in making a commercial movie or theater production.

Thomas Malone, an organizational theorist and professor at the MIT Sloan School, and colleagues at Carnegie Mellon have explored the extraordinary value of teams in their paper, "What Makes Teams Smart." Malone has made the distinction between intelligent individuals and intelligent teams. Though we might assume that smart people make smart teams, his research points to three critical attributes of exceptional teams: social perceptiveness, democratic participation, and the number of women on the team. He suggests that a team's collective intelligence is a stronger predictor of team performance than the ability of individual team members. Collective intelligence includes a group's ability to collaborate, coordinate, and get things done.[13]

Research by Deloitte has found that it is not only individual employees who need to collaborate effectively but managers and leaders as well. Rather than behaving as independent functional experts, the C-suite must operate as a team, or as a "symphonic C-suite." An organization's top executives play together interdependently as a team while also leading their own functional teams. This approach enables the C-suite to understand the many impacts that external forces have on and within the organization—not just on single functions—and formulate coordinated, agile responses.[14]

Team-Based Thinking

In the past several years, Deloitte's annual Global Human Capital Trends report has explored the shift from hierarchies to cross-functional teams that move beyond divide-and-conquer models. In 2019, "Organizational Performance: It's a Team Sport" showcased leaders and teams working together to solve multidisciplinary problems, not to just process and execute transactions. The research showed that adopting team structures improves organizational performance. High-performing organizations promote teaming and

networking. Although they have many senior leaders and functional departments, they are able to move people around rapidly, spin up new initiatives
quickly, and can start and stop projects at need, moving people into new roles
to accommodate.[15]

To tackle these challenges, organizations need to adopt team-based
thinking internally as well as in the broader ecosystem in which today's social
enterprise finds itself. To help accomplish this, there are five layers in which
team-based thinking should be embedded:[16]

1. **The ecosystem**. How the work environment is orchestrated and
   connected: Adaptable organizations exist in purpose-driven ecosystems
   with defined customer-focused missions.
2. **The organization**. How work is configured: Away from deep hierarchy
   and silos toward a network of multidisciplinary teams.
3. **The team**. How work is delivered: High-performing teams adopt
   connected ways of working and an adaptable culture.
4. **The leader**. How work is led and managed: Leaders are inclusive orches-
   trators versus technical task masters in order to unlock the full potential
   of diverse capabilities, experiences, personalities, and skills.
5. **The individual**. How work is executed: By unleashing resilient individuals through adaptive talent programs so that people can learn and develop
   not by "climbing the ladder" but by growing from experience to experience.

Stanley McChrystal's book, *Team of Teams: New Rules of Engagement for
a Complex World*, is a manual for leaders looking to make their teams more
adaptable, agile, and unified in the midst of change. McChrystal, a retired
U.S. Army general, lays out the many ways large organizations can benefit
from the agility of smaller teams. He writes that hierarchical management
techniques no longer work because organizations are too large for any one
person to make all the decisions. The military uses a management style in
which your team operates as a network with a shared consciousness; every
member is empowered to execute. McChrystal says that organizations need
to share information and build genuine relationships and trust.[17] He believes
that leaders should behave like gardeners. "You are not playing a game of
chess where you dictate every move," he said. "You create an environment
where every piece can simultaneously grow like a gardener." [18]

Human–Machine Teams as Superminds

Working as teams extends from colleagues and leaders to teams of people with
machines. MIT's Thomas Malone offers a framework for achieving new forms
of human–machine collective intelligence. In his book *Superminds: The Surprising Power of People and Computers Thinking Together*, Malone defines a

"supermind" as a group of individuals, and increasingly with computers, acting collectively in ways that seem intelligent.[19]

Every company in the world is a supermind, Malone says. So is every democracy, army, neighborhood, scientific community, and club. Realizing this can get us thinking about how we are "in this together," and how we can make our superminds smarter. "Superminds have been around at least as long as people have, and when you learn to recognize them, you realize they run our world," Malone says. "Almost everything we've done has been done by superminds."[20]

Malone identifies five different types of decision-making superminds: hierarchies, markets, democracies, communities, and ecosystems. This is interesting in part because we tend to think that organizations—superminds—make decisions through hierarchies. Recognizing the different types of decision-making provides us with new ways of thinking and approaching how we "organize" work and collective efforts for new and different results. Once you start thinking about these five types of decision-making, you see their usefulness in different situations—and you see their application everywhere.[21]

> **Hierarchies.** In a hierarchy, you follow your boss's orders. Decisions are made by delegating them to specific roles and members in the group.
>
> **Markets.** In markets, decisions are based on mutual transactions. Group decisions are the sum of all of the pairwise agreements made between buyers and sellers.
>
> **Democracies.** In a democracy, group decisions are made by voting or polling.
>
> **Communities.** In a community, you are enabled and constrained by the community's norms. Group decisions are based on a kind of informal consensus based on norms and reputations.
>
> **Ecosystems.** In an ecosystem, group decisions are made by the law of the jungle (whoever has the most power gets what they want) and the survival of the fittest.

Malone's view of ecosystems underscores an interesting point relative to the term *ecosystems*. The word is often used to describe organizational strategies where the focus is on group dynamics *beyond* the organization or enterprise. Tett, talking about silos, and Malone, talking about superminds, both focus our attention on the importance of boundaries and connections, and the mental models we bring to the table in applying these ideas.

> The increasing pace of contextual change means that organizations must also change or die.

Market-Oriented Ecosystems

The primary drivers of organizational evolution are increasingly fast-changing and unpredictable environments, especially those created by technological breakthroughs. When change was predictable, traditional organizational hierarchies were able to support centralized decision-making through functional silos to produce organizational efficiency. However, in our whitewater era of exponential change, traditional organization models fall short.

David Ulrich and Arthur Yeung, in their book *Reinventing the Organization*, describe the context in which organizations increasingly find themselves as volatile, uncertain, complex, and ambiguous, or VUCA. The authors describe a new model for the twenty-first century that they characterize as a market-oriented ecosystem (MOE), in contrast to traditional hierarchies. Yeung, a senior management advisor to Tencent Group, and Ulrich, a professor at the University of Michigan's Ross School of Business, view the evolving organization as a market-oriented ecosystem comprising many forms of collaboration and alliances. "I think that the mental model of an organization as a control system has basically got to shift," Yeung notes. "There's an evolution of the organizational species from hierarchy to systems to capability to MOEs—market-oriented ecosystems," said Ulrich in our interview.[22] To survive and thrive in the era of technological disruption, organizations need to be designed for agility, innovation, and customer centricity. "The increasing pace of contextual change means that organizations must also change or die," Ulrich says. As companies strive to become more agile, they are shifting their structures from traditional, functional models to interconnected, flexible teams.[23]

Yeung said that Tencent is a good example of a market-oriented ecosystem in action. One of the largest companies in China, and the world, Tencent is a social media company and a venture capital and investment firm with holdings in hundreds of companies across media, e-commerce, and gaming. "Structurally, it follows the organizational principle of a platform, plus business teams, plus ecosystem partners," Yeung said. Tencent is able to connect to more than 1 billion active users. This is the core platform that feeds user traffic to all business teams, including online games, music, and videos.[24]

To enrich its product and service offerings, Tencent also develops close partnerships with a large number of ecosystem partners that are able to offer services in dining, transportation, shopping, movie ticketing, food delivery, and even paying taxes or traffic tickets, Yeung says. "They connect into WeChat—a large messaging, social media, and payments system," Ulrich says. "They begin to know what consumers want. They get into JD.com, which is China's largest on-line retailer. And so the knowledge from WeChat (social media) can transfer to what JD.com (on-line retail) can do." Tencent offers an example of an agile organization that is designed to move quickly and is built on connections and extending the reach of an enterprise, through platforms, to a broader ecosystem.[25]

The leader's job at Tencent is not about what they control but how they empower others, Ulrich says. "The traditional mental model of an organization is about power. It's about control. It's about clarifying decision rights. In the MOE organization, it's more about agility, customer, innovation and moving to penetrate market opportunities. I think that mental models of organizations as control systems have basically got to shift."[26] In terms of operating governance, Tencent uses a market-oriented mechanism to govern the relationships between its core platform and business teams, across and among business teams, and between the platform and its ecosystem partners. "Instead of spending a lot of time in internal coordination and negotiation, Tencent creates mechanism for these teams to share revenue or credit through agreed protocols," Ulrich says. "This ensures the efficiency of resource allocation so that the best products or services will get the best resource support inside and outside Tencent ecosystem."[27]

The biggest challenge for leaders when reinventing organizations is a liability of success, Ulrich notes. "When an organization or individual succeeds, they tend to lock into what worked and try to replicate it rather than continue to evolve it." Leaders need to let go of their past assumptions and take a leap into this new organization logic. To help leaders make this leap, Ulrich and Yeung highlight several key questions to be answered by leadership teams:[28]

1. **Do we really need deep changes in our organizational model?** Will we be left behind if we cannot innovate or change fast enough to today's disruptive environment?

2. **What will be the desired organizational model?** Will the MOE model of platform plus business teams plus ecosystem partners work for us? Or does traditional hierarchy or other organizational models make more sense for us?

3. **How can we migrate from our current organizational model to the desired organizational model?** What are the key steps required to lay out a practical roadmap for diagnosis and improvement actions?

4. **How do we increase the chance of success?** Conviction and confidence of the leadership team is critical along the transformation journey. Resources need to be invested to make things happen. Tough decisions in business, organization, and people need to be made. Make sure to effectively communicate to all levels of the organization to keep multiple stakeholders informed and engaged.

5. **What are the implications for business leaders of the new model?** What behaviors and experiences will twenty-first-century leaders need to have to effectively lead market-oriented ecosystems?

Agility and Adaptability for Resilience

Building agile teams and adaptable organizations are critical for success in the dynamic future world of work. If there are three terms extensively used to described future organization strategies, teams, and ecosystems—which we have discussed earlier—agile is at the top of the list. The term *agile* was popularized in the Manifesto for Agile Software Development, published in 2001, which created the agile movement.[29] These ideas have been moving beyond the software and technology corridors for the past decade, but it is useful, given the importance of the concepts behind agile, to revisit its origins.

Agile started as a movement in software almost 20 years ago. In response to the accelerating rate of change in technology—including processing power, then cloud computing and AI—traditional methods for developing and implementing technology solutions and systems were too slow and cumbersome. These models were generally described as "waterfall" methods that organized software projects into linear and sequential phases: requirements gathering, design, development, implementation, security, and support. In a world in which business was more stable and predictable, waterfall projects, which could take years to complete, were effective and successful. Companies would implement a system with the expectation that it would last years—or decades. As the pace of technological innovation continued to speed up, these linear and sequential models, which effectively "froze" requirements once the development of a project started, were not suited for the timeframes and expectations that software and technology teams were challenged to meet. Enter the agile manifesto and movement.

Agile involves approaches to software and technology focused on speed, integrated project teams, iterative design and delivery, customer focus, and collaboration and learning. Early on, agile teams connected design, development, and operations into an approach called DevOps. Then security got in the mix, as it should have from the start, and we saw DevSecOps. The goal was to gather the players in a product on a small, agile team that could collaborate fast, to create a working version—not just prototype—of a technology solution or product. Agile teams developed their own language and routines—like having daily stand-up meetings with all team members to make sure the team was working quickly, moving past obstacles, and getting things done. Another key principle of agile development is the idea of focusing development and delivery on a minimally viable product (MVP). The goal was not to develop a perfect, idealized, version of a product with all the bells and whistles but to get a product that worked and met customer requirements uniquely, out the door as fast as possible. Improvements could be made later on.

The future is being driven by fast changing contexts and technology. Many companies have changed the way they structure and do the work of IT around agile methods and teams. The challenge for us going forward is to build on the experiences and lessons of agile in the technology and software world and ask the question: *How do we build agile, adaptable, and resilient organizations for the work that lies ahead?* We have an idea of what the future looks like; it is organized around teams, networks, and platforms, not as a hierarchy. It is organized around collaboration and distributed decisionmaking, not around centralized command and control. It is organized around responsiveness and constantly changing customer and environmental challenges, not around a world of predictability and scale. The future of work is built for change. It is resilient by design.

CHAPTER 7

Leaders as Coaches and Designers

Moving Beyond Managing Workflows and Controlling Direct Reports to Creating, Influencing, and Building

Without leaps of imagination, or dreaming, we lose the excitement of possibilities. Dreaming, after all, is a form of planning.[1]

—Gloria Steinem, feminist, journalist, and
social political activist

When Daniel Kahneman demonstrated that the decisions consumers make are idiosyncratic, rather than rational, he flipped traditional economic theory on its head, and in the process, won the Nobel Prize in economics.[2] Kahneman was an unlikely recipient of the award. He is a psychologist and admits he has never even taken an economics class.[3] He won the prize by exposing a flaw in a basic tenet of mainstream economic theory. He challenged the reliance on an idealized model of consumer decisionmaking as perfectly thorough and rational, sometimes referred to as "econs."[4] Human irrationality has been a key theme in Kahneman's work, especially the phase with Amos Tversky, his longtime collaborator.[5] Tversky

died in 1996, and could not share the prize Kahneman received in 2002—by the rules of the Nobel committee, you need to be living to receive the honor.[6] With Tversky, Kahneman offered a more realistic view of humans as decisionmakers who do not weigh all the facts and who often defy logic. Kahneman and Tversky's findings have had far-reaching implications, influencing the way government leaders think through foreign policy, investors evaluate financial instruments, consumers choose products, employees select their benefits, and business leaders make decisions.[7] By bringing ideas from the field of psychology to the discipline of economics, Kahneman is one of the pioneers of a new field of knowledge known as behavioral economics.[8]

In response to the new challenges presented by digital disruption and AI, the pace of change, and the gig economy heating up, business leaders have started to think about leading and managing in dramatically different ways. They are starting to embrace the leader's new role in the digital age, realizing that the playbooks they have relied upon are out of date. They are increasingly turning to discipline-crossing approaches, borrowing ideas not only from psychology but also from the fields of design and cultural anthropology. The core set of leadership and management principles that have dominated in the last decades of the twentieth century and start of the twenty-first century is no longer enough. Those principles applied when businesses were predicable, workflows were largely mechanistic, and the rate of change came in repeatable waves. To keep pace with the dynamic nature of business today, leadership is shifting beyond managing employees in highly structured jobs to inspiring and engaging talent in a new, flatter, and more connected ecosystem.

During the latter part of twentieth century, business leaders began to see a number of new approaches to management that extended beyond the core ideas of Alfred Chandler and what had been espoused in the 1930s, 1940s, and 1950s. These new approaches differed from the linear model that structure follows strategy. Wedging its way in were new models including one borrowed from design thinking—design, develop, operate, improve. Indeed design thinking, behavioral economics, and psychology started gathering momentum in the 1980s with their complementary applications to business. That momentum is gathering speed today as business leaders consider their roles as designers and as behavioral economists who understand that human and group dynamics are vital, and that business strategy, structure, process, and operational efficiency may not work in linear and predictable ways. The shift occurring today embraces what were once considered ancillary disciplines as core disciplines. The digital waves of change facing leaders invite a multifaceted approach, beyond traditional management, that includes *designing* the future and understanding the *psychology* and *human dynamics* of complex teams.

I started my MBA at Yale in 1985. My daughter began her MBA studies at Emory in 2019. Despite the 34-year gap between our graduation dates, the core curriculum at her MBA program was almost identical to the one I studied in 1985: finance, accounting, marketing, statistics, operations management, and competitive strategies. But the world has changed dramatically during those 34 years, especially the tech world. When I graduated from business school, there were just under a million cell phones in the United States,[9] and each one carried a $3,000 price tag.[10] Today there are 275 million smartphone users in the United States,[11] and a smartphone costs about $300[12] (and in many cases it's free when you sign up for a year or more of mobile service). A gigabyte of data in the mid-1980s cost about $50,000 (yes, that's not an error), compared with about 10 cents—and dropping—today.[13] Are we preparing managers for the consumer and business world of the last century, or the one we're accelerating through today?

The elephant in the room when discussing the future of work and its impact on leadership and technology, in many ways, *is* technology. The headlines tell us: "Every company is now a tech company,"[14] "Why Software Is Eating the World."[15] Understanding the disruptive impacts of technology is central to shaping and managing businesses and organizations. The challenge is to evolve mental models, management approaches, and their relationship to technology. Gerald Kane, a professor at the management school at Boston College, and the lead author, with colleagues from Deloitte, of the book *The Technology Fallacy*, captures an important dimension of the disruption in management thinking: "The technology fallacy is the mistaken belief that just because an organization's problems are caused by digital technologies that the solution will involve digital technologies as well," Kane said. "But many of the most effective solutions we saw weren't digital and didn't involve technology at all."[16]

A challenge facing managers is determining which parts of management practice to keep, what to discard, and what to add. "It would be easy if you just had to throw out everything and learn it new," Kane said. "Some 20th century practices are still valid, like the need for effective communication," he noted, but the way you communicate effectively has changed dramatically. Managers are charged with teasing out what needs to shift and what does not. Kane notes that "it's just not as simple as having to learn all over again."[17]

Leading as Coaches

The April 2015 cover story of *The Harvard Business Review*, titled "Reinventing Performance Rankings—a Radical New Way to Evaluate Talent," was based on Deloitte's experience redesigning performance management approach for tens of thousands of professionals from a time-intensive evaluation and sorting process to one based on recognizing, seeing, and fueling performance. In some ways, it was the goal of performance management—*fueling performance*—that struck many as radical. How can managers *improve* the performance of individual workers and teams through brief, regular conversations, and check-ins focusing on their near-term work and long-term development opportunities? In other words, how can managers act as coaches for talent, and not just talent scouts?[18]

Shifting the management focus from compliance to coaching involves shifting attention from looking back to setting our managerial sights on the future. Coaching focuses on improvement, progress, and new and better results. It spotlights learning from past experiences—both wins and losses. It zeroes in on what individuals are *capable* of doing—not just what they have done.

Exploring a new approach to performance management, Ashley Goodall, who was the head of leadership development at Deloitte in the United States at the time, and Marcus Buckingham wondered if we could "somehow shift our investment of time from talking to ourselves about ratings to talking to our people about their performance and careers—from a focus on the past to a focus on the future." Although it is useful to measure and reward performance, wouldn't it be better to improve it—or to fuel it they asked?[19]

The Deloitte program has evolved with a focus on actionable data and conversations. Both are critical. To collect data, a performance scorecard was structured around answering four questions at the end of a project milestone.

1. Given what I know of this person's performance, and if it were my money, I would award this person the highest possible compensation increase and bonus. [*Measures overall performance and unique value to the organization on a five-point scale from "strongly agree" to "strongly disagree."*]

2. Given what I know of this person's performance, I would always want him or her on my team. [*Measures ability to work well with others on the same five-point scale.*]

3. This person is at risk for low performance. [*Identifies problems that might harm the customer or the team on a yes-or-no basis.*]

4. This person is ready for promotion *today*. [*Measures potential on a yes-or-no basis.*]

The conversations, or check-ins, occur every few weeks and involve both a review of what is working well and what can be improved. These check-ins provide an opportunity for managers, coaches, and employees to reflect on recent performance and explore ways to learn, alter, and boost for improvement.[20]

Leading as Psychologists

The growing influence of psychology on business leadership can be seen in the rise of behavioral economics and the popularity and impact of the concept of a growth mindset. Both approaches help leaders and managers create the conditions for success by developing the mindset that helps talent thrive in challenging and changing times. Kahneman's work in the area of behavioral economics upended the so-called "homo economicus"—the rational, calculating decisionmaker.[21] Though economists knew that everyone does not act this way all the time, they nevertheless used this framework and this main character in their economic theories.

Kahneman and Tversky's work explored the psychological phenomena around not only decision-making but also judgment. Decision-making is about how we choose, especially when there is uncertainty. Judgment is about estimating probabilities. Kahneman and Tversky showed that, in both cases, human beings do not behave like trained statisticians. In our decisions and judgments, we deviate in identifiable ways from the economic models.[22] Companies have increasingly incorporated their concept of *choice architecture*, recognizing that people have biases, and that it is possible to direct them to make better decisions. That is why in employee or student cafeterias, you see the cut carrots in front, within reach, and the cookies in the back. It is also why many firms automatically enroll their employees in a 401(k) retirement savings plan rather than ask them to sign up.

The importance of Kahneman and Tversky's work lies, in part, in their argument that departures from perfect rationality can be anticipated. They showed that errors are not only common but also predictable.[23] In other words, there are discernable, recognizable patterns for consumer behavior, and it turns out, for employee behavior as well.

Some business leaders have also borrowed from psychology an appreciation of the power of adopting a growth mindset. Carol Dweck, a psychology professor at Stanford, found that people with a growth mindset enjoy challenges, strive to learn, and consistently see potential to develop new skills. In contrast, people who view talent as a quality they either possess or lack as having a fixed mindset. In 2010, she extended her work on mindset beyond individuals to leaders, managers, and organizations. "Can an organization, like an individual, have a fixed or a growth mindset? If so, what are the effects on the organization and its employees?" Dweck and her colleagues Mary Murphy, Jennifer Chatman, and Laura Kray have collaborated with the consulting firm Senn Delaney to explore those questions.[24]

Their findings, reported in *Harvard Business Review*, identified supervisors in growth-mindset companies as expressing significantly more positive views about their employees than supervisors in fixed-mindset companies, rating them as more innovative, collaborative, and committed to learning and growing. Their research suggests that growth-mindset firms have happier employees and a more innovative, risk-taking culture. The growth mindset that embraces change and learning is one that business leaders are increasingly turning to help navigate the uncertainty and changes they face. They are also leveraging the growth mindset to help guide a team that must embrace change to thrive in an employment landscape that in the future world of work could include six or seven careers.[25]

Leading as Cultural Anthropologists

Gillian Tett, whose research has explored the undermining effects of silos in companies, has applied cultural anthropology to business leadership. Tett, who has a PhD in social anthropology, and is editor-at-large, United States, *The Financial Times*,[26] says that silos exist when people in different parts of an organization do not talk to each other or share information. There are also what she calls silos of the mind, which are the categories into which we slot things. In Tett's view, the financial crisis of 2008 was caused both by the silo effect of inadequate communication among departments of giant banks, and by the "mental silos" that resulted in misclassifying credit instruments.[27] When companies have teams or departments operating as silos, she says, it is as if "one hand doesn't know what the other is doing." Her work shows how silos can undermine organizations, and she endorses "silo busting" so that isolation is replaced by greater communication.[28]

Tett recommends that business leaders and managers encourage employees to be fluid and dynamic. "[Employees need to] move between different teams," Tett says, "or be forced to by virtue of working in the gig economy and having to hustle for the next bit of work that forces them to break down siloes and to basically be more fluid." Tett warns against companies that are rigid. "If your company has an excessively rigid internal structure and employees have a rigid mind, they don't just miss dangers and miss risks, they also miss big opportunities," Tett says. "If you want to beat that you need to not just think about how the world's moving outside but look at your own structures and mental taxonomies too." Tett acknowledges that silos can serve a function, and we often need boundaries, but she recommends that the boundaries are porous.[29]

We need to start training and developing managers to think like anthropologists, notes Tett, who is part of a network of business anthropologists who are actively trying to inject anthropology into the discussion. "I'm arguing that anthropology and social science are often like salt," Tett says. "When you add it in, it gives it flavor and binds the ingredients together."[30]

Leading as Designers

Over the past 20 years, design thinking has evolved from applications in the product-development world to user experience, to business design, and even to life design. Design thinking is an innovation methodology that has a track record of success in the field of design on products and services. This approach encourages re-framing, creative thinking, experimentation, curiosity, and collaboration, then going to rapid prototyping, before rolling out a product.[31] Companies have been incorporating design thinking into their practices for decades, including IBM, which has established an innovation lab called the Enterprise Design Thinking lab.[32] Deloitte's own innovation practice, Doblin, uses cross-disciplinary skills, including design thinking, in its work.[33]

Design thinking not only works for designing products but has increasingly been successful as a leadership approach. Since its earliest business applications in the 1980s, design thinking has helped companies solve problems by focusing on collaboration and creativity.[34] For business leaders, design thinking offers new ways to guide teams, innovate, and solve problems. Design thinking focuses on creation and imagination rather than managing or optimization. David Kelley, founder of the design firm IDEO, made design thinking famous and the motivating idea behind the Hasso Plattner Institute of Design at Stanford University, known as the "d.school."[35]

Over the past 30 years, IDEO has tackled everything from the challenge of delivering a needle-free vaccine to rethinking airport-security checkpoints for the TSA.[36] Tim Brown, CEO of IDEO, has explained designed thinking as a human-centered approach to innovation. Though it integrates technology and economics, he says that it starts with what humans need. For business, this means that, regardless of the nature of the challenge you are addressing, your company has to understand where your products and services fit into your customers' lives.

There are five steps to the design thinking process:[37]

1. Empathize: Set aside your own assumptions and understand the problem.
2. Define: Use different activities and exercises to define the problem.
3. Ideate: Choose from a wide variety of techniques to generate ideas.
4. Prototype: Create a simple version of the final product or process.
5. Test: Does the prototype solve the problem?

Design thinking allows business leaders and managers to focus on the person and the experience, not only the process. It puts the employee experience first. Design thinking also casts managers in a new role. They are no longer "process developers" but, rather, "experience architects." One fundamental idea in design thinking is the use of behavioral economics to encourage better decision-making. This concept is referred to as "choice architecture." For example, should a company give people 10 options for 401(k) plans? Behavioral economics suggests that offering a selection of three could result in better overall investment decisions and results.[38]

Some companies are using design thinking to improve learning. For example, Nestlé has used design thinking to develop intuitive, experiential learning programs that begin with the employee's work rather than a model in which the presenter is the focus. Successful design thinking integrates an understanding of human behavior, and asks, *What motivates people? What do they value?* At its core, design thinking is about collaborating. When business leaders prioritize design thinking, they make the most of the power of the collective group brain and cross-functional talent. They bring together unique perspectives from across the organization—and beyond—to find innovative solutions.

The principles of design thinking are beginning to be leveraged in a small number of MBA programs. A leader in this approach is the Rotman School of Management, the business school at the University of Toronto. The redesigned MBA program integrates design thinking and management thinking into the curriculum. Design thinking is not an elective but a critical part of how the Rotman School trains twenty-first-century managers as designers. A former dean of the school, Roger Martin, wrote a book about an approach mostly absent from traditionally analytical MBA programs: design thinking. His book, *The Design of Business*, published in 2009, proposes bringing together both the art and science of management to create better leaders. Martin believes schools need to include design when teaching business. He sought to educate future managers so that they would be equally adept at using tools and frameworks from business, popular culture, and design to solve the challenges of the day. More than a decade later, his ideas about developing integrative thinkers, business leaders who are well grounded in multiple disciplines, has gained traction. Martin was highly influenced by a highly skilled designer he worked with closely. He noticed that the designer tended to view all challenges in a similar way—focusing on new possibilities rather than the application of existing ideas.[39]

Other universities have embraced design thinking. Stanford University's Designing Your Life course was so popular that is spawned a best-selling book. The professors who created the class, Bill Burnett and Dave Evans, believe you can apply design thinking to almost any challenge. With the exception perhaps of weight loss and finding a life partner, the professors claim design thinking can help answer the question, "What do I do with the rest of my one wild and wonderful life?" Though not every student leaves the class knowing what they want to do as a career, they take with them design concepts of prototyping and favoring action that will help them get there.[40]

Core concepts of design thinking connect to agile software development and so-called DevOps, or development and operations. The historically highly structured software development process gave way to a more agile and iterative approach that challenged how long it took to do things in a linear fashion. The result was an integrated, rapid prototyping process in which development teams and operations teams joined one team called the DevOps team. Taking it a step further, security and cyber were added to the mix, so that leaders and managers now face a highly collaborative, integrated development, operations, and security team called DevSecOps, inspired by the interdisciplinary approach fostered by design thinking.

Leading in the Digital Age

In much of the past decade, we have witnessed the steady, and increasing, rise of e-commerce online retail and purchases, relative to traditional, face-to-face shopping. At the end of 2019, about 16 percent of total retail sales were conducted through online shopping—an increase of about 1 percent per year during the decade. In the first half of 2020, this growth has been accelerated by the impact of Covid-19. Some industry analysts predict 25 percent of total retail sales could be online by 2025. The digital economy is on the move.[41]

Business leaders and managers have had to reassess the merits of traditional hierarchical structures and effective leadership as they have surfed two disruptive digital waves, the impact of which continue to reverberate today. The first wave began in 2007, when the iPhone was invented, and was propelled by the convergence of social, mobile, analytics, and cloud technologies (SMAC). Every industry and occupation has been rewired around the first digital revolution. And while we were rewiring, which we are still doing, the second digital wave hit. The second wave began in 2012, and continues today, driven by robotics, cognitive technology (such as voice and sight recognition), and artificial intelligence (AI). Each of these waves has important implications for leaders and managers. The first wave is about connection, including people and machines, while the second is about intelligence and cognition, machines becoming intelligent, and people working with intelligent machines.

In response to the unique challenges leaders and managers face today, Douglas Ready, Senior Lecturer in Organization Effectiveness at the MIT Sloan School of Management, has studied the question of how to choose tools, new and old, and apply them in new, more collaborative management and leadership approaches. He has identified four key mindsets that leaders and managers must adopt to be positioned for success in the digital economy.[42]

- **Producers** who are focused on customers, are digitally savvy, make disciplined decisions, and excel at executing.
- **Connectors** who create trusted partnerships, build relationships, develop networks, and create a sense of belonging.
- **Explorers** who are curious, seek broad input, test, try, learn, repeat.
- **Investors** who pursue a higher purpose, operate sustainably, benefit the community, and develop continuously.

> A great leader in the new economy [is] someone who can build teams, understand the implications of technology on business, adapt to the speed at which business is happening, operate at a high level and a low level simultaneously, and build trust across the organization to get things done.[43]

Dan Shapero, vice president of global solutions at LinkedIn, has summarized the key characteristics of a great leader in the new economy as someone who can build teams, understand the implications of technology on business, adapt to the speed at which business is happening, operate at a high level and a low level simultaneously, and build trust across the organization to get things done.[44] For Ready, the mindsets leadership in the digital age must embrace and encompass "eroding, emerging, and enduring" behaviors. Eroding behaviors are antiquated leadership patterns, such as relying upon hierarchy for influence, command-and-control decision-making, and rigid strategic planning. Enduring behaviors are time-honored ideas about ethics, trust, and integrity, whereas emerging behaviors include digital savviness and collaboration skills.[45] Building on that model, organizations must develop leaders with perennial leadership skills, such as the ability to manage operations, supervise teams, make decisions, prioritize investments, and manage the bottom line. They must also develop leaders with capabilities such as leading through ambiguity, managing increasing complexity, being tech and data-savvy, managing changing customer and talent demographics, and handling national and cultural differences.[46]

Business leaders need to catch up to the challenges wrought by the second digital age. Whereas the first digital wave was about fueling greater connection—accessing computing power, social media interaction, servers that could store vast amounts of data—the second digital wave is about cognition, with machines making predictions and recommendations, rather than simply following orders and talking via chat bots. This movement from connection to cognition has presented vast leadership and ethical challengers for managers and leaders that are still being explored.

Leading in Teams

The dynamic environment these digital waves has swept in has changed the way we lead, no longer in silos, but as a symphony of experts playing in harmony. Indeed, the C-suite itself must now operate as a team. Deloitte calls this trend the "symphonic C-suite," which respondents to their 2018 Global Human Capital Trends survey viewed as among the most pressing issue facing organizations in recent years. Organizations have evolved from functional hierarchies to networked teams, to C-suite leaders themselves realizing that they must move beyond their functional roles and operate as a team. C-suite leaders who *rarely* worked together on projects or strategic initiatives are increasingly engaging in cross-functional teaming to run organizations as agile networks. This cross-functional collaboration is critical at a time when challenges themselves have become multidisciplinary. In the early months of the Covid-19 crisis, we witnessed the shift to a much more collaborative teaming model at the top of most businesses and organizations. No single functional leader, or team, working alone, can solve the complex problems that many organizations are grappling with today.[47]

Leading in an Age of Paradoxes

The author F. Scott Fitzgerald unwittingly summarized a key challenge faced by many business leaders today when he noted that, "The test of a first-rate intelligence is the ability to hold two opposed ideas in mind at the same time and still retain the ability to function."[48] Leaders and managers must continue their day-to-day functions while transitioning to a more integrative approach that not only incorporates ideas from many disciplines but also embraces paradoxes. In Deloitte's 2020 Human Capital Trends report, "The Social Enterprise at Work: Paradox as a Path Forward," they explore how organizations can remain distinctly human in a technology-driven world. The research reveals that the biggest paradox of the decade from 2010 to 2020 might be the competition between technology and humanity. The report called upon organizations to embrace three attributes—purpose, potential and perspective—that characterize what it means to combine people and technology to perform together as a social enterprise at work, not in opposition. The challenge for organizations is to reexamine whether humanity and technology are truly in conflict.[49]

The Covid-19 crisis reminds us that human concerns are not separate from technological advances at all, but integral for organizations looking to capture the full value of the technologies they have put in place. As organizations looked to adapt their ways of working in response to the crisis, they found that, in many parts of the world—though not all—technology was *not* the greatest challenge. In countries where the technology has been available, one of the biggest barriers was the difficulty of building models to integrate humans with those technologies: to create new habits and management practices for how people adapt, behave, and work in partnership with the technology available to them; to fulfill distinctly human needs such as the desire for meaning, connection, and well-being at work; to maximize worker potential through the cultivation of capabilities; and to safeguard ethical values. This crisis also presents a unique opportunity for organizations to overcome the instinct to treat humans and machines on parallel paths and, instead, build connections that can pave a path forward, one that can nurture growth. "In light of Covid-19, the opportunity, and risk, may never be greater for organizations to transcend this paradox and see possibility in what lies ahead."[50]

Embracing paradoxes is a theme for researchers looking at leading in a digital world. Douglas Ready at MIT has explored what he calls "embedded tensions and paradoxes" that make leading effectively much more complicated today. He summarized five paradoxes facing digital leaders:[51]

1. **Revitalization versus Normalization**. How to breathe new life into an organization without employees becoming "change weary." Thus, we find ourselves in the conflicted situation of needing revitalization but desiring normalization.

2. **Globalization versus Simplification**. Leaders struggle with creating organizational responses that address the need to master globalization while offering customers and employees optimal simplification.

3. **Innovation versus Regulation**. Many leaders struggle with the tension between the desire to boost innovation and the need to operate under increasing regulation.

4. **Optimization versus Rationalization**. Leaders are caught in a seemingly endless struggle to reconcile the tension between optimizing benefits to customers while rationalizing their costs of doing business.

5. **Digitization versus Humanization**. Leaders are struggling with how to reconcile the increasing need for the digitization of their business models while trying to create organizational climates that have an authentic sense of humanization—creating an overarching sense of purpose and collective ambition.

Dreaming and Leading in the Language of the Future

In a world where work is being disrupted by new human and technology teams and partnerships, where the workforce continues to move through corporate and ecosystem talent marketplaces, where work is both more team based and fractionalized, and where workplaces are more virtual, remote, connected, digital, and collaborative than ever before, it is no surprise that our mental models of leadership and management need to be updated. Perhaps we can think of it as a management, or leadership, operating system upgrade. For new requirements and new experiences, organizations need new ways of managing and leading. Management, including views of careers and organizations, need to build on resilience emphasizing adaptability, creativity, relationships, meaning, and growth. Management thinking at the start and through much of the twentieth century was predicated on the idea that business and organizational life was predictable, and the goal was to build scale and efficiency. At the end of the late 1990s, the term VUCA (volatile, uncertain, complex and ambiguous) is thought to have been first introduced at the U.S. Army War College to describe the new normal arising from the end of the cold war. We need to add to VUCA exponential speed; global hyper-interconnectedness; social media; a tsunami of data; and machines that learn, talk, and almost drive.[52]

Leading in the twenty-first century involves more than learning a new vocabulary: VUCA, exponentials, AI, superminds, coaching, design thinking, growth mindsets, and choice architecture. As summarized after conducting in-depth interviews on leading in the digital age, Ready reported that "what just jumped out at me from this was that we've learned the *language*. And that's great but it's also scary. The way I like to frame it is that we [have] learned the vocabulary of the language but we haven't [yet] learned to dream in that language. It's like you learn a second language. You know I spent six years learning Spanish, but [perhaps what matters is that] you don't dream in Spanish. Or I didn't dream in Spanish. You know, I haven't gone native with it."[53] While leaders are struggling with balancing new and old management models and disciplines, many leaders are also battling their own "leadership blind spots." In his research, Ready identifies four common leadership blind spots: strategic, cultural, human capital, and personal. These are critical issues for which executives' low levels of self-awareness "disrupt their ability to prepare for the intense and unfamiliar competition brought on by digitalization."[54] His discussion of "personal blind spots" highlights a critical lesson for leaders and managers in the twenty-first century. "The thing that scared me," Ready told us, "Is that in our research, 82 percent of the respondents reported that their leaders need to be at least somewhat digitally savvy. Yet only 13 percent of that population said they strongly agreed that their organizations are currently well-equipped to compete in the new economy. And yet, 71 percent reported that they were *personally ready* [emphasis added]. You know, that math just doesn't work." Ready noted that it takes you back to the performance management studies of years ago when 75 percent of leaders and managers self-reported that they were in the top 25 percent of the organization in terms of performance. Or in a phrase, we see the Lake Wobegon effect, the tendency for most people to believe that they are above average in whatever category is being measured.[55]

The challenge for each of us, as individuals, business leaders, and citizens is to design and create the future—not just manage it. The future needs less arrogance and more self-awareness; less management and more entrepreneurship; less sorting and more coaching. We need to focus less on cost and focus more on value, meaning, and impact. Embracing these shifts and proceeding with less rigidity and more adaptability will fuel the leadership and management resilience that the future requires.

PART III

Playbooks for Growth

Charting Paths Forward for Individuals, Leaders, Citizens, and Society

CHAPTER 8

Carpe Diem

As Individuals, Strengthen Adaptability and Choice to Face Great Opportunities and Disproportionate Responsibilities

It is not the most intellectual of the species that survives; it is not the strongest that survives; but the species that survives is the one that is able best to adapt and adjust to the changing environment in which it finds itself.

—Charles Darwin,[1] geologist and biologist

W e've all heard of the greenhouse effect and the placebo effect, but the Etsy effect? Not so much. The Etsy effect refers to the platform's remarkable track record for propelling female entrepreneurship. Etsy now connects about 1.9 million sellers of handmade creations with buyers around the world.[2] In contrast to the ride-sharing apps, which employ more men than women,[3] and mostly in urban areas, Etsy is fueled by women, who make up 87% of the sellers, most in rural locations.[4] Etsy sellers report earnings that satisfy their full-time salary aspirations. These micro-businesses, often consisting of only one person, have provided sellers with an opportunity to be creative and self-determined, and for a handful, to become millionaires.

Etsy is part of a dynamic digital platform economy that is increasingly offering opportunities for self-employment and independent work. Since its launch in Brooklyn, New York, in 2005, the platform has received

two unexpected boosts.[5] During the 2009 recession, at the time of the most severe economic and financial meltdown in the United States since the Great Depression, Etsy sales spiked due to consumer interest in less expensive, more personalized products.[6] Etsy sales spiked again in 2020 during the novel coronavirus (Covid-19) pandemic. The company saw its stock surge in contrast to the losses and turmoil in the broader market. As an online marketplace, Etsy was able to dodge the negative impact of the spreading coronavirus that hit many other companies, in part, because it did not have to worry about its supply chain. Etsy creators already worked from home. *Mad Money* host Jim Cramer endorsed Etsy as a "stay-at-home" tech stock that could outperform in the novel Covid-19 environment.[7]

Not without its detractors, Etsy has been criticized for selling items that were not handmade, for exploiting sellers who do not earn as much from their creations as they should, and more. Still, it's hard to argue with CEO Josh Silverman's characterization of Etsy as among the easiest paths to entrepreneurship today. "With 20 cents and creative energy," Silverman has said, "you can start a shop on Etsy and you can run it from your living room and sell it to the entire world." Etsy generated revenue of more than $818 million in 2019, up from more than $603 million the previous year.[8]

Etsy entrepreneurs embody many of the mindsets that individuals will need to embrace regardless of what direction they choose in the future world of work. Each of us will benefit from developing a growth mindset, a plan that acknowledges that careers will take many twists and turns, a willingness to fold learning and reinvention into our life, and an appreciation of the many ways to leverage technology. Of course, we will need social and institutional support and regulations to ensure that the gig economy does not create a class of "digital serfs." Yet this is not a time to rely solely on solutions from employers or government institutions, because many are not moving quickly enough. Individuals need to take charge and direct their own career paths. Although the future of work will bring great opportunities, it will also present disproportionate responsibilities to us as individuals. To help navigate the opportunities and challenges ahead, we need new playbooks.

Seven Key Mindset Shifts for Individuals

1. Develop a Growth Mindset versus a Fixed Mindset[9]

Carol Dweck found the focus of her life's work as a young researcher when she began studying the very different ways people handle failure. She observed how differently students grappled with hard problems. Some felt discouraged, while others actually enjoyed the challenge and did not even seem to think they were failing. They thought they were learning. These early observations led Dweck, a researcher and professor at Stanford University, to introduce the groundbreaking idea that two types of mindsets exist: fixed and growth. You are not stuck with the mindset you were born with, Dweck explains. A fixed mindset can prevent us from reaching our potential, while a growth mindset can open us up for possibility. People with a fixed mindset believe their intelligence and talents cannot change or improve. They also believe that talent leads to success, and effort perhaps less so. In contrast, people with a growth mindset believe their learning and intelligence can grow. They put in extra effort, which leads to higher achievement.

Dweck's work is part of a tradition in psychology that explores the power of people's mental models and beliefs. Whether they are conscious or unconscious, these beliefs influence whether we succeed in getting what we want. A growth mindset provides a significant advantage because the need to adapt and shift careers will require a willingness to learn new things and persevere.

Actions:

- To cultivate a growth mindset, keep learning. Take on new challenges, and if you can, new experiences. Don't be too quick to interpret setbacks or difficulties as a lack of ability—often they are the natural side effects of learning and growing.

- Be open to intradisciplinary education and work models that encourage learning across disciplines. To appreciate new ways of learning that better prepare students for today's marketplace, look no further than Erica Muhl, the founding director of the USC Iovine and Young Academy.[10] The Academy's unique education model, which teaches critical thinking and nurtures creativity, has emerged at the forefront of the drive to expand the reach of higher education beyond traditional disciplinary silos, and toward new ways of learning. The approach embraces the intersection of arts and design, engineering and computer science, business and venture management, tech savvy, and communications. The Academy reminds us, "it's not what you know, *it's how you think*."[11]

- Seek out new connections through personal and professional development and networking efforts. The opportunity to cultivate professional relationships may crop up in unexpected places, such as when you join a local book club, volunteer in your community, or participate in team sports.

2. Plan for a Long and Winding Career with Multiple Chapters, Rather Than Today's One-and-Done Career Model

Workers must set their sights on longer careers with multiple stages, involving ongoing training and reskilling. The Bureau of Labor Statistics reports that

Americans will have 12 to 14 jobs in their lifetime.[12] We need to shift from the mindset that "you are what you do," because we will be doing many things in a more varied career than ever before. Part of the challenge will be to continue to expand our capabilities and experiences to be able to pivot to a new job or career. The multiple chapters of our work lives will involve some transitions that will be to adjacent opportunities or to new roles in new organizations, and others that will involve wholesale reinvention. Expect these shifts. Prepare for them.

Actions:

- To build a resilient career, make adaptability your safety and transition net. Because many mainstream organizational models, community programs, and education opportunities are not yet designed for the number of career transitions ahead, it will be up to each of us to curate our own reinvention portfolio.
- Gain support from friends, family, and personal networks to drive ongoing reinvention. Starting with our first transition from education to work, to subsequent career moves and training, our personal networks will need to supply the encouragement, support, financial help, and sometimes tough love.
- Integrate exploring and preparing for your next chapter, or gig, while working on your current one. Anticipate future moves and opportunities.
- Build relationships via platforms like LinkedIn and connect on social media, such as Facebook, Instagram, and Twitter to forge relationships that can serve you professionally. Find ways to do the same across local communities, such as visiting and participating in makerspaces, local lectures, and meet-ups.

3. Hone the Mindset of a Team Player Rather Than the Solo Star

Increasingly, much of the work we do will be accomplished through interactions and contributions on teams. These teams will include diverse groups from across our organizations and ecosystems, teams working in the same location, and groups collaborating remotely and virtually. Teams will involve combinations of people as well as combinations of people and machines working together. In each of these situations, team dynamics will need to support the different roles people can play, the need for connection, and the opportunity for each member of a team to make a meaningful and recognized contribution.

Actions:

- Understand, develop, and practice team and group dynamics. Teaming is a uniquely human capability and perhaps among the most critical for us to develop. The ability to communicate, listen, express empathy, motivate, influence, and sometimes direct and take direction—and to do so in continually changing situations and contexts will be increasingly important for our professional and personal lives.

- Work on building connections with colleagues. "How well you're [socially] connected may be as important . . . as how smart you are and what your experiences are," says Michael Arena, the leader of talent at Amazon Web Services.[13] "You can have a bunch of brilliant people on a team, but if they're not socially connected with each other and they're not in sync, you're going to lose benefits on output."[14]

- Develop your personal capabilities to effectively lead, participate, and support the teams you are part of, formally and informally. The research that Tom Malone, at MIT, and his colleagues, conducted on group intelligence versus individual intelligence reinforces the view that team intelligence and performance are the result of factors beyond the technical capabilities of the individual team members. Instead, team intelligence is a function of the team's ability to understand the emotional state of team members, how actively and democratically team members participate in team activities, and the percentage of women on the team. Teams with more women tend to perform more effectively.[15]

- To accelerate learning, find ways to connect through networks to work groups, which John Hagel, former co-chairman of the Deloitte's Center for the Edge, defines as "a small group, of at most 15 people, who are working tightly every day together. Not just coming together on Fridays to do an update." These work groups are going to be the core unit of organization. A reason for the focus on workgroups, Hagel says, is the belief that learning is most effective when you are with a small group of people with whom you have trust-based relationships and where you are all committed to achieving more and to both challenging and supporting each other to learn faster.[16]

4. Race with the Machines, Not Against Them

Once we accept the fact that if tasks within a job are routine, they can often be done better and faster by a machine, we can shift our focus to developing capabilities that are complementary to and take advantage of machines rather than those that can be substituted by technology. Machines do not yet excel at tasks that require creative thinking, problem solving, critical thinking, or judgment (such as entrepreneurship or scientific discovery, or curiosity and questioning), interpersonal relationships (such as writing, communicating, leading, managing, influencing, entertaining, and negotiating) and combinations of intellectual, physical, and emotional flexibility and dexterity (illustrated by parts of jobs as diverse as nursing and plumbing).

Most of us will experience a growing interdependence with machines. Members of our teams and working groups will include robots, robotic process automation—software that automates specific work processes, and AI. Humans and machines will work together to find solutions for many of our most complex and pressing problems. Consider examples ranging from the renaissance radiologist, computers and people playing freestyle chess, and the ATM and bank tellers expanding the scope of banking services at local branches.

For many of us, this interdependence with machines will involve a significant redesign of our work. Some of the tasks that make up our jobs will be replaced by technology, some tasks will be augmented by technology, and others will involve deep human work that is focused on relationships, creativity, and imagination. The ability to code, manage complex data, and build algorithms (computer programs which can make predictions based on data and machine learning) will be important skills to develop. We will see an increase in jobs that involve building and maintaining the technologies— hardware, software, data, and algorithms—that enable the work of human– machine teams.

Actions:

- Recognize that our work will involve dynamic relationships with rapidly evolving technologies. Eric Topol, the cardiologist, scientist, and author, challenges organizations and individuals to cultivate the gift of time we will have in our work through the combination of substitution and augmentation.[17] Focus on the capabilities that can complement or be augmented by technologies. This will require both ongoing learning, capability development, and reskilling, and also an expanded focus on how to work with smarter tools and teams.

- Gain tech and data fluency, which will be required of all workers, regardless of occupation.

- Develop computational thinking, also known as statistical and algorithmic thinking, and our ability to see the world through data, statistics, predictions, and their visualizations—more commonly referred to as charts and graphs and increasingly data dashboards.

- Take the time, especially through learning platforms like online courses (MOOCs) and YouTube, to explore how the latest technologies work and how we work with them. John Seely Brown, JSB, former co-director of

Deloitte's Center for the Edge, and a leading thinker on learning and thriving in an age of exponential technologies, is a proponent of YouTube's ability to reflect the latest thinking in the rapidly changing field of artificial intelligence. "I get most of my new ideas every night by spending time reviewing posts on YouTube, Medium, etc." he says. "There are always two or three sources on the web that are pushing the very boundaries of new AI techniques. There is no way I can wait for a paper that's going to be published after six months of preparation, or wait to go to a lecture at Stanford that could already be two years out of date."[18]

5. Nurture Capabilities to Be an Explorer by Leveraging Your Curiosity and Love of Learning

The World Economic Forum identified an urgent need for humans to develop social and emotional capabilities to add value where machines fall short.[19] John Hagel and JSB, former co-chairs of the Deloitte Center for the Edge, have written extensively about the ability of individual learners to leverage an ecosystem of "semi-structured, unorthodox learning providers at the 'edges' of the traditional higher educational system."[20] Their work focuses on the importance of building capabilities, not just skills, and creating new knowledge, not just sharing practices and insights.[21]

Hagel highlights the critical difference between skills and core human capabilities as involving context. "Skills are very context specific," Hagel says. "If you're operating a certain type of machine in a certain environment or processing a specific kind of paperwork in a specific environment, you need a set of skills to do that. What we're talking about are capabilities that are helpful in any environment, that are *context independent*."[22]

One of these capabilities, curiosity, is often crushed in a scalable, efficiency world, Hagel notes. "You're asking questions? Go back and read the manual. Don't get distracted. You've got tasks to do," Hagel says, mimicking a manager with a thing or two to learn about leading. In contrast, in the future world of work, it will be essential to be able to anticipate unseen problems and opportunities, he says. "If you're not curious, you're not going to see them."[23]

Capabilities, not just skills, are critical to building multichapter lives, but Hagel and Brown's research also focuses on what motivates us to perform and grow, especially in environments of extreme pressure. "We identified a very specific form of passion, the passion of the explorer," Hagel says. "It's this constant drive to learn. You're not just doing it because you're going to lose your job or because you're told to learn." Their work has found that passion and capabilities are tightly related. People who have cultivated the passion of the explorer are innately curious and imaginative. "We believe if you can cultivate that passion, bring out that passion," Hagel says, "you'll at the same time lead to a much richer set of capabilities in the workforce."[24]

Actions:

- Develop and invest in your own enduring human capabilities as your foundation: curiosity, imagination, creativity, empathy, problem solving, teaming, and social intelligence.
- Secure a strong foundation in computational thinking. The key is building capabilities upon which you can acquire and update skills, such as knowledge of a computer program, or a specific process or type of technology, which are valuable in the spot job market.
- Invest in continual learning to develop skills through specialized programs, such as coding-intensive boot camps (for example, Dev Bootcamp, Hack Reactor, and Codecademy), Meetups, and MOOCs.

6. Own the Longevity Dividend Rather Than *Endure* Decades of Retirement

As we live 100-year lives, and work for 50 to 60 years, remember that the work will not be uninterrupted or full-time at the same job. It will involve a mix of work, learning, time off, and personal pursuits. For those who are complacent about their careers, thinking they are stable, the future of work tells us otherwise. Research from the U.S. Department of Labor shows that by 2024, *one in four* workers in the United States will be 55 or older. To put this in context, in 1994, *one in 10* workers were 55 or older.[25] Ongoing personal reinvention is the name of the game. Women and working mothers have been leading the way in recent decades in career reinvention. So have those challenging the idea of traditional retirement as a time in our lives traditionally characterized by "not working." Retirement, which might span decades from our mid-50s to our 90s, will involve threads combining work, leisure, learning, and public and community service.

Actions:

- Shift your mental model to plan for a long life. A 100-year life and 60-year career are different models than going to school for 20 years, working for 25 years, and then retiring.
- Choose employers where learning and work are highly integrated. Some companies offer employees subsidies for additional learning or the opportunity to transfer to other divisions internally to develop new skillsets. Do everything you can to continue to learn so you are ready for career reinvention—always.

- Your way forward involves viewing your life as a portfolio of careers and chapters.
- Family, friends, networks, and relationships, in and across communities, will be part of proactively building lives planning for and incorporating the longevity dividend.

7. Exercise Agency Whenever Possible, versus Waiting for Our Communities, Society, Companies to Come Up with the Solutions. Take Charge of Your Future

There is no denying that institutional challenges, financial inequities, and systemic racism exist. It is for these reasons, and more, that all of us might be well advised to combine pushing for institutional solutions (considered in more detail in Chapter 10) while exercising personal initiative. A critical personal course of action is to do everything within one's power to continue learning and reinventing throughout longer work lives. "Agency is defined as the capacity of individuals to act independently and to make their own free choices,"[26] says Gary Bolles, whose father wrote *What Color Is Your Parachute?*, one of the most popular books on finding a job. He believes among the most important skills to build in the future of work is personal reinvention, "the ability to let go of who you are today and recreate yourself as jobs around you change."[27]

Actions:

- Find your next new thing. Don't wait for it to come to you.
- Make choices. While we may lack institutional support for our actions, the future of work, our careers, and our lives will in part be about personal investments, experiments, and explorations.
- Leverage online courses—many are free—to explore and build skills via MOOCs (massive open online courses), nano courses, micro-credentials, or community college.
- Be open to new options by searching for jobs online, on community boards, and through your networks. Recognize that your next job might not be full time but a combination of gigs or your own new business.
- Realize that though it is critical to be self-motivated to look for solutions to the challenges you face, you are not in it alone. Continually build new relationships throughout your life that you nurture and can leverage for support. Make your voice heard in community and societal

discussions about investments and policies in the future of work public policy agendas.

Preparing for the Open Road

Never before have we had so many different ways to learn and explore new career options, thanks to the availability of online tutorials, classes, and even degrees, some free of charge. Stanford professor Andrew Ng has made it his mission to provide free education to the masses. Coursera, the online learning platform he co-founded in 2012, offers massive open online courses (MOOCs) at no charge. Partnering with universities and colleges, Coursera also offers fee-based offerings, including certifications and degrees in subjects such as engineering, data science, machine learning, computer science, and digital marketing. More than 47 million students use Coursera, which is just one example of MOOCs, growing in popularity for almost a decade.[28]

While students in the United States pursue an education primarily to attain a degree or certification to get a better job, for Mette Buchman, a lifelong pursuit of an education has been an extension of her interests and passions, exemplifying the concept of learning in the flow of life that will become increasingly important in the future world of work.

Buchman, who lived in Denmark for most of her life, has earned four master's degrees during a career that began and continued at the Danish Broadcasting Corporation until recently when she joined the New York Public Library as a senior operations advisor. Buchman has had more than a few stops along the way. After she earned a bachelor's degree in information science, she wanted to try something new. Her first master's degree was in film and media studies. Next, she earned a master's in women's studies, followed by a master's in culture studies, and finally a master's degree in organizational psychology.[29]

"The why's of each degree were very different but they were all more driven by intrinsic motivation than extrinsic motivation," Buchman says. "There is more support of an intrinsic motivation for learning in Denmark than you have in America." This support has been both cultural and financial. One degree was paid for by the Danish government and two by her employers. The only degree she paid for was the one she earned while living in the United States.[30]

The greatest value of these advanced degrees to Buchman has been acquiring what she calls a big toolbox. "I come to the table with analytical approaches and a method to tackle any issue," Buchman says. "In a modern workplace, agility, transformation, getting people to work together are very important."[31]

The United States is just starting to educate students to reflect the new needs of the future world of work. When music producer Jimmy Iovine and rapper-producer Dr. Dre co-founded Beats Electronics in 2006, they had trouble finding the right people to hire. Each had already launched highly successful companies in the music industry.[32] Now they were making a move from creating and engineering music to developing what they promised would be world-class consumer headphones. Their reputation as strategic innovators and future-thinking entrepreneurs meant they could attract any talent they wanted. But what they wanted was in short supply.[33] "When we started Beats, we tried to hire people and we would get either engineers or people from the creative community," Iovine said. "There weren't people who understood both languages."[34]

This shortage of ideal employees, however, didn't slow them down. In fact, it fueled another idea. Within four years, Beats Electronics captured a 20% market share of the headphones industry. Two years later, Apple bought the company for $3 billion, one of the largest acquisitions in Apple's history. This meant Iovine and Dr. Dre, whose real name is Andre Young, were able to do what most business leaders cannot. "I said to Dre, why don't we start a school that teaches people how to combine all this," Iovine recalled. They decided to fund a new model of education that would produce the kind of students they had wanted to hire when they launched Beats. Their $70 million endowment to the University of Southern California (USC) created the USC Jimmy Iovine and Andre Young Academy for the Arts, Technology, and the Business of Innovation. The first class graduated in 2018.[35]

In a world that tends to separate creative, intuitive right-brain learners from logical, analytical left-brain learners, Iovine and Dr. Dre seek to integrate both approaches. They wanted future generations to explore the intersection of disciplines that generally have little overlap: art and design with engineering and technology, and then couple those approaches with entrepreneurship and venture management. Fluency in more than one way of thinking, they believe, will equip graduates with the capabilities and tools they need to succeed in today's increasingly complex and collaborative marketplace. Also on the roster: teaching students to learn and work in teams and to adapt to uncertainty.[36]

Another academic dean who is shaking things up, Charles Isbell, has spent his academic career furthering AI and computing. A professor at Georgia Tech, and dean of the College of Computing, Isbell believes academia needs to prepare students for a different economy. That's why he made some big changes at Georgia Tech, such as offering an online Master of Science degree in Computer Science.[37] By putting a $7,000 price tag on the degree, Isbell made his Top-10 ranked program more widely available. Isbell noted that typical students are working adults in their 30s, many of whom would not have been able to pursue a graduate degree if this option did not exist. Isbell sees tremendous value in more students taking computer science classes. He believes that just as a liberal arts degree gives you a way of thinking, so does computer science.[38]

While the USC Jimmy Iovine and Andre Young Academy offers a very high-touch approach, Georgia Tech allows a more mass-appeal and scaledup approach, closer to the Coursera model. These two examples represent different ends of the spectrum. There will likely be more experimentation and diverse forms of innovation in higher education, continuing education, and distance learning.

> Just as a liberal arts degree gives you a way of thinking, so does computer science.

Tips for the Open Road

When we asked experts for the advice they would offer to individuals at the start and middle of their careers to prepare for the future of work, here is some of what we heard:

"The ability to learn, and learn fast, is really important," says Micha Kaufman, founder and CEO of Fiverr. "It's more important than actually gaining specific knowledge. If you asked me what the best programming language is to learn these days, it doesn't matter. It doesn't matter because by the time you master it, it's going to be obsolete. Right? So I think that

The Aging Workforce: A Business Leader's Bookshelf[39]

In the past 30 years, a great deal has been written about the aging workforce. Five key books frame much of this literature:

1. *Age Wave*

   by Ken Dychtwald, PhD[40]

   Based on 15 years of research by a leading expert on aging, this is the first comprehensive analysis of the consequences of the aging baby-boomer population on society.

2. *The 100-Year Life*

   by Lynda Gratton and Andrew Scott[41]

   Drawing on the unique pairing of psychology and economics, this book offers an analysis to help us all rethink retirement, finances, education, career, and relationships to create a fulfilling 100-year life.

3. *The New Long Life: A Framework for Flourishing in a Changing World*

   by Andrew Scott and Lynda Gratton[42]

   In this sequel to the 100-year life, the authors explore the factors that will lead to longer lives, the challenges for working and financing longevity, and the impact on health, technology, and governance.

4. *Encore*

   by Marc Freedman[43]

   Stories of baby boomer career pioneers, who are not content or affluent enough to spend their next 30 years on the golf course.

5. *The Longevity Economy*

   by Joseph F. Coughlin[44]

   Coughlin challenges myths about aging with groundbreaking multidisciplinary research into the concept of old age (hint, we made it up) and what older people actually want—not what conventional wisdom suggests they need—while focusing on the significant economic opportunities ahead for older workers as consumers and employees.

the ability to learn, and the ability to understand basic science, is important. Things that nurture your curiosity are important. Curious people succeed more."[45]

"In the increasingly computerized world, there will be an increasing demand for things that are consciously noncomputerized," says Tom Malone, professor at MIT's Sloan School of Management. "In the same way that we value handmade clothing and locally grown food, and there's something cool about watching a football game or a play live instead of watching it on TV, I think there's also an opportunity for people who are really good at the non-computer things. I'll give you a somewhat personal example from my own family. My son was an art major in college. His field is comics and graphic art. In spite of my efforts to influence him otherwise, he never really liked the idea of computer-generated animation. He does use computers a little bit in his comic art but I think he thinks of himself as an old-school type of artist. And I think there's a place for people like that. Or people who are really good at the pure human relationships that are needed. They might even resist using computers in places where they could because they want to maximize the interpersonal value of the relationships they establish. I think there's an opportunity for that, too."[46]

"My students know how to use Excel but I tell them to make sure to grow over the course of their lives, which is in some ways harder," says Louis Hyman, a historian of work and business at the ILR School of Cornell University, where he also directs the Institute for Workplace Studies. "When I meet with alums, the ones that are a year out, they say, 'I really wish I had some more time learning [data analytics programs like] Python.' The ones that are 10 years out, say, 'I wish I had some more time thinking about teaming.' But the ones that are like 20 or 30 years out say, 'I wish I had some more time reading history and philosophy.' Because when you're moving along in your career, you realize the hardest part of change is not that specific skill. It's how you think about transition and change. Because if you learn how to learn, you can pick up any skill on the way."[47]

"We need to boost entrepreneurship—we need to invent new ways of using technology to create value," says Erik Brynjolfsson, professor, MIT Sloan School of Management. "What skills and capabilities do we need to develop in our workforce so we're moving beyond optimization and cost, and into creating value? That's entrepreneurship. We need to create and be an entrepreneur. We need to develop the capabilities that machines have not yet mastered. It's useful to think about, what are the kinds of things that machines can do well now and will be able to do well in the next five, ten, twenty years? And what are the things where humans have a comparative advantage? There's no shortage of work that only humans can do. Machines are obviously very good at routine information processing, memorizing facts. On the other hand machines for now and I think for the foreseeable future are not very good at interpersonal dynamics, emotional intelligence, connecting with other people. So there are a lot of caring professions, and teamwork, leadership, persuasion, these are things that people look to other people for. Also another big category is creative work, whether that's scientific work or entrepreneurship or the arts, literature, other kinds of arts, performance, these are things that machines are not very good at and probably won't be for a very long time. So as someone charts their career, they should emphasize those kinds of things where humans have a comparative advantage."[48]

"What advice would I have for a student entering college today? Study history. And pick up the practices of a research historian," says John Seely Brown (JSB), former co-chairman of Deloitte's Center for the Edge and former research director of Xerox PARC. "Why? Because historians understand how everything gets entangled with everything else. That no simple explanation is real. You learn how to deal with situations that are profoundly entangled and you develop strategies and comfort in trying to untangle them. Research historians become trained in how to do that. So there's a certain . . . disdain for radical reductionism and squeezing problems into little tiny boxes—and defining anything that spills out of the box as an external anomaly."[49]

"Here's what I told my 23-year-old daughter about how to prepare for the future of work: Go discover what you love. And try to create something," says Michael Arena, head of talent at Amazon Web Services. "If a company won't let you do that, then fire the company and go someplace else. The last thing you want to do is double down on something that you don't love. It's a giant exploration. And by the way, we rarely have to tell that to young people, because that's the way they're thinking already. But that would be the first wave. Once you find that passion, dive deep. The learning comes by doing today. It's in the flow of work. The people that are incredibly successful today are the people that fall in love with something. Fall in love with the problem, and then go figure out what they need to learn to solve that problem. It's much more in the flow of work and the flow of passion and much less about applying what you've learned. It's both discovery, first in your passion and second in what you need to find to solve the problems that matter most to you."[50]

> "The people that are incredibly successful today are the people that fall in love with something. Fall in love with the problem, and then go figure out what they need to learn to solve that problem. It's much more in the flow of work and the flow of passion and much less about applying what you've learned."

Taking Advantage of the Open Road

One might argue that there has never been a better time to be a life-long learner or an entrepreneur with a great idea. We live in an era of the "University of Everything" as Kevin Carey writes in his book, *The End of College*, and you can team with amazing technology to leverage your inventions.[51] For the MIT team that put together the fourth annual Inclusive Innovation Challenge in 2019, the goal was to empower entrepreneurs who are making the economy work for more people. Erik Brynjolfsson, a professor at the MIT Sloan School of Management, who was involved in the innovation challenge, saw it as a way "to move the dial and change things by recognizing all these organizations that are doing amazing things, and give them the resources to thrive."[52]

Through the innovation challenge, start-ups working to broaden economic opportunities around the world were awarded $1.6 million in prizes. One of the $250,000 prize winners was JobGet, a mobile platform that matches low-income job seekers with employers. The company has helped nearly 10,000 people, primarily in blue-collar fields, improve their employment options and job security. JobGet offers a job-seeking process with no resumes, no cover letters, no interview questions. After job seekers set up a profile, which takes under five minutes, they can apply to hundreds of jobs.[53]

Rather than focus on automation taking everyone's jobs away, the innovation competition shifts the conversation to the people who are doing the opposite by leveraging technology to bring economic opportunity to people. Whether it's JobGet or Etsy, technology can help to create new opportunities for individuals to land jobs or create their own.

CHAPTER 9

Create Opportunity

As Business Leaders, Unlock Value by Reimagining Jobs and Partnering with Workers to Build Resilience and Dynamic Careers

Everyone is talking about the future of work. But few are asking the most fundamental question: What should that work be?

—John Hagel,[1] management consultant and author

If you have ever experienced whitewater rapids, you know the exhilarating sensation of making hairpin turns to avoid rocks; changing direction every few seconds; and trusting your team, your very wet, adrenaline-pumped team, as you cut through rushing currents. Few have navigated the treacherous Covid-19 rapids as deftly as Eric Yuan, CEO of Zoom, the now ubiquitous video conferencing technology company. Zoom was founded in 2011 when the video conferencing market was already in full swing. That same year, Microsoft bought Skype for $8.5 billion.[2] Four years earlier, Cisco, the Internet networking giant, bought WebEx, another leading videoconferencing company, for $3.2 billion.[3] Yet when the world went into quarantine, and businesses and schools relocated to living rooms, everyone learned to Zoom.

Though Yuan and his team had trained on responding to natural disasters in the run-up to going public in 2019, they never imagined they would face the size of the surge in demand. But they were prepared: Zoom's data centers were set up to handle traffic surges of 10 to 100 times normal, Yuan says. Zoom did not miss a beat when, overnight, everybody realized they needed a tool like Zoom to connect their people. In a typical day early in the pandemic, 343,000 people globally downloaded the Zoom app, compared with 90,000 people worldwide just two months earlier, according to mobile intelligence firm Apptopia. That's almost four times as many downloads in a single day. With engineering teams across the globe, Zoom was able to remotely monitor its systems around the clock.[4]

The job of business leaders today can resemble navigating in unpredictable, turbulent, crowded, and even dangerous waters. Whitewater is named for the bubbly, unstable, aerated, frothy water that appears white. As John Seely Brown (JSB), former co-chair of Deloitte's Center for the Edge, has reminded us, "we are living in a whitewater world. It's a world that is rapidly moving in often surprising and unforeseen ways." Like a whitewater kayaker, business leaders must learn to skillfully read the currents and disturbances of the context around them, "interpreting the surface flows, ripples, and rapids for what they reveal about what lies beneath the surface."[5]

Navigating the rapids also involves the occasional crash into rocks or capsizing. Yuan, the entrepreneur, experienced such challenges early in the quarantine, including security and privacy breaches. He responded by acknowledging the problems and working harder to address them. He also learned more about his customer base, always a prime focus for Yuan. The typical Zoom client had been a company's chief information officer who had been introduced to the product's functionality, including privacy features, and leveraged them. With the pandemic came many first-time users who thought nothing of posting on social media a gallery view from a Zoom call, which they did not realize included their meeting room and password. Suddenly, complaints of "Zoom bombing" arose, with strangers crashing video conferencing calls. Yuan and his team quickly realized that the Covid-19 crisis brought a different user base to his product, one that did not know about Zoom's security features. As a result, Zoom shifted to focus on "how to make it easier for first-time users," Yuan explains. "We changed our practice."[6]

Companies poised to thrive in today's whitewater world, and the future world of work, are organized to facilitate quickly creating new products, services, and experiences. They are sensing and building, responding and growing, as they focus on continual improvement. They work in highly integrated teams, with a dedicated customer focus, and the ability to deliver in sprints. Agile by design, the next MVP (minimum viable product) is their touchstone.

The rapid rise of Zoom during the first half of 2020 is likely to be a case taught in business schools. And well it should. While Zoom will attract its fans and critics, it is hard to argue that there is not something essential to learn from this evolving story. In uncertain and volatile markets, nimble, entrepreneurial companies can take on corporate giants and reorder industries. This is the growth opportunity of leading in the whitewater world through maintaining an almost fanatical focus on usability and customer experience ("it's so easy to use"), building for scalability, investing in resilience, and managing a team focused on continual improvement and unseen problems. The Zoom team's ability to navigate the whitewater environment illustrates the types of challenges in which humans excel, and AI, so far, does not.

Seven Key Mindset Shifts for Business Leaders

1. Create Value, Meaning, and Impact, Moving Beyond Cost Reduction and Efficiency as the Main Goal

"Everyone is talking about the future of work. But few are asking the most fundamental question: what should that work be?" John Hagel and John Seeley Brown (JSB), former co-chairmen of Deloitte's Center for the Edge since

2007, have been asking questions like this in their work to identify emerging opportunities and big shifts in the business landscape.[7] In their recent research, they dive deeply into this question: The future of work to what end? Their research points out that "far too many initiatives are focused on incremental gains or efficiency-boosting activities." They call robotic process automation, AI, and machine learning "shiny new tools" that companies can implement to cut costs and work faster with less human labor. However, they caution that "when organizations subscribe to this narrow perspective, the work of tomorrow will be the same as the work of today." As Hagel and JSB point out, the opportunity is greater than doing more of the same, only faster and cheaper. The big opportunity is to expand notions of value beyond the cost to the company. Companies have additional levers to explore new sources of value and meaning to remain competitive amid rapidly changing market dynamics.[8] Companies that successfully redefine work to focus on our human qualities enable their employees to engage in four types of activities: Identifying unseen problems and opportunities; developing approaches to solve problems and address opportunities; implementing new approaches; and iterating and learning based on the impact achieved. The Zoom example powerfully illustrates human beings excelling in each of these four types of activities.

Actions:

- Shift the objective of work beyond efficiency to expand the value and impact delivered to customers, workers, and communities.
- Fundamentally redefine work from executing routine tasks to creatively addressing unseen problems and opportunities.
- Cultivate work to use our human qualities, shifting from skills to capabilities.
- Build relationships within and across teams so that managers and workers can focus on output and impact, not just on workflow and transactional activities. Connect teams so they consider the impact and think about what's important to customers and workers.
- Instill a culture of tolerance for heterodox ideas and risk-taking.

2. Focus on Redefining Work as the Way Forward, Not Just Redesigning Jobs

The application of robots, robotic process automation, and cognitive and AI technologies offers unprecedented opportunities to improve efficiency and productivity. Unfortunately, many companies are aiming their future of work efforts narrowly at *job redesign* for efficiency and cost savings, which will only get them so far, rather than at *redefining work*. In the limited view of redesigning jobs, workers represent cost savings rather than the capacity to create new value for the business and the customer. When most companies redesign jobs, their narrow focus is on productivity—the same work outputs, only faster and cheaper, with fewer errors. The challenge is not only to redesign jobs but to expand the focus to redefining work, including product strategies and business models.

By *redefining work*, employees at all levels focus on finding and addressing unseen problems and opportunities. "The unseen is a key aspect of redefining work," Hagel and JSB have noted in their research. "Addressing a hidden problem or opportunity has the potential to create more value because it has been neither considered nor understood; there is room for far more learning, and impact, by trying to better understand a brand-new situation than from making incremental improvements on a well-defined issue."[9]

A critical shift for business leaders is to balance the focus on efficiency and productivity on the one hand with innovation and value on the other. Innovation does not arise from productivity and efficiency unless work teams, managers, and employees are challenged to recognize that better work is not just more of the same. It is something new: new value, products, new services, new experiences—also known as entrepreneurialism. It is a fusion of value for the customer and well-being for the workforce.

Expanding Opportunity: from Redesign to Redefine

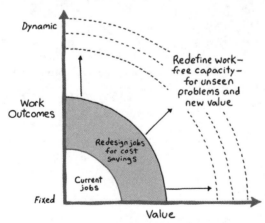

Source: "Defining Work for New Value." *Deloitte Insights*, December 2019.

Cost savings and efficiency *can* have larger and longer lasting value when business leaders use the cost savings to fund investments in new products and strengthening customer relationships and experiences. As we have noted, the proliferation of ATMs resulted in redesigning the jobs of retail bankers so that they offered a different service from the machines. Retail bankers were no longer simply dispensing cash but they could spend more time with customers, introduce them to new products and services, and extend the bank's ability to offer a higher level of customer interaction and service. Doing more of the same, and doing it faster, is *not* where the magic happens—the magic is when workers and teams can solve new problems and create new value, services, and relationships.

Actions:

- Integrate job redesign—for speed and improved output through automation—with work redefinition to create new value with freed capacity.
- Challenge work groups and teams to focus on uncovering unseen problems—not just cost savings.
- Create work group agency so teams have the focus and the flexibility to both produce the product *and* improve the product. As we have learned from the Toyota factory line, among the world's most productive *and* innovative manufacturers, the job of the workgroup on the line is not just to execute production but to improve production and quality.[10]
- Build work groups and teams around the relationships that will drive innovation, contribution, and well-being, not just efficiency. Design and connect work groups and teams in networks, within and beyond the enterprise, to create value and opportunity for workers and customers.[11]

> Doing more of the same, and doing it faster, is *not* where the magic happens—the magic is when workers and teams can solve new problems and create new value, services, and relationships.

3. Leverage the Entire Open Talent Continuum, from Full-time Workers to Freelancers, Crowds, along with Virtual and Digital Workplace Options

Work and workforces have been increasingly separated from companies as we have witnessed with the expansion of the alternative workforce—managed services, contractors, freelancers, gig workers, and crowds. As the workforce has expanded to a much broader continuum of employment models who are working in new ways, and in new places, the traditional talent management mindset of "attract, develop, retain" employees is giving way to new approaches. Historically, the employee lifecycle has focused on recruiting the employees we need; developing them with prescribed, linear, career paths; and holding on to them—especially the "critical talent"—as long as possible.

Deloitte Consulting LLP's Workforce Transformation practice is developing a new approach, beyond the traditional employee lifecycle, to a workforce ecosystem cycle, shifting to a new mindset: *access, curate, engage.*[12]

> **Access:** How do you tap into capabilities and skills across your enterprise and your broader ecosystem? This includes sourcing from internal and external talent marketplaces and leveraging and mobilizing on- and off-balance-sheet talent.
>
> **Curate:** How do you provide employees—ecosystem talent—and teams with the broadest and most meaningful range of development? This includes work experiences that are integrated into the flow of their work, their careers, and their personal lives.
>
> **Engage:** How do you interact with and support your workforces, business teams, and partners, to build compelling relationships? This includes multidirectional careers, in, across, and outside of the enterprise; and for business leaders and teams, providing insights to improve productivity and impact while taking advantage of new ways of working and teaming and new digital technologies.[13]

Actions

- Integrate talent and workforce strategies and programs to access, curate, and engage capabilities from within and across the enterprise and ecosystem.
- Explore how to use talent and opportunity marketplaces, not just HR managers and administrators, to deploy people by giving them agency to choose full-time and part-time jobs, gigs, and assignments across your organization. Watch workforce engagement rise and the quality of workforce information and analytics improve.
- Develop an organizational culture, as well as manager and team incentives, to encourage development and stretch assignments. Reinforce the concept that employees work for the company, not just one division or one manager.
- Build relationships across the entire talent ecosystem for your industry to be able to broadly access talent and create opportunities for people to move in and out of your organization for jobs and projects.

- Create an environment providing the comfort, connection, and opportunity to contribute that workers are seeking, where they feel they are part of the organization's mission, purpose, and team.[14]

- Recognize that work and teams are increasingly structured around projects. A number of creative industries, including films and media, have moved from vertically integrated studios and companies to a portfolio of projects—where each project can be crafted and constructed to access capabilities and talent, from almost anywhere to create unique results.

- Understand that the relationship between work and workplaces are in the midst of fundamental shifts. These changes have been accelerated globally by the Covid-19 pandemic. During the public health crisis, a record number of workers shifted almost overnight to remote and virtual work. MIT research reported that in the first week of April 2020, just under 50 percent of workers surveyed in the United States were working remotely.[15] A survey of CFOs during that same time period reported that 74 percent of organizations surveyed expected to move at least 5 percent of their workers to *permanently* remote positions post Covid-19, and a quarter of organizations surveyed were planning to move at least 20 percent of workers to permanent remote work.[16] Redesigning work for remote and hybrid ways of working is a key action and opportunity for business leaders.

> If at this critical juncture, insufficient attention is devoted to inventing and creating demand for, rather than just replacing, labor, that would be the "wrong" kind of AI from the social and economic point of view.

4. Build Superminds, Superteams, Superjobs, Investing in Capabilities for a Resilient Workforce, Beyond a Narrow Focus on Skills and Reskilling

The future of work is about new combinations of teams of people and machines. These "superteams" will leverage the three ways people and machines work together: through substitution, augmentation, and unleashing people to spend more time on work that is uniquely human. The same three approaches can be applied to individual jobs to create "superjobs"—taking over some tasks, or parts of some tasks; extending workers' capacity to do more work, often faster, more accurately, and at higher levels of complexity; and providing the gift of time to focus on uniquely human work and capabilities.[17]

Focusing on the opportunities of new combinations of human and machine intelligence, Superminds, as framed by Tom Malone at MIT, represents a shift for many business leaders beyond the pressure to focus on short-term efficiencies and costs. Daron Acemoglu, a leading economist, warns of the dangers of what he calls the wrong kind of AI. "If at this critical juncture, insufficient attention is devoted to inventing and creating demand for, rather than just replacing, labor, that would be the 'wrong' kind of AI from the social and economic point of view," Acemoglu notes. "Rather than undergirding productivity growth, employment, and shared prosperity, rampant automation would contribute to anemic growth and inequality."[18]

In a whitewater world with 100-year lives and a 60-year portfolio of careers, businesses have a unique responsibility to build the capabilities of the workforce. Deloitte's 2020 Global Human Capital Survey reported that the entities viewed as primarily responsible for workforce development were organizations and businesses, first (73 percent), and individuals, second (54 percent). Both far exceeded the next three on the list: educational institutions (19 percent), governments (10 percent), and unions and professional associations (8 percent). Only 45 percent of respondents in the same report said that their organizations reward workers for developing skills and capabilities. Even fewer (39 percent) are rewarding leaders for developing skills and capabilities on their teams.[19]

In addition to reskilling the workforce for near-term needs, leaders should consider an approach that treats workforce development as a strategy for building worker and organizational *resilience*—equipping workers, and the organization, with the tools and strategies to adapt to a range of uncertain futures. Through a resilience lens, workforce reinvention shifts from something that could threaten worker security to the very thing that defines it. Workers who are able to refresh their skills and learn new ones are those who will be most able to find employment in our rapidly shifting job market.[20]

Actions:

- Expand the focus for workforce development beyond tactical skilling and reskilling. While these programs may help mitigate short-term needs, a critical priority is shifting to a focus on developing enduring human capabilities and recognizing and investing in workforce resilience and adaptability. Creating the societal support—including transition nets, healthcare, opportunities for training and continuing education—will be critical steps.

- Design teams and jobs to take advantage of the unique combinations of humans and machines, leveraging the power of automation and substitution, the opportunity in augmentation with technological tools and algorithms, and unleashing human workers—with the gift of time and the challenge to focus on unseen problems—to focus on deep human work.
- Balance capabilities *and* skills when recruiting and accessing talent.
- Build talent marketplaces to more effectively deploy workers and to create the opportunity for workers to invest and own their career portfolios and progressions. Talent markets can create better information and analytics on both the workforce and workforce requirements, more dynamically allocate workers across full-time and part-time projects and gigs, and strengthen workforce agency and choice.
- Grow relationships with community, and leverage online education and technical institutes to build skills and capabilities through nano certifications and new combinations of learning badges and programs.

5. Develop the Agility to Lead in Whitewater Conditions, in Real Time, Shifting from Leading in Still Water, in Linear Ways

One of the fundamental business and organizational shifts for leaders in the accelerated future of work is to move beyond mindsets based on static, linear, and predictable strategies and workflows. In a volatile, uncertain, complex and ambiguous world, with technologies continuing to accelerate at exponential speed, leaders need to be prepared to sense and adapt for real time changes. The heart of this challenge is to build adaptable organizations and agile ways of working.

Leading in whitewater involves shifting from a focus on hierarchy and workflows to a focus on teams, networks, and continual improvement and new outcomes. Teams can reconfigure quickly for new challenges and play offense and defense when required. As Tom Friedman, the global columnist for *The New York Times* has reminded us, teams, and individual players, have to prepare "like someone who is training for the Olympics but doesn't know what sport they are going to enter."[21]

Actions:

- Cultivate a managerial and leadership mindset based on a whitewater, VUCA world. Prepare yourself, your teams, and your networks for change and focusing on unseen, unpredictable, problems.

- Make teams and networks the unit of management, action, and analysis for your business and organization.
- Understand the importance of how to design and deploy teams and what makes for and high performing teams. Remember the three characteristics of intelligent teams: high levels of social perceptiveness, high levels of democratic participation, and higher percentages of women.[22]
- Develop a team leader mindset and portfolio with the flexibility to lead as a coach, a designer, a social scientist (behavior economist, cultural anthropologist, and a psychologist), a teacher, and a manager.
- Lead beyond organizational hierarchy and boundaries through adopting an agile, project, initiative focus and mindset.

6. Adapt a Symphonic C-suite Mindset That Integrates Leaders, People, Teams, and AI, Rather Than Focusing on Functional Silos and Technology Alone

In their effort to navigate the Covid-19 pandemic, business and public sector executive teams around the world found that most of their challenges did not fit neatly into organizational lines. They involved workforce (HR) *and* customer (sales and service) *and* finance *and* technology (IT). They involved research and development, *and* supply chain, *and* business operations unit leaders. They often required collaboration and response in almost real time. In Deloitte research in 2018, this team response was described as the "symphonic C-suite," or teams of leaders. In this construct, C-suite executives combine business unit and functional ownership with cross-functional teaming to run the organization as an agile network.[23]

Senior leaders must emerge from their silos to work with each other. To address cross-disciplinary challenges, a company's top leaders must work as teams of leaders. In 2020, Deloitte extended this research in a tenth annual Global Human Capital Trends report, challenging business leaders with the question, "Is it possible to remain distinctly human in a technology-driven world?" The report presents an integrated approach for merging the historically disconnected tracks of technology and human performance over recent decades.[24]

Actions:
- Identify business priorities that require cross-functional collaboration among leaders for their success. For example, most future of work

projects (human–machine collaboration, new workplace strategies), digital transformation, and innovation efforts all require combinations of leaders to be involved in their design and execution. Bring teams of leaders together to tackle these challenges.

- Develop performance management and career paths for leaders that provide the cross-disciplinary experience required for integrative issues.
- Evaluate leaders on their ability to influence, network, and collaborate, as well as their track record exercising authority.
- Shift the executive agenda *beyond* a competition between people and technology. Reframe business challenges as team challenges and expect that every project and priority will involve a combination of people and technology to achieve improved and new business results.
- Extend the symphonic C-suite and teams of leaders to access leaders and influencers in the ecosystem—beyond the enterprise—including suppliers, customers, and business partners.

7. Co-create and Partner with the Workforce by Leveraging the Role of Talent Markets and Platforms—Moving Beyond the Traditional Approach of Managing Work and Workforces as Prescribed Administrative Functions

One of the most interesting new ways of working is the introduction of talent marketplaces as mechanisms for matching the growing demand to staff full-time jobs, short-term gigs, and projects of every size, with employees and alternative workers. Recent research on opportunity marketplaces from *MIT Sloan Management Review* and Deloitte report on the growing use of opportunity marketplaces, defined as "systems and platforms that enable talent to access strategically valuable opportunities while building skills and capabilities for themselves." These marketplaces can facilitate better and faster exchanges between organizations and their workers "by empowering and encouraging workers to evaluate, choose, and act on opportunities important for the organization and for themselves."[25] Similar shifts are occurring on platforms, like GitHub[26] for programmers, and InnoCentive[27] for competitive problem solving. The shift is beyond one of managing work to an approach whereby self-organizing communities and competitions can facilitate new types of cooperation and co-creation.

Co-creation, teaming, and collaboration are not designed to be managed or controlled in the same way work was supervised through much of the last century. As work is less mechanized, less process based (because process-based work can largely be automated), and less standardized (because standard work can also be significantly automated), work becomes a team sport. The focus moves from control, to connection, context, and co-creation. The future of work is as much about new ways of people, teams, and managers collaborating to solve new problems as it is about new combinations of people, robots, AI, and machines working together.

Actions:

- Change the language. Integrate combinations of people and machines moving beyond people versus technology; move from models of managerial control to team coordination; shift from managing for cost efficiency—alone—to cost, and value, and meaning.

- Introduce talent and opportunity marketplaces to facilitate the ability of both employees and alternative workers to access and be matched to a complex portfolio of options including jobs, gigs, assignments, and projects.

- Organize work around platforms to facilitate the sharing of knowledge and tools (e.g., GitHub) and competitions to create and access new solutions (e.g., Innocentive).

- Extend teams to co-create within and across the enterprise and the ecosystem.

- Focus on the horizontal nature of work, careers, teams and ecosystems moving beyond a vertical—control—oriented view of how work is done.

Choosing Value Creation and Impact

In the decade ahead, business leaders face the opportunity to shift their focus from increasing efficiency and cost savings to creating value. Hagel reminds us that the road to greater value is not from cost. Instead, we are challenged to redefine work for new value. Hagel asks leaders to consider how to deliver more value, meaning, and impact to the marketplace, to customers, and to each other within a company. Finding answers to these questions "would translate into rapid growth and profit improvement for companies," Hagel says.[28]

What companies like Zappos, Airbnb, and Uber, and major tech innovators like Apple, Amazon, and Google have in common is a core business philosophy focusing on creating new value in new ways: a shoe company without shoe stores; a hospitality company without buildings; a transportation company without cars; retailers without stores. They are all in the business of creating new value by exploring and executing new ways of working—leveraging new combinations of people and technology.

There was a time when many believed the one business that would never move online was shoe sales. Consumers were convinced that you could not buy shoes online. How can you buy shoes if you cannot try them on? Returning ill-fitting shoes by mail is too expensive. Enter Tony Hsieh and his innovative solution. Hsieh, the CEO of Zappos, the groundbreaking online shoe retailer, decided to address those concerns head on by making them part of the core business strategy. Zappos has a return policy that allows customers to ship back merchandise *for free* for 365 days from date of purchase. That's quite a promise. It helped grow Zappos to more than $1 billion in gross annual merchandise sales. Customers choose from a large selection of shoes they can try on in their living room with their favorite outfit and ship back at no charge. The selling point was not a better shoe; it was top customer service coupled with a new shoe-shopping experience.[29]

The goal has indeed flipped from scalable efficiency to organizations that can learn and create value. In their research, Hagel and JSB have charted the move from scalable efficiency to scalable learning. Scalable learning is about organizations focusing on creation and unseen problems. "We've come to believe that all our institutions will need to make a fundamental shift from a scalable efficiency model to a scalable learning model," Hagel says, noting that the scalable efficiency model has driven the growth and success of large institutions around the world over the past century. In this model, the primary focus is on performing complex tasks efficiently and reliably at scale. However, in a world that is evolving at an accelerating rate with growing uncertainty, customers are less willing to settle for standardized, mass-market products and services. "The combination of these two forces creates a paradox: scalable efficiency is becoming less and less efficient," Hagel says.[30]

The alternative is what Hagel calls scalable learning, the ability to learn faster at scale. "I'm talking about learning in the form of creating new knowledge by confronting situations that have never been seen before and developing new approaches to create value," he explains. "It's learning through action, not just sitting and reading books or thinking great new thoughts." Rather than standardize all tasks, the most efficient way to respond to rapidly changing contexts will be to learn faster about the new approaches that will deliver the most value efficiently.[31]

Leaders have an opportunity to remind workers, including the 55-year-old worker, to use muscles that may have atrophied in order to learn, adapt, and thrive, Hagel says. "The key, we believe, is to create environments now that will not only encourage you but make it easier to exercise those muscles," he says. "How do you redefine the work environment? How do you define a new set of practices for workers and coach them in adopting those practices? And then at the leadership level, how do you get leaders to embrace a different way of leading?" Hagel suggests that asking powerful questions as a leader "is huge in terms of its impact on the workers. How would I solve that? How would I address that? And by the way, it's not only okay but expected to ask questions. And it's okay to ask for help. That's a powerful message."[32]

A recent survey conducted in the United States found that during the Covid-19 pandemic, in some economies, nearly 50 percent of the workforce is working remotely.[33] Thus, a new challenge has emerged for leaders amidst the pandemic and the move to remote work. Leaders must design ways of working so that the percentage of their workforce working remotely is engaged, productive, and innovative. Technology brought us to this point. We need to find the opportunities in an economy in which a large percentage of the workers are not in the traditional workplace.

Whether you believe you will be returning to work or returning to the future of work, we will not be returning to where we were pre-Covid-19. Business leaders will be charged with developing management strategies and practices that can engage the workforce in its broadest sense—to create value and improve at faster rates. This is not done by efficiency, compliance, and sheer will alone. This is accomplished by harnessing the creative and social energies and impulses of people and technology working in teams and solving problems together.

> Business leaders face critical choices that will determine whether their workers are marginalized or empowered, and whether their organizations are creating value or merely cutting costs.

Preparing the Workforce for the Transition

Business leaders face critical choices that will determine whether their workers are marginalized or empowered, and whether their organizations are creating value or merely cutting costs.[34] A pressing challenge facing corporate leaders is how to support employees in their work transitions, according to Lynda Gratton, professor of management practice.

"Why aren't adults taking gap years the way that students do before starting colleges?" Gratton asks. "One reason is that they are penalized by their companies for taking time out. Women see their careers stall when they take time out to raise children. Men, too. But the ability to move in and out of the workforce will become increasingly important in the future, especially as we have longer careers. More businesses need to recognize this."[35]

Gratton notes that neither individuals nor businesses tend to excel at transitions. "We find them very challenging," she says, pointing to a race between how quickly technology is changing and our ability to learn enough to keep up and keep our jobs. However, our value lies in innately human capabilities, such as creativity, curiosity, and empathy. "Robots and AI don't have them," she notes. "Ironically, we have taken a lot of that out of the workplace. I think it's crucial that we bring being human back to work."[36]

The way that most companies are adopting AI appears to fly in the face of the spirit of corporate citizenship. Daron Acemoglu, a professor of economics at MIT, believes the kind of AI many companies focus on prioritizes automation over the worker. In his work with Pascual Restrepo, Acemoglu notes that automation is not making workers more productive, it is enabling employers to substitute cheaper capital for workers. Acemoglu challenges the focus on automation, noting that "the best minds in the current generation are gravitating towards computer science, AI and machine learning, but with a heavy emphasis on automation." Instead of focusing on automation, Acemoglu believes that the approach that would "create the tide that lifts all boats" is to use new technologies to create new tasks, new occupations, new industries, new ways of organizing production so that we reinstate workers into new jobs in which they can have high productivity.[37]

> At this critical juncture . . . executives can choose to use advances in technology to drive more efficiency and cost reduction, or they can consider more deeply the ways to harness these trends and increase value and meaning across the board . . .

At this critical juncture, we are redefining what it means to work and to be an employer. Chief executives can choose to use advances in technology to drive more efficiency and cost reduction, or they can consider more deeply the ways to harness these trends and increase value and meaning across the board—for businesses, customers, and workers.[38]

Leading Through Paradoxes

In an interview in an *MIT Sloan Management Review* report, Ronald de Jong, a member of the executive committee at Royal Philips, identified several trade-offs—or, more precisely, cultural tensions—that leaders must address. These include digitization and humanization; speed, focus, deliberateness, and integration; analytics and intuition; and purpose and profits.[39] When we asked several leaders for their business strategies and insights that address some of the paradoxes inherent in leading work, workforces, and workplaces in today and tomorrow's dynamic world, here is some of what we heard.

"What makes a great leader in this new economy?" asked Dan Shapero, vice president of global solutions at LinkedIn. "In a way, it boils down to a few things: Do they build great teams? Do they understand the implications of technology on the business? Are they able to adapt to the speed at which business is happening? Can they operate at a high level and a low level simultaneously? And do they have the ability to build trust across the organization to get things done? In other words: Great leaders use a new playbook."[40]

"It's time for leaders to take a stand. It's time for them to be bold, to articulate . . . their own powerful leadership narrative," said Doug Ready, senior lecturer at MIT Sloan School of Management, and co-author of *The New Leadership Playbook for a Digital Age.* "To be crystal clear about the fact that a) they don't have all the answers, but b) they're in pursuit of those answers and they're going to reach out and ask for help. Understanding that if you tie a lot of these things together, asking for help can set you free. People are dying to make their contributions to the organization. Most people pop out of bed in the morning wanting to do good things for their customers and their companies. And yet they're often just not asked. I think by being clear, and asking for help, you get more power by giving it away. Building this notion of a community of leaders is energizing in an organization."[41]

"The world is getting more complex. The problems that the world is dealing with, that society is dealing with, are more complex. And therefore I think it's a natural assumption that the solutions will have to be more complex as well," commented Erica Muhl, dean of the USC Iovine and Young Academy. "Our recent interim president Wanda Austin, who is literally a rocket scientist, said to me once, 'Erica, you know, the world's most difficult problems have rarely been solved by a single discipline.' And it was a really concise but I think kind of accurate thing to say in that if we think about some of the things that we've had to deal with as a society, that is generally true. But I think it's even more true as we go forward today that solving some of the things we are facing will naturally take multiple approaches, multiple problem-solving approaches, all of which may include an ability to understand the human component of those problems in a way that is deeper and more profound maybe than has been applied by some of the disciplines in the past."[42]

"If as a company you've created an amazing structure and team and set of ideas that dominated in one era, inevitably if you cling onto that old cloth the rest of the world outside you will move on," noted Gillian Tett, editor-at-large, United States, of the *Financial Times.* "If you want to beat that, you need to not just think about how the world's moving outside but look at your own structures and mental taxonomies too. There are lots of ways of doing that. I generally believe that learning to look at yourself afresh through someone else's eyes is one of the most powerful tools that you can use to see your taxonomy because it's very hard for us, most of us, to see our taxonomies because it's what we live every day. It's how our minds are shaped. It's like asking a fish to think about water. Because you know, they're just in it. They can't see it. So we all think it's entirely natural to put sales in one department, marketing in another, IT in a third department. Just as to Sony, in 1999, it seemed obvious to have hardware, software, and content in different departments. That wasn't obvious once the iPod took off. So the reason I come back to anthropology is because it gives us the ability to look back at ourselves."[43]

"There's a recurring pattern throughout history that even the most amazing . . . especially the most amazing technologies, take a surprisingly long time to have an impact on productivity and performance," commented Erik Brynjolfsson, professor, MIT Sloan School of Management. "That's because . . . you have to rethink the way work is organized, the incentive systems, the business processes, decision rights, the hiring and the training and human capital. As managers learn which new organizational forms broadly define better work, there's a lag. That's what we're going through right now with AI and these other technologies as we rethink work. Hopefully we can tighten that lag a little bit and speed up the adoption of the more successful business models and organizational forms."[44]

Navigating the Future by Creating It

How do we chart the road ahead? By leading with human capabilities. Research by Deloitte has identified three actions for leaders to consider as they confront the uncertain future of work.[45] Each critical action, by design, is based on a uniquely human capability and characteristic: imagination, composition, or activation. In a world of paradoxes, speed, complexity, and machines, we need to lead by doing uniquely human things. People imagine the future; people compose music, work, businesses; and people activate curiosity, passion, connectedness, and belonging. We sometimes need to be reminded that we invented all this technology. This is our technology and it is in the service of us. Business leaders can set goals that reach beyond cost and efficiency to include value and meaning. They have the chance to analyze, redesign, and redefine work, workforce, and workplace options that take advantage of the value of automation, alternative talent sources, and collaborative workplaces. And they can align the organization, leadership, and workforce development programs to access skills, curate next-generation experiences, and engage the workforce of the future in long-term relationships and business leaders in new ways of working. This creative process involves trial and error. Tim Harford, author of *Adapt: Why Success Always Starts with Failure*, notes our difficulty accepting the error part of trial and error. "[We need to] take problems in our stride when a decision doesn't work out, whether through luck or misjudgment. And that is not something human brains seem to be able to do without a struggle."[46]

Stewart Butterfield, the Canadian entrepreneur and businessman best known for co-founding the photo-sharing website Flickr and the team platform Slack, recognizes the value of trial and error when creating, whether he is making software or an omelet.[47] "I like to cook," he said at the *MIT Technology Review*'s EmTechNext 2020 conference. "I taste. I decide if I need to reduce or add water. Is it overdone or underdone? I make adjustments until I like the results." Butterfield knows that most people do not like to operate that way. We tend to prefer to be armchair philosophers who try to think things through before doing them. The drawback of that approach, however, is that "none of us is smart enough to model every possibility in our head," Butterfield said.[48] As leaders, we need to allow ourselves to experiment, try things out, and make adjustments. Leaders navigating the future of work will find themselves experiencing the uncomfortable stages of the creative process. They may also be surprised by what they discover is possible.

The Covid-19 crisis presented not only a stress test but an opportunity to explore the limits of what we can achieve. "If you asked any CEO with more than 100 employees if you could you get their whole organization remote in a one week, the answer would have been no," Butterfield said. Yet companies around the world found ways to stay in business and operate remotely during the Covid-19 pandemic. "We thought this was impossible; it wasn't," Butterfield said. "What other things that we thought were impossible are not?"[49] Business leaders can take advantage of this pivotal moment by making choices that lead to greater value, not only greater profits, and by opting, when faced with a fork in the road, to pick the path that leads to creating something new.

Note: This chapter includes summaries and excerpts from the research by the Deloitte Center for the Edge, previously published in Deloitte Insights, *"Redefine Work—The Untapped Opportunity for Expanding Value," and in* MIT Sloan Management Review, *"Reframing the Future of Work" and "Redefining Work for New Value."*

CHAPTER 10

Set New Agendas

As Citizens and Communities, Reset Education, Labor Regulations, Job Transitions, and Societal Norms to Reflect Our Values

Through the [Coronavirus], we can rediscover what is possible and what we are capable of as a nation. We can use this crisis to create a better America.[1]

—Anne-Marie Slaughter, lawyer, foreign policy analyst, political scientist, and public commentator

The citizen and community agendas for the future of work can start with one person. Take Yves Cooper. He was more than happy to say goodbye to his part-time gig driving a van when he landed an IT position that promised, at long last, a career path. Though highly motivated and a quick study, Cooper had been stuck in dead-end jobs. He found a way out—and up—when he gained skills that made a difference through the nonprofit Merit America, while continuing to work his day job. Merit America offers training in skills that are in high demand for the 50 million working adults without college degrees. After Cooper learned Office 365; dove into networking, security, and system administration; and earned a Google IT Certificate, he was hired for a full-time position, with benefits, as an IT helpdesk technician.[2] Google's professional certificate in IT automation was updated in early 2020 to include Python, the most in-demand programming language today. More than 530,000 U.S. jobs, including 75,000 entry-level jobs, require Python proficiency.[3]

Historically, reskilling and upskilling workers has not been a strength in the United States. If we look back to strategies used to help workers displaced by technology and globalization in the 1980s, they were largely failures. The Job Training Partnership Act (JTPA) was the federal response to the 1980 recession. At the time, President Ronald Reagan warned that seven million Americans were experiencing "the personal indignity and human tragedy of unemployment." After studying JTPA and job-retraining programs for more than 20 years, economist Gordon Lafer concluded that they did not work very well.[4] One of the weaknesses of many job retraining programs is that they frame reskilling as a crisis management response. Reskilling takes place when jobs are lost, as factories and businesses close or relocate, creating pools of displaced workers. When job retraining swoops in during such a crisis, it functions like a band-aid rather than a long-term solution. The crisis management approach to reskilling is not an integral part of a life constructed around a portfolio of careers and jobs. In longer lives with ongoing career reinvention, crisis management may not be a sustainable solution. Other countries may offer strategies for paths forward.

In France, Germany, and Sweden, for example, a growing number of job training programs are organized around *ongoing* reskilling. Generally, Swedish workers replaced by machines are able to land another job as good as their old ones. There, the federal unemployment agency also runs retraining and counseling programs. Skills most in demand are tracked so that programs can adapt to market changes. A network of job security councils is run by industries and unions that retrain workers in the skills most in-demand. During the period that workers are trained, they are supported by a safety net that includes jobless benefits. Germany has also been successful helping the job-less find new work. Its national unemployment agency offers a job-matching service, provides career advice, and issues vouchers to cover retraining costs.[5] What distinguishes these programs from those in the United States, in part, is their integrated nature—job skills training, safety net support, and job match-ing. All three are offered—the trifecta for workers in transition.

In the United States, organizations like Merit America offer a bright spot. Indeed, some people will find training options through programs like theirs that make it possible to keep your day jobs while gaining new skills. Merit America boasts an impressive track record: Graduates see an average annual wage gain of $18,000. Of their graduates who seek work, 89 percent receive job offers within six months of graduation.[6] Other U.S. workers may reskill by taking a "gap year" with programs like Year Up, a nonprofit that offers low-income adults training that focuses on skills companies seek, including those in technology, healthcare, and finance.[7] The prevalence of MOOCs (massive open online courses) and free online training through programs like Coursera make it easier to acquire specific skills than ever before. However, we need more upward-mobility programs that offer well-rounded support, many of which currently rely on charitable, corporate, and some government funding.

To prepare for the types of careers and lives ahead, we need easy to access and affordable ways to gain new skills and receive support at the same time. I call these transition nets. These transitions nets would pick up where our current social safety nets leave off, helping us make transitions in the flow of our lives as our jobs change and we need to reskill to remain employable. Among the key public and community challenges when navigating the future of work will be education, job transitions, regulation, and ethics. The two that we are bringing to the fore here, education and transition nets, address our need for life-long learning to support the dozen or so different jobs many of us will have in our careers, and transition nets to support life-long reinvention. My goal in this final chapter, albeit an ambitious one, is to identify citizen, community, and society-level actions and institutions needed for us to thrive in the future world of work. Given the scale of public policy and institutional changes required across the landscape of the future of work, I will undoubtedly miss some issues and concerns. I am willing to take that risk in pursuit of the goal of sketching a starting

> We have to decide what we want and what our values are as a society.

point for a citizen and community future-of-work agenda. These conversa-tions are just beginning, around our dinner tables, in our backyards, and in our communities—everywhere.

Seven Key Mindset Shifts for Citizens and Communities

1. Reimagine the Social Contract and Public Institutions to Reflect Evolving Values and Priorities in Our Work, Education, and Lives, Recognizing That the World Is Changing

As the nature of work, workforces, workplaces, careers, organizations, and management are in the midst of dramatic technological, social, and political changes, including recent movements in the United States concerning racial equity and inclusion, we face the opportunity, and need, to revisit our social and public institutions and programs to ask whether they are up to the task and reflect our values and aspirations as citizens, communities, and societies. Associated questions of minimum and living wages and universal basic incomes (UBI) have become a growing part of the citizen and political discussion on the future of work. So has a Senate bill that proposes to shorten the workweek to 32 hours from 40 hours to provide more jobs.[8] A government guarantee of employment through the public sector has been proposed as a way to eliminate involuntary unemployment by creating jobs in the communities where they are most needed through a federally funded public service employment program.[9]

It is time to reset public and social questions around the future of work, including what we value, how we recognize and reward work, and how we will support ourselves through the many transitions we will make during longer lives with more twists and turns.

Actions:

- Educate ourselves on the effectiveness of our public institutions and broader social responsibilities. These issues include the social contract, the expected support between citizens and public institutions and programs; the metrics; the regulations; the laws for work, health, well-being, and education; and the commitments to sustainability in and across generations.

- Deepen our understanding of historical and global solutions to such social challenges as occupational safety measures, minimum wages, and universal primary and secondary education to identify the most promising approaches going forward.

- Participate in public and political mechanisms, including voting, to register concerns to influence the speed and direction of the policy debate on the range of future-of-work issues.
- Expect that progress on resetting the social and public agenda, in part, will be a function of the choices we make as citizens, business leaders, and individuals.

2. Update Legal and Regulatory Frameworks for Work and Jobs to Reflect the Realities of the Twenty-first Century Rather Than Their Roots in the Nineteenth and Twentieth Centuries

Many of our laws and rules for work, social protections and insurance, and education may be out of date and out of synch with the nature of jobs and careers today, and in the future. Labor laws and rules should be reviewed and adapted to reflect the growing trend of people working multiple jobs—at any one time and through their lives—rather than the historical precedent of one full-time job for a prolonged period of time. New rules and norms are needed to guide, measure, and regulate new ways of working.

Most labor statistics and regulatory bodies do not capture the portfolios of jobs and gigs many people assemble every week and every month to get by. Louis Hyman, professor at Cornell University's School of Industrial & Labor Relations, reminds us there are challenges in how we measure employment today and going forward. Although it is easy to find out if someone is working a traditional full-time job, it becomes more complex when asking a rideshare driver, for example, if they are a full-time, part-time, or temporary worker. Different people will provide different answers, Hyman says. "The way we even conceptualize work itself doesn't fit neatly into our surveys, which the Bureau of Labor Statistics is fully aware of, and they're trying to figure out how to ask these [most basic questions]," he says.[10] This question becomes more complex as an increasing number of people work a combination of full-time and gig work.

Our current policies for deciding who can receive benefits do not reflect the way many people work today, and will likely work tomorrow. They also do not provide "portable benefits" that belong to the worker regardless of their full-time or part-time work status. According to Anne-Marie Slaughter, president of the New America Foundation, "we fundamentally are going to have to blow up the distinction between employee and contractor."[11]

Actions:

- Review and update labor standards and classifications to capture the diverse nature of employment models in which an increasing percentage of people work portfolios and combinations of full time, part time, and gig work. Without more accurate and actionable information and data, it will be difficult to monitor and formulate the new regulations and data we require.

- Recognize different types of work and different types of work contributions. This can start by considering that the primary unit of analysis for many of us is not, in fact, a full-time job but a portfolio of jobs, gigs, and social and personal commitments. Work is more transactional and likely requires systems to capture, at the hour or gig level, the work performed. This approach could facilitate payments systems for benefits, healthcare, and unemployment insurance to be calculated and funded for all types of work—no matter how small. Other options might include developing systems of electronic job records (EJRs), which could be linked to networks and recommendation engines.

- Innovate how we regulate and report on work. Many types of work constitute a workweek: full-time, part-time, and social and not-for-profit work. Perhaps in addition to a 1099 (a tax statement capturing hours worked as an independent worker), that work and those hours can be tied to a micropayment benefits system for healthcare, retirement, and retraining. What if we also captured hours spent working part-time and volunteering for not-for-profit and social agencies? Could we capture, report, and provide tax and retirement benefits based on these hours? Could we produce a social 1099 (or a 1099-S) to report on these contributions and include them in government benefit programs as well? The 1099-S is just one example of the type of innovation organizations might explore to capture the changing nature of work and jobs.

3. Review Public Investments and Tax Policies to Reflect Changing Policy and Political Priorities for Investment in Education, Training, and Infrastructure

Public investments in education, training, equipment, machinery, and infrastructure shape the landscape and direction of careers and development across societies. The introduction and funding of elementary, secondary, and post-secondary—technical, college, and university education—have reshaped education and work across countries and across history. Tax incentives and disincentives for savings, as well as investment in equipment, education, and research all have consequences for the future of work. While resisting the temptation to make recommendations on specific policies and programs, we raise some of the questions and categories for review for public investment and tax policies. These include investment and financing for education at all levels throughout our lives.

One recent example in the United States: the federal government's investment in higher education has been $180 billion, while the investment in worker education and training has been in the range of $12 billion. That is 15 times more for higher education in the first chapter of our lives than throughout our working lives. Compounding this, state government support for public higher education has been decreasing.[12] Other examples include the need for investments to access high speed Internet in both rural areas and urban deserts, which have been underserved. One of the refrains during the first months of the Covid-19 health crisis was the importance of broadband Internet access through the country, and the world, to support virtual work and education. And finally, tax and accounting policies can influence the timing and level of investments in human capital, technology, and other categories.

Actions:

- Review investment in education financing considering the requirements for lifelong education beyond K–12, as well as technical and college training.
- Consider and plan for twenty-first-century infrastructure including high-speed broadband Internet—and the next generations of these and other technologies. Just as governments invested in access to electricity throughout the twentieth century, citizens and communities will need investments and access to Internet and new technologies to learn, work, compete, and live.
- Evaluate the balance and impact of tax and accounting subsidies and incentives on the investments in combinations of human and technological capital and R&D (research and development) at different levels—down to the individual and community levels. The goal should be to ensure that incentives are provided and shared equitably across stakeholders in the company and individual workers as well as countries, states, counties, and cities and towns.

4. Develop Transition Nets, Not Only Social Safety Nets, to Support Ongoing Job Changes and Education for Working Adults Throughout Multichapter Careers and Longer, More Varied Lives

A theme of the accelerated future of work is the realization that we will all undergo multiple career and work–life transitions through 100-year lives— and 60-plus-year careers. One of the major challenges, of course, is that our mental default model and most of our institutions and social norms are wired for traditional education–work–retirement models that are long outdated. Instead, we will all likely have multiple jobs and career shifts, and most of them will not be the education-to-work transitions of our teens or our twenties. The challenge is to create new public- and private-sector strategies, financing, norms and support for ongoing transitions and the multiple challenges for adults reskilling while working or between jobs.

Actions:

- Explore the idea of transition nets to support longer lives with multiple work and education moves. Broaden our thinking about ongoing job and career transitions—recognizing that the typical working life will involve multiple education and work transitions beyond those at the start or end of careers and careers in crisis.

- Challenge community and public leaders at different levels to consider integrated programs to support transition nets—leveraging and combining safety nets for healthcare, housing, food security, and income support with a focus on the challenges of reskilling while working or moving between jobs and careers.

- Explore with public officials, at the state and federal levels, proposals for financing strategies including micro and portable benefits, including healthcare, and life-long training accounts.

5. Refresh the Foundation in K–14+ Education with a Focus on the Range of Skills—Soft and Hard—Required for Success in a Rapidly Evolving Work and Career Landscape

Education in the first 20 or so years of our lives is generally recognized as both critical and often a major determinant of future success in life. But what are the key capabilities and skills young people need to be prepared for their lives and careers? David Deming, at Harvard's Graduate School of Education, told us that he thinks "that the big skill deficit in the labor market is actually more of a soft skilled deficit," and that these fundamental skills—which might be labeled capabilities—include the ability and habits to learn and explore.[13]

A key capability we need to instill and develop in our educational system is curiosity, exploration, and the motivation, habits, and discipline, to learn on our own. The technical term is an autodidact—a person who is self-taught or motivated to learn on his or her own without formal or institutional support. As John Hagel, formerly at Deloitte's Center for the Edge, reminds us, that is what we naturally do as children.[14] But often education crushes the motivation for self-learning and curiosity for behaviors focusing on compliance and repetition. Hagel's former co-chairmen at the Center, John Seely Brown, in talking about how he stays current on trends in AI, told us that he relies on YouTube videos of talks and lectures, which often are available before formal papers and books.[15] Erica Muhl, Dean of the Iovine and Young Academy at USC, told us that the school actively recruits and depends on autodidacts given the interdisciplinary nature of their program.[16] Perhaps we need to challenge ourselves as parents, family members, and communities to ask if our educational institutions, from kindergarten through the first years of technical and higher education are developing these lifelong "soft skills" and enduring human capabilities.

Actions:

- Take a fresh look at what we require of our educational institutions and investments for young people in the first 20 years of their education. Are our curriculum and requirements in line with the types of lives and careers our children and grandchildren can expect to live in 2045, 2070, and the year 2100?

- Have a point of view on what capabilities and soft skills will be required in the future. Investigate the enduring human capabilities that will be required in a world of waves of digital transformation—mobile, cloud, drones, and AI.

- Discuss with community, education, and public policy leaders what you think are the critical skills, capabilities, and dispositions to be deeply rooted in our K–14 educational institutions. And let's hold ourselves responsible for making this happen.

6. Commit to Workforce Development and Education to Reflect Life-long Learning and Work Transitions Through Longer Lives

In the long and winding careers and lives of the twenty-first century, we need to expand our mental models of development and education beyond the first part of our lives. Lifelong education will require new frameworks, institutions, and financing mechanisms. These approaches likely need to embrace the ongoing nature of career reinvention and transition beyond workforce development in times of crisis. Anne-Marie Slaughter, at New America, summarized the challenge: "Already the economy is changing so fast. I tell my children and everybody I mentor, your education in your 20s in either technical, college, or graduate school is just round one. You should be thinking about rounds two, three and four over the course of your lifetime. And yet we're not set up beyond a few executive education programs to do that."[17]

There are some promising proposals, such as the one put forth by Mark Hagerott, the chancellor of North Dakota University. He suggests a digital land grant act, building on the historical precedent of the Morrill Land Grant Act in the United States in 1862, which set aside proceeds from the sale of federal lands to support the creation of colleges, institutes for agriculture, and the mechanical arts.[18] This led to the founding of a new stable of colleges across the country, including Kansas State University, the University of Wisconsin, the Massachusetts Institute of Technology, and parts of Cornell University.[19]

The digital land grant act proposal is an example of the type of innovation that may be a bridge to building the twenty-first-century educational institutions we need. Hagerott's proposal suggests that since the government created the Internet, in the United States, we might consider a variety of digital taxes and taxes on digital transactions that could create a new generation of digital land grant universities that would focus on the kinds of digital skills and education and training that people will need in the future.

Actions:

- Create a new set of expectations, institutions, and financing strategies for lifelong learning. Our current models, which are heavily weighted toward education in the first 20, or so, years of life will not get us there.

- Explore the multiple channels that will unfold as lifelong learning evolves. Some might be government supported, perhaps like Mark Hagerott's digital land grant proposal; others might be driven by institutional innovation, like the integrated programs at USC for design, technology, business, and the arts, along with commercial channels, including the convergence of education and entertainment.

- Set expectations with community and education leaders, and government officials and representatives on the importance of investment, innovation, and new institutions to support the lifelong learning.

7. Address the Ethical Concerns the Future of Work Raises and Engage in Dialogue and Reform at All Levels

The future of work involves new combinations of people and technology in every job and every industry. The speed of these disruptions will continue to raise ethical issues at many levels. In Deloitte's 2020 Global Human Capital Trends Report, ethics and the future of work was front and center as one of 10 key trends for the next year and the next decade.[20] The ethical discussion extends to the impact of technology on employment, including the relationship among minimum wages, worker bargaining power, the substitution effect of automation, the humanity of human–technology working conditions in physical settings (i.e., factories and distribution centers) and micro-tasks (i.e., ghost workers reviewing offensive and graphic material), and the role, treatment, and wages of essential workers.[21]

In a world as hyper-connected as ours is today, we need to shift our mindsets to consider the implications and consequences of rapidly changing work, human–machine partnerships, workforce and employment relationships, and workplace strategies. The challenge is to find the combinations of "can we" and "how should we," which reflect our personal, communal, and societal values.

Actions:

- Reflect on the direction and speed of change we want for new ways of working. The goal, perhaps, is not to go faster or slower, but rather to deliberate about where we are going, how quickly, and the implications.

- Examine the impact of future work and education arrangements in the communities and cities. The future of work is a personal and local issue as well as a national and global one.

- Encourage research, debate, and the development of norms and policies that reflect the values and direction we would like to see in the future of work.

> Transition nets are designed to help develop careers in the flow of life . . . They reflect the challenges of lives that include a dozen jobs, and that are not static or predictable.

Bridges to the Future

As we reset agendas and our institutions to focus on the new realities of work, we must take into account longer lives and shorter, more numerous, and more varied careers. Our new portfolio of careers may offer even less security and stability than today. For many, work is becoming more project based.[22] Our challenge is to explore how we can make our journey in an economy of transactional work provide a livable wage and a good quality of life. What can we do to help reskill low-wage earners so they can transition into family-sustaining jobs? Investments to support and expand nationally the local success stories of organizations like Merit America and Year Up that are aligned with in-demand careers may be a good place to start.

The bridges to the future must support millions of Americans who need to move from low-wage work to stable careers that offer a path to advance.[23] Creating transition nets will underwrite this critical support throughout our lifelong process of reskilling and reinvention. Our existing social safety nets alone are not sufficient. By extending our discussion beyond the necessity of social safety nets to transition nets, we recognize the multiple dimensions of support that communities will need to provide to adults when they move between one of the many shifts in a multi-chapter career.

Transition nets are designed to help develop careers throughout the flow of life. They do not frame job transitions as crises but opportunities and next acts. They reflect the challenges of lives that include a dozen jobs, and that are neither static nor predictable. We need safety nets to ensure that everyone has access to basic necessities, such as health insurance and food security. We need transition nets to provide access to training and skills development, and cost-of-living support such as housing or transportation allowances, while we reskill, which will vary at different points in our lives. A working parent in his or her 30s will need a different level of support than a 55-year-old with children out on their own.

The challenges of worker development, reskilling, and wages for low wage workers are significant and not to be understated. During the first months of the COVID-19 health crisis, questions arose about the wages and treatment of those identified as "essential workers." Salary surveys for essential employees—including retail salespeople, postal service mail carriers, light truck drivers, cashiers, janitors, and cleaners—showed that these workers earn an average of *18.2% less* than employees in other industries: an average annual salary of $32,474 versus $39,810.[24] Wendy Edelberg, a director of the Hamilton Project, an economic policy initiative within the Brookings Institution reflecting on this situation commented, "the pandemic has shone a spotlight on the critical importance of low-skill work. As a society, we must choose to value all workers—particularly those who are keeping essential services going right now on the front lines while so many others work remotely in the safety of our homes."[25]

David Deming of the Harvard Graduate School of Education notes the similarities between this idea of transition nets and flex security. "Many of the Scandinavian countries have this model where benefits are much more generous for people who want to get retrained or who are out of work through no fault of their own," Deming said. A part of the hardship many gig workers face is that they lack health insurance because, in the United States, healthcare benefits are tied to full-time employment. "I think about it as a social insurance system that allows people to take risks and invest in themselves," he adds. "The United States is among the most advanced economies and about the worst there is in terms of allowing people to [retrain with financial support]. We have a lot of work to do."[26]

To have teeth, transition nets would need the support of government policies organized around transitions from school to work (young adults entering workforce), job transitions prompted by crises (a plant closing, the relocation of a plant or office), and the increasingly common transition of adults between jobs and careers throughout their lives. Government policies would have to recognize that these transition nets would be needed throughout our careers as we move through multiple different careers and jobs. Transition nets would provide the array of financial, institutional, and community support. We imagine the day when, considering or preparing for a job or career transition, you could open an app and access everything you needed to start a period of reskilling, retooling, and re-inventing: access to educational financing as well as healthcare, housing, and childcare support. Our society is not yet oriented to the masses retooling their careers. Thomas Friedman, the columnist and author, has recognized in his book, *Thank You for Being Late*, the power of communities in an age of accelerating global interdependence, in which "the bridges of understanding that we have to build are longer," while "the chasms they have to span much deeper."[27] We have our work cut out for us.

Advice for Twenty-first-century Citizens and Communities

In my interviews with thought leaders, I asked for insights regarding the challenges arising from the future of work and the larger public and social agendas. Here is some of what I heard:

"The hard part is the cultural transition," says Louis Hyman, professor at Cornell University's School of Industrial & Labor Relations. The hard part about that transition is not the technology; it's not the policy. That's something that technocrats can do in a room. "How do we create an educational system that teaches people to be curious rather than teaches them to obey as we did in the industrial age? One that teaches people to be compassionate rather than just look out for themselves. And values people. What's interesting about all of this is that it forces us to confront the value of being a human. And some people have lived their entire lives training to be robots. So how do we actually cultivate the human values of people? And when I say that, people often say, 'well, not everyone's going to be a research scientist.' I'm like, yeah, I know that but that's not what humans are valuable for. We're valuable for caring for each other."[28]

"If nothing else comes out of [the coronavirus] crisis, it surely has to bring us to nationwide, high-quality broadband [for rural areas and urban digital deserts]," says Anne Marie Slaughter, CEO of New America, reminding us of the rural electrification investments of the late 1930s and the United States passing the Rural Electrification Act in 1936.[29] "It is the electricity of our time. You cannot learn without it, just like you couldn't learn if you still had to work by candlelight. You couldn't study after the sun went down. It's comparable in so many ways. So that one just seems as the most obvious thing that has to come out of the crisis because government can't provide other services that it's bound to provide like public education if we don't have that."[30]

"I think that the big skill deficit in the labor market is actually more of a soft-skill deficit," commented David Deming, U.S. economist and professor of education and economics at the Harvard Graduate School of Education. "The first part of your life will probably always be more intensive in investments and skills. And I think it becomes all the more important to learn how to learn new things and to develop frameworks for thinking about managing change. Okay, I've got a set of data or I've got some sort of abstract problem I'm trying to solve. How do I go about even thinking about it? Who do I ask? How do I approach a problem? . . . There is a skill which is the ability to be flexible and adaptable, to understand your strengths and weaknesses relative to other workers. I think that the early part of life is for building those fundamental skills."[31]

"The French have been recognized internationally as having among the most sophisticated systems for managing lifelong learning and financing for education," notes Susan Winterberg, a fellow at Harvard's Kennedy School of Government. "The international best practice that's cited for that is France's Individual Training Accounts Program. Similar to a 401(k) contribution [retirement savings]. . . employers contribute to an individual's training account. It's portable. So if they leave employers, they can bring the account with them. That allows them to pursue education throughout their career."[32]

"We have to decide what we want and what our values are as a society," commented Erik Brynjolfsson, professor at MIT Sloan School, on the expectations of citizens in the future world of work. "Which kinds of tasks and professions we'd like to have more well rewarded. I certainly could make a case that we should reward better people who are teaching our children or taking care of people. There are opportunities here to do more to reward those kinds of tasks."[33]

The Social Enterprise

The evolving citizen and community future of work agenda is part of larger societal shifts around the world. In the past several years, individuals have increasingly expected businesses to broaden their focus to include wider social and environmental concerns.[34] In 2018, Deloitte, in its annual report on global human capital trends, re-introduced, reframed, and expanded the idea of the social enterprise. "What is a social enterprise: An organization whose mission combines revenue growth and profitmaking with the need to respect and support its environment and stakeholder network. This includes listening to, investing in, and actively managing the trends that are shaping today's world. It is an organization that shoulders its responsibility to be a good citizen (both inside and outside the organization), serving as a role model for its peers and promoting a high degree of collaboration at every level of the organization."[35]

In turn, business leaders have recognized that they have growing stakes in social and public responsibility. As we explore the challenges of the future of work agenda reset, we recognize the opportunity for individuals to work with businesses, and community and public agencies, to address broader social issues. Companies that have made it a priority to align meaning and value as well as profit and purpose may have distinct advantages over those that focus only on narrow perspectives of corporate profits. The world's biggest investor, BlackRock CEO Larry Fink, has been a leader on this issue. Fink made headlines in 2018 when he used his annual letter[36] to chief executives to urge CEOs to do more than make profits. He asked them to run their companies in a way that makes a positive contribution to society.[37]

"Profits are in no way inconsistent with purpose," Mr. Fink wrote. "Purpose is not the sole pursuit of profits but the animating force for achieving them."[38] When Fink, who oversees nearly $6 trillion at BlackRock, speaks, people take notice. Chief executives began to talk about their companies' purpose.

Linking purpose and profits is at the heart of Leena Nair's mission at Unilever, the global consumer goods company with products available in 190 countries.[39] As Unilever's chief human resources officer, Nair argues that now, more than ever, business must become "more human."[40] Like Fink, she believes that businesses must evaluate their

> The social . . . imperative we face to invest in education and transitions will allow us to build a more productive economy and a fair society.

actions based on their impact on society, not only on the bottom line. Nair notes employees want to work with companies with purpose just as consumers are paying attention to how companies run their business.[41] A recent Nielsen study found that 67 percent of employees prefer to work for socially responsible companies, and 55 percent of consumers will pay extra for products sold by companies committed to positive social impact. For the first time, in 2018, most U.S. public companies were required to disclose their CEO pay ratio, which compares the CEO's compensation to employees' median pay.[42]

The business imperative to balance purpose and profits was echoed at a recent Business Roundtable meeting where 181 chief executives committed to "improving society," by leading their companies with a long-term view benefiting all stakeholders—customers, employees, suppliers, communities, and shareholders. The business leaders specifically noted their commitment to investing in their employees. "This starts with compensating them fairly and providing important benefits," they wrote. "It also includes supporting them through training and education that help develop new skills for a rapidly changing world."[43] The business leaders at the roundtable redefined our collective responsibility to our employees and those in our communities who need the skills and support to maintain their livelihood.

The citizen's agenda for the future of work involves exploring and expanding the intersection of market value with communal and social values. This agenda, at this intersection, will help shape and create the educational, institutional, regulatory, and ethical directions citizens and communities seek to pursue in the future. Our work arrangements are complex combinations of economic, political, and social forces. Their direction and priorities should reflect our values and aspirations, not only the interplay of unfettered market and technological forces. The challenge is to integrate these values and aspirations as the touchstones for resetting the citizen and community future of work agenda to achieve broad-based equitable and sustainable growth.

Start Where We Live

The social and communal imperative we face to invest in education and the transitions that training entails will allow us to build a more productive economy and a fair society. When U.S. Supreme Court Justice Louis Brandeis wrote that our states can act as laboratories of democracy, he highlighted our ability to start to solve global and national challenges in our local communities. Brandeis writing in 1932 stated that it is "one of the happy incidents of the federal system that a single courageous state may, if its citizens choose, serve as a laboratory; and try novel social and economic experiments without risk to the rest of the country."[44] Indeed, our communities can serve as laboratories for innovation, where we can develop and test reskilling programs, explore the creation of transition nets, and reset local agendas as a precursor to resetting national policies and programs. Louis Hyman of Cornell University reminded us that the future of work is about the choices we make. As we reset the agenda for the future of work with the actions we take in our towns and communities, let them reflect our values and the future we want. Let's start the conversation. Let's begin the reset.

Acknowledgments

Writing a book, contrary to popular belief, is far from a solitary pursuit.

Work Disrupted has been a team project from the start. Suzanne Riss, a talented writer, editor, researcher, and author, has patiently worked with me every week for the past 18 months to help me craft my ideas, observations, and analysis into the stories and narrative that comprise this book. Tom Fishburne, the Marketoonist, a unique cartoonist and illustrator, and irrepressible personality, worked with us for more than a year to create the 25 cartoons that bring the stories in this book to life.

Jim Guszcza, Deloitte's chief data scientist, has been an amazing partner in developing my ideas on human–machine collaboration. He reviewed every chapter of the book and provided invaluable feedback. John Hagel, John Seely Brown (JSB), and Maggie Wooll, the leaders of Deloitte's Center for the Edge, were sources of insights and inspiration throughout the process; their ideas flow through many of the chapters in this book. Others, including Bill Eggers, of Deloitte, and Rob Norman, the former global chief digital officer of Group M, reviewed and provided comments on chapters in the book.

I am grateful to more than two dozen leading thinkers and pioneers in the future of work who generously participated in interviews for the book and I thank them for hours of dynamic, thought-provoking conversations, and for sharing their unique insights in this book. My thanks to this group, which included Michael Arena, John Seely Brown, Erik Brynjolfsson, Mette Buchman, Allan Cooke, Tom Davenport, Dave Deming, Bill Eggers, Lynda Gratton, John Hagel, Mark Holmstrom, Louis Hyman, Jerry Kane, Micha Kaufman, Gideon Lichfield, Thomas Malone, Erica Muhl, Doug Ready, Anne-Marie Slaughter, Kristen Swanson, Gillian Tett, Eric Topol, Dave Ullrich, Susan Winterberg, Amy Wrzesniewski, and Arthur Yeung.

This book grew out of my roles in Deloitte Consulting, in the United States and globally, as a senior partner in our Human Capital consultancy, a leader in the creation of our future of work offerings, and a senior advisor in our workforce transformation practice. Special thanks to Erica Volini, Heather Stockton, and Brett Walsh, the global leaders of our Human Capital practice, for their leadership in working to develop these ideas and their generous, ongoing support as co-creators of our future of work practice. Robin Jones and David Brown, leaders of our workforce transformation practice, and Steve Hatfield, the global leader of our future of work practice, have been amazing teammates and collaborators. And my thanks to Juliet Bourke, a partner in Deloitte Australia, for shaping our early perspectives on work, worker, and workplace, a key component of the scaffolding underlying my research and this book.

For the past several years, this book has been supported by Deloitte Consulting's leadership as one of our firm's Signature Issues. Thanks to Michael Stephan, U.S. leader of Human Capital; Andrew Blau, the managing director of the Signature Issues program; and our U.S. Consulting CEO, Dan Helfrich.

Over the past year, I have benefited enormously from project management provided by Lissa Tucker and Krista Bassett. In the first months of Covid-19, Lissa kept us on track and focused to deliver the manuscript. Rohini Menezes and Caitlin Pike, consultants on our Workforce Transformation team, provided indispensable support as this book grew from idea, to proposal, to manuscript, to the book you're reading today. Researchers from Deloitte in the United States and South Africa assisted with research and fact-checking. My thanks to Isabel Hayes, Sabrina Knott, Shaune Littleton, Talitha Muller, Blake Winters, and Sam Yarnis. Their focus on the myriad details and notes in this book was invaluable. At the end of the day, I accept and am responsible for any errors and omissions.

Thanks to Richard Narramore, our executive editor, and Victoria Anllo at John Wiley & Sons, who guided me, as a first-time author, through the publishing process.

Finally, a personal note of thanks and appreciation to my partner, Kate Marber. Anyone who has written a book understands the sacrifices and strains on relationships and family. For all those weekends, and there were many, and all those late nights, and there were many of those too, and for all her encouragement and support, thank you.

Jeff Schwartz
New York

Notes

Chapter 1 From Fear to Growth

1 Coelho, Paulo. "A Quote from *The Devil and Miss Prym*." Goodreads, n.d. https://**www.goodreads.com/quotes/62867-when-we-least-expect-it-life-sets-us-a-challenge**.

2 Slaughter, Anne-Marie. "Forget the Trump Administration. America Will Save America." *The New York Times*, March 21, 2020.

3 Wall, Mike. "NASA Chief Orders Agency Employees to Work from Home amid Coronavirus Pandemic." **Space.com**, March 18, 2020. **https://www.space.com/nasa-employees-work-home-coronavirus-pandemic.html**.

4 Albergotti, Reed, and Faiz Siddiqui. "Ford and GM Are Undertaking a Warlike Effort to Produce Ventilators. It May Fall Short and Come Too Late." *The Washington Post*, April 4, 2020. **https://www.washingtonpost.com/business/2020/04/04/ventilators-coronavirus-ford-gm/**.

5 Slaughter, "Forget the Trump Administration."

6 "Forces of Change: The Future of Work." *Deloitte Insights*, n.d. **https://www2.deloitte.com/content/dam/insights/us/articles/4322_Forces-of-change_FoW/DI_Forces-of-change_FoW.pdf**.

7 Slaughter, "Forget the Trump Administration."

8 Levitan, Richard. "The Infection That's Silently Killing Coronavirus Patients." *The New York Times*, April 20, 2020. **https://www.nytimes.com/2020/04/20/opinion/sunday/coronavirus-testing-pneumonia.html**.

9 "Planet Money: The Parable Of The Piston." *Morning Edition*. NPR, April 2, 2020.

10 Morris, David Z. "Glow Sticks to Surgical Masks: Businesses Pivot to Tackle Coronavirus Shortages." *Fortune*, March 26, 2020. **https://fortune.com/2020/03/26/coronavirus-businesses-pivot-n95-masks-ventilators-shortage/**.

11 Fleming, Sean. "How Big Business Is Joining the Fight against COVID-19." World Economic Forum, March 20, 2020. **https://www.weforum.org/agenda/2020/03/big-business-joining-fight-against-coronavirus/**.

12 "The Coronavirus Pivot." *The Indicator From Planet Money*. NPR, April 2, 2020.

13 Ibid.

14 O'Brien, Sara Ashley. "Instacart Hired 300,000 Workers in a Month. It Plans to Hire 250,000 More." CNN, April 24, 2020. **https://www.cnn.com/2020/04/23/tech/instacart-hiring-workers/index.html**.

15 Wood, Charlie. "Uber Will Broaden Out beyond Ride Hailing and Food Delivery during the Pandemic to Courier Packages, Medicine, and Pet Supplies." *Business Insider*, April 20, 2020. **https://www.businessinsider.com/uber-launches-courier-coronavirus-2020-4**.

16 "19 Businesses Pivoting in Response to COVID-19." *Maddyness UK*, April 15, 2020. **https://www.maddyness.com/uk/2020/03/31/19-businesses-pivoting-in-response-to-covid-19/**.

17 "A Quote by William Gibson." Goodreads, n.d. **https://www.goodreads.com/quotes/681-the-future-is-already-here-it-s-just-not-evenly**.

18 Seitz, Patrick. "What Are FANG Stocks, and Should You Invest in Them?" *Investor's Business Daily*, April 27, 2020. **https://www.investors.com/news/technology/what-are-fang-stocks-faang-stocks/**.

19 Brynjolfsson, Erik, and Andrew McAfee. *Race against the Machine: How the Digital Revolution Is Accelerating Innovation, Driving Productivity, and Irreversibly Transforming Employment and the Economy*. Lexington, MA: Digital Frontier Press, 2012.

20 Malone, Thomas W. *Superminds: The Surprising Power of People and Computers Thinking Together*. New York: Little, Brown Spark, 2019.

21 Callaham, John. "The History of Android OS: Its Name, Origin and More." Android Authority, February 19, 2020. **https://www.androidauthority.com/history-android-os-name-789433/**.

22 Hyman, Louis, interview with Suzanne Riss and Jeff Schwartz, January 13, 2020.

23 Schwartz, Jeff, John Hagel, Maggie Wooll, and Kelly Monahan. "Reframing the Future of Work." *MIT Sloan Management Review*, February 20, 2019. **https://sloanreview.mit.edu/article/reframing-the-future-of-work/**

24 Somers, Meredith. "Are We Encouraging the Wrong AI?" *MIT Sloan Management Review*, May 8, 2019. **https://mitsloan.mit.edu/ideas-made-to-matter/are-we-encouraging-wrong-ai**.

25 "Disruptive Innovation." Clayton Christensen, October 23, 2012. **http://clayton-christensen.com/key-concepts/**.

26 Moeller, Leslie H., Nick Hodson, and Martina Sangin. "The Coming Wave of Digital Disruption." *Strategy Business*, November 30, 2017. **https://www.strategy-business.com/article/The-Coming-Wave-of-Digital-Disruption?gko=b9726**.

27 Christensen, Clayton M. *The Innovator's Dilemma*. New York, NY: Harper Business, 2011.

28 Reier, Sharon, and *International Herald Tribune*. "Half a Century Later, Economist's 'Creative Destruction' Theory Is Apt for the Internet Age : Schumpeter: The Prophet of Bust and Boom." *The New York Times*, June 10, 2000. **https://www.nytimes.com/2000/06/10/your-money/IHT-half-a-century-later-economists-creative-destruction-theory-is.html**.

29 Ibid.

30 Strohmeyer, Robert. "The 7 Worst Tech Predictions of All Time." *PCWorld. IDG*, December 31, 2008. **https://www.pcworld.com/article/155984/worst_tech_predictions.html**.

31 Sorrel, Charlie. "More Ballmer Madness: 'There's No Chance That the iPhone Is Going to Get Any Significant Market Share.'" *Wired*, May 1, 2007. **https://www.wired.com/2007/05/more-ballmer-ma/**.

32 Strohmeyer, Robert, and *PC World*. "The 7 Worst Tech Predictions of All Time." ABC News, December 31, 2008. **https://abcnews.go.com/Technology/PCWorld/story?id=6558231**.

33 "Old Maps—A Brief History of Cartography." Maps International, April 16, 2019. **https://www.mapsinternational.co.uk/blog/old-maps/**.

34 Larsen, Reif. "A Quote from *The Selected Works of T.S. Spivet*." Goodreads. **https://www.goodreads.com/quotes/360748-a-map-does-not-just-chart-it-unlocks-and-formulates**.

35 "Eight Climbers Die on Mt. Everest." **History.com**. A&E Television Networks, November 13, 2009. **https://www.history.com/this-day-in-history/death-on-mount-everest**.

36 "Everest 1953: First Footsteps—Sir Edmund Hillary and Tenzing Norgay." *National Geographic*, March 3, 2013. **https://www.nationalgeographic.com/adventure/ features/everest/sir-edmund-hillary-tenzing-norgay-1953/#close**.

37 Parker, Kim, Rich Morin, and Juliana Menasce Horowitz. "The Future of Work in the Automated Workplace," Pew Research Center, December 31, 2019. **https://www.pewsocialtrends.org/2019/03/21/the-future-of-work-in-the-automated-workplace/**.

38 Lichfield, Gideon. "EmTech Digital 2019." MIT *EmTech Next 2019*.

39 "The Future of Jobs Report 2018." World Economic Forum. **http://www3.weforum.org/docs/WEF_Future_of_Jobs_2018.pdf**.

40 Allen, Katie. "Technology Has Created More Jobs than It Has Destroyed, Says 140 Years of Data." *The Guardian*, August 18, 2015. **https://www.theguardian .com/business/2015/aug/17/technology-created-more-jobs-than-destroyed-140-years-data-census**.

41 "The Exponential Primer—Exponential Growth—SU." Singularity University, n.d. **https://su.org/concepts/**.

42 Ings, Ted. "Henry Ford Disrupted and Reshaped American Society." Center for Performance Improvement, July 18, 2019. **https://www.centerforperformance improvement.com/blog/2017/11/26/henry-ford-disrupted-and-reshaped-american-society**

43 Pethokoukis, James. "What the Story of ATMs and Bank Tellers Reveals about the 'Rise of the Robots' and jobs." AEIdeas, June 6, 2016. **https://www.aei.org/ economics/what-atms-bank-tellers-rise-robots-and-jobs/**

44 Bessen, James. "Learning by Doing." The Library of Economics and Liberty, May 23, 2016. **https://www.econtalk.org/james-bessen-on-learning-by-doing/**.

45 Ibid.

46 Bessen, James. "Will Robots Steal Our Jobs? The Humble Loom Suggests Not." *The Washington Post*, January 25, 2014. **https://www.washingtonpost.com/news/ the-switch/wp/2014/01/25/what-the-humble-loom-can-teach-us-about-robots-and-automation/**.

47 Kessler, Sarah. "Over the Last 60 Years, Automation Has Totally Eliminated Just One US Occupation." Quartz, May 15, 2017. **https://qz.com/932516/over-the-last-60-years-automation-has-totally-eliminated-just-one-us-occupation/**.

48 Fuller, Joseph B., Manjari Raman, Judith Wallenstein, and Alice de Chalendar. "Future Positive." Harvard Business School, BCG Henderson Institute, May 2019. **https://www.hbs.edu/managing-the-future-of-work/research/Documents/ Future%20Positive%20Report.pdf**.

49 Kessler, "Over the Last 40 Years."

50 Wrzesniewski, Amy, interview with Suzanne Riss and Jeff Schwartz, June 17, 2019.

51 Maynard Keynes, John. "Economic Possibilities for our Grandchildren (1930)." In: *Essays in Persuasion*. New York: Harcourt Brace, 1932. **https://assets.aspeninstitute.org/content/uploads/files/content/upload/Intro_and_Section_I.pdf**.

52 Brynjolfsson, Erik, and Andrew McAfee, *Race against the Machine*.

53 Hiipakka, Julie, David Mallon, Denise Moulton, and Kathi Enderes. "Capabilities and Skills: The New Currency for Talent." Deloitte Development LLC, November 27, 2019.

54 Gratton, Lynda, and Andrew Scott. *The 100-Year Life*. London: Bloomsbury Information, 2016.

Chapter 2 People and Machines Working Together

1 Grosz, Barbara J., "The AI Revolution Needs Expertise in People, Publics and Societies." *Harvard Data Science Review* (2019). **https://hdsr.mitpress.mit.edu/pub/wiq01ru6**.

2 Stewart, Jack. "Don't Freak Over Boeing's Self-Flying Plane—Robots Already Run the Skies." *Wired*, June 12, 2017. **https://www.wired.com/story/boeing-autonomous-plane-autopilot/**.

3 Frey, Carl Benedikt, and Michael A. Osborne. "The Future of Employment: How Susceptible Are Jobs to Computerization?" *Technological Forecasting and Social Change* 114 (January 2017): 254–280. **https://doi.org/10.1016/j.techfore.2016.08.019**.

4 Frey, Carl Benedikt, and Michael A. Osborne. "The Future of Employment: How Susceptible Are Jobs to Computerisation?," Oxford Martin: 1–72.

5 Google Trends, May 8, 2020. **https://trends.google.com/trends/explore?date=all&geo=US&q=**"future of work".

6 Kutarna, Chris. "Map #37: (Whose) Future of (What) Work." Chris Kutarna (blog), November 26, 2018. **https://kutarna.net/map-37-whose-future-of-what-work/**.

7 Frey and Osborne, "The Future of Employment."

8 Brynjolfsson, Erik, and Andrew McAfee. *Race against the Machine: How the Digital Revolution Is Accelerating Innovation, Driving Productivity, and Irreversibly Transforming Employment and the Economy*. Lexington, MA: Digital Frontier Press, 2012.

9 Chui, Michael, James Manyika, and Mehdi Miremadi. "Four Fundamentals of Workplace Automation." McKinsey Digital, November, 2015. **https://www.mckinsey.com/business-functions/digital-mckinsey/our-insights/four-fundamentals-of-workplace-automation**.

10 Long, Tony. "Jan. 25, 1921: Robots First Czech In." *Wired*, January 2011. **https://www.wired.com/2011/01/0125robot-cometh-capek-rur-debut/**

11 Rosen, Rebecca J. "Unimate: The Story of George Devol and the First Robotic Arm." *The Atlantic*, August 16, 2011. **https://www.theatlantic.com/technology/archive/2011/08/unimate-the-story-of-george-devol-and-the-first-robotic-arm/243716/**

12 Davids, Mariane. "A Brief History of Robots in Manufacturing." *ROBOTIQ* (blog), July 17, 2017. **https://blog.robotiq.com/a-brief-history-of-robots-in-manufacturing**.

13 Rosen, "Unimate."

14 Guszcza, Jim, Jeff Schwartz, and Joe Ucuzoglu. "Superminds, Not Substitutes: Enabling Human–Machine Collaboration for a Better Future of Work." *Deloitte Review*, no. 27. (2020).

15 Lynch, Shana. "Andrew Ng: Why AI Is the New Electricity." *Stanford Business*, March 2017. **https://www.gsb.stanford.edu/insights/andrew-ng-why-ai-new-electricity**.

16 Autor, David H. "Why Are There Still so Many Jobs? The History and Future of Workplace Automation." *Journal of Economic Perspectives* 29, no. 3 (2015): 3–30. **https://economics.mit.edu/files/11563**

17 Chowdhry, Amit. "Artificial Intelligence to Create 58 Million New Jobs by 2022, Says Report." *Forbes*, September 18, 2018. **https://www.forbes.com/sites/ amitchowdhry/2018/09/18/artificial-intelligence-to-create-58-million-new- jobs-by-2022-says-report/#5eeb56364d4b**.

18 Topol, Eric J. *Deep Medicine: How Artificial Intelligence Can Make Healthcare Human Again*. New York: Basic Books, 2019.

19 Ibid.

20 Wrzesniewski, Amy, interview with Suzanne Riss and Jeff Schwartz, June 2019.

21 Ibid.

22 Guszcza et al., "Superminds, Not Substitutes."

23 Malone, Thomas W. *Superminds: the Surprising Power of People and Computers Thinking Together*. New York: Little, Brown Spark, 2019.

24 Guszcza et al., "Superminds, Not Substitutes."

25 "Deep Blue." IBM100 – Deep Blue, n.d. **https://www.ibm.com/ibm/history/ ibm100/us/en/icons/deepblue/**.

26 **History.com** Editors. "Chess Champion Garry Kasparov Defeats IBM's Deep Blue." **History.com**. **https://www.history.com/this-day-in-history/kasparov- defeats-chess-playing-computer** (accessed May 8, 2020).

27 Greenemeier, Larry. "20 Years after Deep Blue: How AI has Advanced Since Con- quering Chess." *Scientific American*, June 2, 2017.

28 Ibid.

29 Guszcza et al., "Superminds, Not Substitutes."

30 "Advanced Chess." Wikipedia, April 30, 2020. **https://en.wikipedia.org/wiki/ Advanced_chess**.

31 Guszcza et al., "Superminds, Not Substitutes."

32 Kasparov, Garry. "The Chess Master and the Computer." *The New York Review of Books*. February 11, 2010. **http://www.nybooks.com/articles/2010/02/11/the- chess-master-and-the-computer/** .

33 Guszcza et al., "Superminds, Not Substitutes."

34 Guszcza, Jim, and Jeff Schwartz. "Superminds: How Humans and Machines Can Work Together." *Deloitte Insights*, January 28, 2019. **https://www2.deloitte.com/ us/en/insights/focus/technology-and-the-future-of-work/human-and- machine-collaboration.html**.

35 Thompson, Derek. "Health Care Just Became the U.S.'s Largest Employer." *The Atlantic*, January 9, 2018. **https://www.theatlantic.com/business/ archive/2018/01/health-care-america-jobs/550079/**.

36 Walker, Joseph. "Why Americans Spend so Much on Health Care—in 12 Charts." *The Wall Street Journal*, July 31, 2018. **https://www.wsj.com/articles/why- americans-spend-so-much-on-health-carein-12-charts-1533047243**.

37 Edwards, David. "Healthcare Assistive Robot Market to Surpass $1.2 Billion by 2024." *Robotics & Automation News*, January 21, 2019. **https://roboticsandau- tomationnews.com/2019/01/21/healthcare-assistive-robot-market-to-sur- pass-1-2-billion-by-2024/20618/**.

38 Chris Caulfield RN, NP-C. "Council Post: The Gig Economy Has Arrived in the World of Nursing." *Forbes*, September 27, 2019. **https://www.forbes.com/sites/ forbestechcouncil/2019/09/27/the-gig-economy-has-arrived-in-the-world- of-nursing/#28e069526274**.

39 CBS. "Dallas Hospital Has 'Moxi'; First in Country to Use A.I. Robot." CBS Dallas/ Fort Worth, September 20, 2018. **https://dfw.cbslocal.com/2018/09/20/the-robot-will-see-you-now-skynet/**.

40 "Table 8. Occupations with the Largest Projected Number of Job Openings due to Growth and Replacement Needs, 2012 and Projected 2022." U.S. Bureau of Labor Statistics, December 19, 2013. **https://www.bls.gov/news.release/ecopro.t08.htm**.

41 "Workforce." ANA, n.d. **https://www.nursingworld.org/practice-policy/workforce/**.

42 Nasser, Haya El. "The Graying of America: More Older Adults Than Kids by 2035." The United States Census Bureau, October 8, 2019. **https://www.census.gov/library/stories/2018/03/graying-america.html**.

43 "2020 NSI National Health Care Retention & RN Staffing Report." NSI Nursing Solutions, Inc., March 2020. **https://www.nsinursingsolutions.com/Documents/Library/NSI_National_Health_Care_Retention_Report.pdf**.

44 "Diligent Robotics." Diligent Robotics, n.d. **https://diligentrobots.com/**.

45 "Moxi." Diligent Robotics, n.d. **https://diligentrobots.com/moxi**.

46 "What Is Collaborative Robot (Cobot)?—Definition from Techopedia." **Techopedia.com**, n.d. **https://www.techopedia.com/definition/14298/collaborative-robot-cobot**.

47 Topol, *Deep Medicine*.

48 Ibid.

49 "What Is Diagnostic Error?" *Improved Diagnosis*, September 27, 2019. **https://www.improvediagnosis.org/what-is-diagnostic-error/**.

50 Kubota, Taylor. "Algorithm Better at Diagnosing Pneumonia than Radiologists." *Stanford Medicine*, November 15, 2017. **https://med.stanford.edu/news/all-news/2017/11/algorithm-can-diagnose-pneumonia-better-than-radiologists.html**.

51 Johnson, Khari. "Google's Lung Cancer Detection AI Outperforms 6 Human Radiologists." *VentureBeat*, May 20, 2019. **https://venturebeat.com/2019/05/20/googles-lung-cancer-detection-ai-outperforms-6-human-radiologists/**.

52 Pearson, Dave. "Artificial Intelligence in Radiology: The Game-Changer on Everyone's Mind." *Radiology Business*, October 13, 2017. **https://www.radiologybusiness.com/topics/technology-management/artificial-intelligence-radiology-game-changer-everyones-mind**.

53 Topol, *Deep Medicine*.

54 Guszcza et al., "Superminds, Not Substitutes."

55 Thompson, Clive. "May A.I. Help You?" *The New York Times*, November 14, 2018. **https://www.nytimes.com/interactive/2018/11/14/magazine/tech-design-ai-chatbot.html?mtrref=www.google.com&gwh=2A100D89219975BB4B34C48E8B775EAD&gwt=pay&assetType=REGIWALL**.

56 Muro, Mark, Robert Maxim, and Jacob Whiton. "Automation and Artificial Intelligence: How Machines Are Affecting People and Places." Brookings, January 2019. **https://www.brookings.edu/wp-content/uploads/2019/01/2019.01_BrookingsMetro_Automation-AI_Report_Muro-Maxim-Whiton-FINAL-version.pdf**.

57 Gray, Alex. "The 10 Skills You Need to Thrive in the Fourth Industrial Revolution." World Economic Forum, January 16, 2016. **https://www.weforum.org/**

agenda/2016/01/the-10-skills-you-need-to-thrive-in-the-fourth-industrial-revolution/.

58 Muro, Mark, Robert Maxim, and Jacob Whiton. "Automation and Artificial Intelligence: How Machines Are Affecting People and Places." Brookings, November 25, 2019. **https://www.brookings.edu/research/automation-and-artificial-intelligence-how-machines-affect-people-and-places/**.

59 Chowdhry, "Artificial Intelligence to Create 58 Million New Jobs by 2020."

60 Ibid.

61 Harvard Business School, May 23, 2019. **https://www.hbs.edu/news/releases/Pages/hbs-future-positive-tap-employee-optimism.aspx**.

62 Gross-Loh, Christine. "Don't Let Praise Become a Consolation Prize." *The Atlantic*, December 16, 2016. **https://www.theatlantic.com/education/archive/2016/12/how-praise-became-a-consolation-prize/510845/**.

63 "Research Proves That Mindsets Can Be Changed." *Mindset Works*, n.d. **https://www.mindsetworks.com/science/Changing-Mindsets**.

64 Gross-Loh, "Don't Let Praise Become a Consolation Prize."

65 Hagel, John, Maggie Wooll, and John Seely Brown. "Skills Change, but Capabilities Endure." *Deloitte Insights*, August 30, 2019. **https://www2.deloitte.com/us/en/insights/focus/technology-and-the-future-of-work/future-of-work-human-capabilities.html**.

66 Hagel, John, interview with Suzanne Riss and Jeff Schwartz, June 2019.

67 Volini, Erica, Indranil Roy, and Jeff Schwartz. "From Jobs to Superjobs." *Deloitte Insights*, April 11, 2019. **https://www2.deloitte.com/us/en/insights/focus/human-capital-trends/2019/impact-of-ai-turning-jobs-into-superjobs.html**.

68 Volini, Erica, Brad Denny, Jeff Schwartz, Yves Van Durme, Maren Hauptmann, Ramona Yan, and Shannon Poynton. "Superteams: Putting AI in the Group." *Deloitte Insights*, May 15, 2020. **https://www2.deloitte.com/us/en/insights/focus/human-capital-trends/2020/human-ai-collaboration.html**.

69 Schwartz, Jeff, John Hagel, Maggie Wooll, and Kelly Monahan. "Reframing the Future of Work." *MIT Sloan Management Review*, February 20, 2019. **https://sloanreview.mit.edu/article/reframing-the-future-of-work/**.

Chapter 3 Making Alternative Work a Meaningful Opportunity

1 Schwartz, Jeff, Amy Wrzesniewski, Michael H. Jordan, and Kelly Monahan. "Creating Meaning and Structure for Independent Work." *Deloitte Insights*, December 19, 2018. **https://www2.deloitte.com/us/en/insights/focus/technology-and-the-future-of-work/amy-wrzesniewski-interview-independent-work.html#**.

2 Katz, Lawrence, and Alan Krueger. "The Rise and Nature of Alternative Work Arrangements in the United States, 1995–2015." Princeton University, September 13, 2016. **http://arks.princeton.edu/ark:/88435/dsp01zs25xb933**.

3 Volini, Erica, Jeff Schwartz, Indranil Roy, Maren Hauptmann, Yves Van Durme, Brad Denny, and Josh Bersin. "The Alternative Workforce: It's Now Mainstream." *Deloitte Insights*, April 11, 2019. **https://www2.deloitte.com/us/en/insights/focus/human-capital-trends/2019/alternative-workforce-gig-economy.html**.

4 Katz, Lawrence, and Alan Krueger. "Understanding Trends in Alternative Work Arrangements in the United States." The National Bureau of Economic Research, January 2019. **https://www.nber.org/papers/w25425**.

5 Mitic, I. "Gig Economy Statistics for 2020: The New Normal in the Workplace." *Fortunly*, January 28, 2020. **https://fortunly.com/statistics/gig-economy-statistics**.

6 Chakrabarti, Meghna, and Louis Hyman. "The Origin Story of the Gig Economy." WBUR, August 20, 2018. **https://www.wbur.org/onpoint/2018/08/20/gig-economy-temp-louis-hyman**.

7 Hyman, Louis, interview with Suzanne Riss and Jeff Schwartz, January 13, 2020.

8 Szalai, Jennifer. "How the 'Temp' Economy Became the New Normal." *The New York Times*, August 22, 2018. **https://www.nytimes.com/2018/08/22/books/review-temp-louis-hyman.html**.

9 Marsh, Laura. "What Happened to All the Good Jobs?" *The Nation*, October 25, 2018. **https://www.thenation.com/article/archive/what-happened-to-the-steady-job/**.

10 "Who Chooses Part-Time Work and Why?" U.S. Bureau of Labor Statistics, March 2018. **https://www.bls.gov/opub/mlr/2018/article/who-chooses-part-time-work-and-why.htm**.

11 "Deloitte Global Millennial Survey 2019." Deloitte, May 24, 2019. **https://www2.deloitte.com/global/en/pages/about-deloitte/articles/millennialsurvey.html**.

12 Chakrabarti and Hyman, "The Origin Story of the Gig Economy."

13 Volini et al., "The Alternative Workforce."

14 Gray, Mary L., and Siddharth Suri. *Ghost Work: How to Stop Silicon Valley from Building a New Global Underclass*. Boston: Houghton Mifflin Harcourt, 2019.

15 Mitic, "Gig Economy Statistics for 2020."

16 Chakrabarti and Hyman, "The Origin Story of the Gig Economy."

17 Mas, Alexandre, and Amanda Pallais. "Valuing Alternative Work Arrangements." *American Economic Review* 107, no. 12 (2017): 3722–3759.

18 Ibid.

19 Irwin, Neil. "To Understand Rising Inequality, Consider the Janitors at Two Top Companies, Then and Now." *The New York Times*, September 3, 2017. **https://www.nytimes.com/2017/09/03/upshot/to-understand-rising-inequality-consider-the-janitors-at-two-top-companies-then-and-now.html**.

20 Moore, Monika. "The Changing Landscape of Tenure-Track Positions." HigherEdJobs, May 30, 2019. **https://www.higheredjobs.com/Articles/articleDisplay.cfm?ID=1952**.

21 "Background Facts on Contingent Faculty Positions." AAUP, n.d. **https://www.aaup.org/issues/contingency/background-facts**.

22 Chan, Daisy, Freek Voortman, Sarah Rogers, and Bart Moen. "The Rise of the Platform Economy." Deloitte, December 2018. **https://www2.deloitte.com/content/dam/Deloitte/nl/Documents/humancapital/deloitte-nl-hc-reshaping-work-conference.pdf**.

23 Volini, Erica, Jeff Schwartz, Indranil Roy, Maren Hauptmann, Yves Van Durme, Brad Denny, and Josh Bersin. "Talent Mobility: Winning the War on the Home Front." *Deloitte Insights*, April 11, 2019. **https://www2.deloitte.com/us/en/ insights/focus/human-capital-trends/2019/internal-talent-mobility.html**.

24 Schrage, Michael, Jeff Schwartz, David Kiron, Robin Jones, and Natasha Buckley. "Opportunity Marketplaces: Aligning Workforce Investment and Value Creation in the Digital Enterprise." *MIT Sloan Management Review*, April 28, 2020. **https:// sloanreview.mit.edu/projects/opportunity-marketplaces/**.

25 Volini et al., "The Alternative Workforce."

26 Hyman, interview.

27 Younger, Jon. "Will Companies' Internal Freelance Platforms Replace Upwork and Fiverr?" *Forbes,* November 13, 2018. **https://www.forbes.com/sites/ jonyounger/2018/11/13/will-company-digital-talent-platforms-like- pwcreplace- upwork-and-fiverr/**.

28 Kaufman, Micha, CEO, Fiverr, interview with Suzanne Riss and Jeff Schwartz, February 2020.

29 Ivanovs, Alex. "Top 18 Most Popular Freelance Marketplaces 2020." Color-lib, December 18, 2019. **https://colorlib.com/wp/popular-freelance- marketplaces/**.

30 "GrabCAD: Design Community, CAD Library, 3D Printing Software." Grabcad, n.d. **https://grabcad.com/**.

31 "Experfy—AI Products | Big Data Consulting | AI Consulting." Experfy, n.d. **https://www.experfy.com/**.

32 "In-Demand Talent on Demand.™ Upwork Is How.™" Upwork, n.d. **https:// www.upwork.com/**.

33 "TaskRabbit—Get Your Groceries Delivered, Errands Done . . ." TaskRabbit, n.d. **https://www.taskrabbit.com/**.

34 "Freelancer." n.d. **https://www.freelancer.com/**.

35 "Fiverr—Freelance Services Marketplace for Businesses." n.d. **https://www. fiverr.com/**.

36 "Toptal—Hire Freelance Talent from the Top 3%." n.d. **https://www.toptal.com/**.

37 Kaufman, Micha, CEO Fiverr, interview with Suzanne Riss and Jeff Schwartz, February 2020.

38 Brown, Molly. "'Ghost Work' Explores the Ups and Mostly Downs of the Hidden Gig Economy." *GeekWire*, May 14, 2019. **https://www.geekwire.com/2019/ ghost-work-explores-ups-mostly-downs-hidden-gig-economy/**.

39 Gray and Suri, *Ghost Work*.

40 Gray, Mary L., and Siddharth Suri. "Ghost Work: How to Stop Silicon Valley from Building a New Global Underclass." *Kirkus Reviews*, May 7, 2019. **https://www. kirkusreviews.com/book-reviews/mary-l-gray/ghost-work/**.

41 Schwartz et al., "Creating Meaning and Structure for Independent Work."

42 Ibid.

43 Ibid.

44 Ibid.

45 Charalampous, Maria, Christine A. Grant, Carlo Tramontano, and Evie Michailidis. (2018). "Systematically Reviewing Remote e-Workers' Well-Being at Work: A Multidimensional Approach." *European Journal of Work and Organizational Psychology* 28, no. 1 (November 1, 2018): 51–73. **https://doi.org/10.1080/13594 32X.2018.1541886**.

46 Conger, Kate, and Noam Scheiber. "California Bill Makes App-Based Companies Treat Workers as Employees." *The New York Times*, September 11, 2019. **https://www.nytimes.com/2019/09/11/technology/california-gig-economy-bill.html**.

47 Flamm, Matthew. "TLC Approves Historic Pay Rules for App-Based Drivers." *Crain's New York Business*, December 4, 2018. **https://www.crainsnewyork. com/transportation/tlc-approves-historic-pay-rules-app-based-drivers**.

48 Pelta, Rachel. "California AB5 and Freelancers: What It Means for You." FlexJobs Job Search Tips and Blog, April 1, 2020. **https://www.flexjobs.com/blog/post/ california-ab5-freelancers/**.

49 "Unemployment Insurance Relief During COVID-19 Outbreak." U.S. Department of Labor, n.d. **https://www.dol.gov/coronavirus/unemployment-insurance**.

50 Pardes, Arielle. "This Pandemic Is a 'Fork in the Road' for Gig Worker Benefits." *Wired*, April 9, 2020. **https://www.wired.com/story/gig-worker-benefits-covid-19-pandemic/**.

51 "Origins and Evolution of Employment-Based Health Benefits." Employment and Health Benefits: A Connection at Risk. U.S. National Library of Medicine, January 1, 1993. **https://www.ncbi.nlm.nih.gov/books/NBK235989/**.

52 Hyman, interview.

Chapter 4 Working from Almost Anywhere

1 Branson, Richard. "Give People the Freedom of Where to Work." *Virgin*, February 25, 2013. **www.virgin.com/richard-branson/give-people-the-freedom-of-where-to-work**.

2 DeVaney, James, Gideon Shimshon, Matthew Rascoff, and Jeff Maggioncalda. "Higher Ed Needs a Long-Term Plan for Virtual Learning." *Harvard Business Review*, May 5, 2020. **https://hbr.org/2020/05/higher-ed-needs-a-long-term-plan-for-virtual-learning?utm_campaign=hbr&utm_medium=social&utm_source=twitter**.

3 Nixey, Catherine. "Stories of an Extraordinary World: Death of the Office." *The Economist*, May 5, 2020. **https://www.economist.com/news/2020/05/05/ death-of-the-office**.

4 Zaveri, Paayal. "These Charts Show How Use of Microsoft Teams, Slack, and Zoom Has Skyrocketed Thanks to the Remote Work Boom." *Business Insider*, May 2, 2020. **https://www.businessinsider.com/microsoft-teams-slack-zoom-usage-charts-increased-remote-work-pandemic-2020-4?IR=T**.

5 "Lesson 1, What is Slack?" *Slack*. **https://slack.com/intl/en-za/resources/ slack-101-lesson-1-what-is-slack**.

6 Swanson, Kristen, interview with Suzanne Riss and Jeff Schwartz, April 2020.

7 Ibid.

8 Levy, Nat. "Google Glass Takes on Microsoft HoloLens with New Augmented Reality Eyewear for Businesses." *GeekWire*. May 20, 2019. **https://www.geekwire.**

com/2019/google-glass-takes-microsoft-hololens-new-augmented-reality-eyewear-businesses.

9 Carey, Scott. "How Microsoft HoloLens Is Being Used in the Real World." *Computerworld*. May 16, 2018. **https://www.computerworld.com/article/3412263/how-microsoft-hololens-is-being-used-in-the-real-world.html**.

10 *Inc*. Editorial Staff. "Your Office in 2020: A Glimpse into the Future," *Inc*. **https://www.inc.com/comcast/your-office-in-2020-a-glimpse-into-the-future.html**.

11 Levy, Steven. "The Race for AR Glasses Starts Now." *Wired*, December 16, 2017. **https://www.wired.com/story/future-of-augmented-reality-2018/**.

12 Darlin, Damon. "How the Future Looked in 1964: The Picturephone." *The New York Times*, June 16, 2014. **https://www.nytimes.com/2014/06/27/upshot/how-the-future-looked-in-1964-the-picturephone.html**.

13 "The History, Evolution and Future of Remote Work." WWR. **https://wework remotely.com/history-of-remote-work**.

14 Kowalski, Steve. "WFH." Kowalski Heat Treating, April 24, 2020. **https://www.khtheat.com/wfh/**.

15 Francis, Ejiofor. "Virtual Reality Is Already Changing How We Work and Communicate." *Entrepreneur*, April 20, 2018. **https://www.entrepreneur.com/article/311735**.

16 Chokshi, Niraj. "Out of the Office: More People Are Working Remotely, Survey Finds." *The New York Times*, February 15, 2017. **https://www.nytimes.com/2017/02/15/us/remote-workers-work-from-home.html**.

17 Topol, Eric J. *Deep Medicine: How Artificial Intelligence Can Make Healthcare Human Again*. New York: Basic Books, 2019.

18 Topol, Eric, interview with Suzanne Riss and Jeff Schwartz, July 2019.

19 Browne, Ryan. "70% of People Globally Work Remotely at Least Once a Week, Study Says." CNBC, Make It, May 30, 2019. **https://www.cnbc.com/2018/05/30/70-percent-of-people-globally-work-remotely-at-least-once-a-week-iwg-study.html**.

20 "The Benefits of Remote Work-for Both Employees and Managers." WeWork, May 4, 2020. **https://www.wework.com/ideas/worklife/benefits-of-working-remotely**.

21 Holmstrom, Mark, interview with Suzanne Riss and Jeff Schwartz, November 12, 2019.

22 Schwartz, Jeff, Heather Stockton, Mary Ann Stallings, and Stephen Harrington. "Beyond Yahoo: Breaking Down the 'Virtual' Versus 'Campus' Debate." *Deloitte Review, Deloitte Insights*, January 14, 2014. **www2.deloitte.com/us/en/insights/deloitte-review/issue-14/dr14-beyond-yahoo.html**.

23 Bishop, Caitlin. "What Is Hot-Desking and What Are the Benefits?" WeWork, November 21, 2019. **www.wework.com/ideas/office-design-space/what-is-hot-desking**.

24 Schwartz et al., "Beyond Yahoo."

25 "What Is a Makerspace?" Makerspaces, March 15, 2017. **https://www.maker-spaces.com/what-is-a-makerspace/**.

26 Levy, "The Race for AR Glasses Starts Now."

27 Schwartz, Jeff, Steve Hatfield, Robin Jones, and Siri Anderson. "What Is the Future of Work?" *Deloitte Insights*, April 1, 2019. **https://www2.deloitte.com/us/**

en/insights/focus/technology-and-the-future-of-work/redefining-work-workforces-workplaces.html.

28 "Build Software Better, Together." GitHub, n.d. **https://github.com/**.

29 "How Businesses Use Crowdsourcing to Disrupt and Avoid Disruption." Inno-Centive, June 13, 2019. **https://www.innocentive.com/how-businesses-use-crowdsourcing-to-disrupt-and-avoid-disruption/**.

30 Engelbert, Cathy, John Hagel, and Thomas Friedman. "Radically Open: Tom Fried-man on Jobs, Learning, and the Future of Work." *Deloitte Insights*, July 31, 2017. **https://www2.deloitte.com/us/en/insights/deloitte-review/issue-21/tom-friedman-interview-jobs-learning-future-of-work.html**.

31 Schwartz, Jeff, Amy Wrzesniewski, Michael H. Jordan, and Kelly Monahan. "Creating Meaning and Structure for Independent Work." *Deloitte Insights*, December 19, 2018. **https://www2.deloitte.com/us/en/insights/focus/technology-and-the-future-of-work/amy-wrzesniewski-interview-independent-work.html#**.

32 Petriglieri, Gianpiero, Susan J. Ashford, and Amy Wrzesniewski. "Agony and Ecstasy in the Gig Economy: Cultivating Holding Environments for Precarious and Personalized Work Identities." Sage Journals, February 6, 2018. **https://journals.sagepub.com/doi/abs/10.1177/0001839218759646**.

33 Schwartz, Wrzesniewski, et al., "Creating Meaning and Structure for Inde-pendent Work."

34 Ibid.

35 Ibid.

36 Arthur, Charles. "Yahoo Chief Bans Working from Home." *The Guardian*, Febru-ary 25, 2013. **https://www.theguardian.com/technology/2013/feb/25/yahoo-chief-bans-working-home**.

37 Lee, Mara. "Aetna to Cut Workforce, Reduce Work-at-Home Policy." *Hartford Cou-rant*, October 11, 2016. **http://www.courant.com/business/hc-aetna-work-at-home-20161010-story.html**

38 Swanson, interview.

39 Brandon, John. "This Is Huge: Twitter CEO Says Employees Can Work from Home 'Forever.'" *Forbes*, May 12, 2020. **https://www.forbes.com/sites/johnbbrandon/2020/05/12/this-is-huge-twitter-ceo-says-employees-can-work-from-home-forever/#2b4ec4134382**.

40 Christie, Jennifer. "Keeping Our Employees and Partners Safe during #Coronavirus." Twitter, May 12, 2020. **https://blog.twitter.com/en_us/topics/company/2020/keeping-our-employees-and-partners-safe-during-coronavirus.html**.

Chapter 5 Plan for Many Careers, Not One

1 Friedman, Thomas L. *The World Is Flat: A Brief History of the Twenty-First Century.* Bridgewater, NJ: Distributed by Paw Prints/Baker & Taylor, 2009.

2 Kittrels, Alonzo. "Back in the Day: Time Has Passed on the Gold Watch Retirement Gift." *The Philadelphia Tribune*, July 29, 2017. **https://www.phillytrib.com/lifestyle/back-in-the-day-time-has-passed-on-the-gold/article_5e853ac1-aa1a-5f2b-9bd2-f3b09dd9cd34.html**.

3 Pelster, Bill, Dani Johnson, Jen Stempel, and Bernard van der Vyver. "Careers and Learning: Real Time, All the Time." *Deloitte Insights*, February 28, 2017. **https://www2.deloitte.com/us/en/insights/focus/human-capital-trends/2017/learning-in-the-digital-age.html**.

4 "Number of Jobs, Labor Market Experience, and Earnings Growth: Results from a National Longitudinal Survey." Bureau of Labor Statistics, August 22, 2019. **https://www.bls.gov/news.release/pdf/nlsoy.pdf**.

5 Gratton, Lynda, interview with Suzanne Riss and Jeff Schwartz, July 2019.

6 Gratton, Lynda. "The 100-Year Life: Reframing Longevity as a Gift." *Future of Work*, March 30, 2016. **https://lyndagrattonfutureofwork.typepad.com/lynda-gratton-future-of-work/2016/03/the-100-year-life-reframing-longevity-as-a-gift.html**.

7 Pelster et al., "Careers and Learning."

8 Schwartz, JeffSpeech presented at the MIT Future of People Conference, MIT Media Lab, December 2016.

9 Gratton, Lynda, and Andrew Scott. *The 100-Year Life*. London: Bloomsbury Information, 2016.

10 Thomas, Douglas, and John Seely Brown. *A New Culture of Learning: Cultivating the Imagination for a World of Constant Change*. Lexington, KY: CreateSpace, 2011.

11 Brynjolfsson, Erik, and Andrew McAfee. *The Second Machine Age: Work, Progress, and Prosperity in a Time of Brilliant Technologies*. Vancouver, BC: Langara College, 2014.

12 Ford, Martin R. *Rise of the Robots: Technology and the Threat of a Jobless Future*. New York: Basic Books, 2015.

13 Ford, Martin. *Architects of Intelligence: The Truth about AI from the People Building It*. Birmingham, UK: Packt Publishing, 2018.

14 Ford, Martin. *The Lights in the Tunnel: Automation, Accelerating Technology and the Economy of the Future*. Charleston, SC: Acculant, 2009.

15 Friedman, Thomas L. *Thank You for Being Late: An Optimist's Guide to Thriving in the Age of Accelerations*. Penguin Books, 2017.

16 Benko, Cathleen, and Molly Anderson. *The Corporate Lattice: Achieving High Performance in the Changing World of Work*. Boston, MA: Harvard Business Press, 2010.

17 Benko, Cathleen, and Anne Weisberg. *Mass Career Customization: Aligning the Workplace With Today's Nontraditional Workforce*. Harvard Business Review Press, 2007.

18 Hoffman, Reid, Chris Yeh, and Ben Casnocha. *The Alliance: Managing Talent in the Networked Age*. London: HarperCollins, 2014.

19 Pink, Daniel H. *A Whole New Mind: How to Thrive in the New Conceptual Age*. London: Cyan, 2006.

20 Burnett, Bill, and Dave Evans. *Designing Your Life: How to Build a Well-Lived, Joyful Life*. New York: Alfred A. Knopf, 2016.

21 Gratton, interview.

22 Gratton, Lynda. *The Shift: The Future of Work Is Already Here*. HarperCollins Publishers, 2014.

23 Engelbert, Cathy, John Hagel, and Thomas Friedman. "Radically Open: Tom Friedman on Jobs, Learning, and the Future of Work." *Deloitte Insights*, July 31, 2017. **https://www2.deloitte.com/us/en/insights/deloitte-review/issue-21/tom-friedman-interview-jobs-learning-future-of-work.html**.

24 Englebert et al., "Radically Open."

25 LaPrade, Annette, Janet Mertens, Tanya Moore, and Amy Wright. "The Enterprise Guide to Closing the Skills Gap." IBM, n.d. **https://www.ibm.com/downloads/cas/EPYMNBJA**.

26 Brown, John Seely, interview with Suzanne Riss and Jeff Schwartz, June 2019.

27 Wired staff. "The Debriefing: John Seely Brown." *Wired*, August 1, 2000.

28 Brown, interview.

29 Ibid.

30 Ibid.

31 Ibid.

32 Brown, John Seely. Pardee RAND Commencement Speech, June 16, 2018. **http://www.johnseelybrown.com/JSBpardeerand.html**.

33 Mahdawi, Arwa, and Mona Chalabi. "What Jobs Will Still Be around in 20 Years? Read This to Prepare Your Future." *The Guardian*, June 26, 2017. **https://www.theguardian.com/us-news/2017/jun/26/jobs-future-automation-robots-skills-creative-health**.

34 Ibid.

35 Deming, David. "In the Salary Race, Engineers Sprint but English Majors Endure." *The New York Times*, September 20, 2019. **https://www.nytimes.com/2019/09/20/business/liberal-arts-stem-salaries.html**.

36 Ibid.

37 LaPrade et al., "The Enterprise Guide."

38 Pelster et al., "Careers and Learning."

39 Muhl, Erica, interview with Suzanne Riss and Jeff Schwartz, July 2019.

40 Ibid.

41 "To Future-Proof Your Career, Start by Embracing Cross-Disciplinary Thinking." *Quartz*, December 19, 2019. **https://qz.com/1589490/to-future-proof-your-career-start-by-embracing-cross-disciplinary-thinking/**.

42 Muhl, interview.

43 "To Future-Proof Your Career."

44 Muhl, interview.

45 Lichfield, Gideon, and Charles Isbell. EmTech Next, MIT Media Lab, Cambridge, MA, 2019.

46 Ibid.

47 Ibid.

48 "Massive Open Online Course." Wikipedia, May 27, 2020. **https://en.wikipedia.org/wiki/Massive_open_online_course**.

49 Khan, Salman. *The One World Schoolhouse: Education Reimagined*. New York, NY: Twelve, 2012.

50 Tom. "The History of Online Education." *Peterson's*, November 29, 2017. **https://www.petersons.com/blog/the-history-of-online-education/**.

51 DeVaney, James, Gideon Shimshon, Matthew Rascoff, and Jeff Maggioncalda. "Higher Ed Needs a Long-Term Plan for Virtual Learning." *Harvard Business Review*,

May 5, 2020. **https://hbr.org/2020/05/higher-ed-needs-a-long-term-plan-for-virtual-learning?utm_campaign=hbr**.

52 "Coursera." Wikipedia, May 25, 2020. **https://en.wikipedia.org/wiki/Coursera**.

53 Carey, Kevin. *The End of College: Creating the Future of Learning and the University of Everywhere*. New York: Riverhead Books, 2016.

54 Jovanovic, Boyan, and Peter L. Rousseau. "General Purpose Technologies." In: *Handbook of Economic Growth*, 2005, 1181–1224. **https://doi.org/10.1016/s1574-0684(05)01018-x**.

55 "Timeline of Steam Power." Wikipedia, April 19, 2020. **https://en.wikipedia.org/wiki/Timeline_of_steam_power**.

56 "Models." *Blended Learning Universe*, September 12, 2019. **https://www.blendedlearning.org/models/?gclid=CjwKCAjwqpP2BRBTEiwAfpiD-_w5sINumOFRN-WHMu-cJBkzptAMBDBqPnPTOLXpGB2SDbCrxre2CoRoCkPgQAvD_BwE**.

57 "Khan Academy Part of 'Flipped' Classroom Trend." | *Education World*, n.d. **https://www.educationworld.com/a_curr/vodcast-sites-enable-flipped-classroom.shtml**.

58 "TED Organization Unveils New Online Education Platform, TED-Ed |." *EdTech Times*, March 13, 2012. **https://edtechtimes.com/2012/03/12/ted-organization-unveils-new-online-education-platform-ted-ed/**.

59 Hagel, John, interview with Suzanne Riss and Jeff Schwartz, June 2019.

60 Ibid.

61 Pelster et al., "Careers and Learning."

62 Centre for the New Economy and Society. "The Future of Jobs Report 2018." World Economic Forum. **http://www3.weforum.org/docs/WEF_Future_of_Jobs_2018.pdf**.

63 Ibid.

64 Pate, Deanna. "The Skills Companies Need Most in 2020—And How to Learn Them." LinkedIn Learning, January 13, 2020. **https://learning.linkedin.com/blog/top-skills/the-skills-companies-need-most-in-2020and-how-to-learn-them**.

65 Deming, David, and Kadeem Noray. "STEM Careers and the Changing Skill Requirements of Work." NBER Working Paper Series, 2018. **https://doi.org/10.3386/w25065**.

66 "Job Outlook 2019." National Association of Colleges and Employers (NACE), November 2019. **https://www.odu.edu/content/dam/odu/offices/cmc/docs/nace/2019-nace-job-outlook-survey.pdf**.

67 Miller, Claire Cain. "Why What You Learned in Preschool Is Crucial at Work." *The New York Times*, October 16, 2015. **https://www.nytimes.com/2015/10/18/upshot/how-the-modern-workplace-has-become-more-like-preschool.html**.

68 Hyman, Louis, interview with Suzanne Riss and Jeff Schwartz, January 13, 2020.

69 Gratton, interview.

70 Ibid.

71 Volini, Erica, Jeff Schwartz, Indranil Roy, Maren Hauptmann, Yves Van Durme, Brad Denny, and Josh Bersin. "Learning in the Flow of Life." *Deloitte Insights*, April 11, 2019. **https://www2.deloitte.com/us/en/insights/focus/human-capital-trends/2019/reskilling-upskilling-the-future-of-learning-and-development.html**.

72 Ibid.

Chapter 6 The Rise of Teams

1 Tett, Gillian, interview with Suzanne Riss and Jeff Schwartz, February 2020.

2 Shinal, John. "Steve Wozniak Is Still on Apple's Payroll Four Decades after Co-Founding the Company." CNBC, January 18, 2018. **https://www.cnbc. com/2018/01/18/steve-wozniak-still-on-apple-payroll-jokes-he-still-reports-to-jobs.html**.

3 Rahnema, Amir, and Tara Murphy. "The Adaptable Organization Harnessing a Networked Enterprise of Human Resilience." Deloitte, n.d. **https://www2. deloitte.com/global/en/pages/human-capital/articles/the-adaptable-organization.html**.

4 Rhodes, Mark. "Strategy First . . . Then Structure." Blog: Strategic Planning. Free Management Library, January 23, 2011. **https://managementhelp.org/blogs/ strategic-planning/2011/01/23/194/**.

5 Nixey, Catherine. "Death of the Office." *The Economist*, May 5, 2020. **https:// www.economist.com/news/2020/05/05/death-of-the-office**.

6 Ibid.

7 Tett, Gillian. *The Silo Effect: The Perils of Expertise and the Promise of Breaking Down Barriers.* New York: Simon & Schuster, 2016.

8 Tett, Gillian, interview.

9 Ibid.

10 Ibid.

11 Ibid.

12 Ibid.

13 "What Makes Teams Smart." *MIT Sloan Management Review*, October 4, 2010. **https://sloanreview.mit.edu/article/what-makes-teams-smart/**.

14 Brodie, John. "The Symphonic C-Suite: Teams Leading Teams." Deloitte, n.d. **https://www2.deloitte.com/za/en/pages/human-capital/articles/the-symphonic-c-suite.html**.

15 Volini, Erica, Jeff Schwartz, and Indranil Roy. "Organizational Performance: It's a Team Sport 2019 Global Human Capital Trends." *Deloitte Insights*, April 11, 2019. **https://www2.deloitte.com/us/en/insights/focus/human-capital-trends/2019/team-based-organization.html**.

16 Ibid.

17 McChrystal, General Stanley, Tantum Collins, David Silverman, and Chris Fussell. *Team of Teams: New Rules of Engagement for a Complex World.* New York, NY: Penguin Publishing Group, 2015.

18 Gordon, Beau. "Key Takeaways from Team of Teams by General Stanley McChrystal." *Medium*, March 27, 2017. **https://medium.com/@beaugordon/key-takeaways-from-team-of-teams-by-general-stanley-mcchrystal-eac0b37520b9**.

19 Guszcza, Jim, and Jeff Schwartz. "Superminds: How Humans and Machines Can Work Together." *Deloitte Review*, no. 24 (January 28, 2019). **https://www2. deloitte.com/us/en/insights/focus/technology-and-the-future-of-work/ human-and-machine-collaboration.html**.

20 Ibid.

21 Malone, Thomas W. *Superminds: The Surprising Power of People and Computers Thinking Together.* New York: Little, Brown Spark, 2019.

22 Ulrich, David, and Arthur Yeung, interview with Jeff Schwartz.
23 Ibid.
24 Ibid.
25 "How Companies Like Google and Alibaba Respond to Fast-Moving Markets." *Harvard Business Review*, April 8, 2020. **https://hbr.org/podcast/2019/10/how-companies-like-google-and-alibaba-respond-to-fast-moving-markets**.
26 Ibid.
27 Ulrich and Yeung, interview.
28 Ibid.
29 Nyce, Caroline Mimbs. "The Winter Getaway That Turned the Software World Upside Down." *The Atlantic*, December 8, 2017. **https://www.theatlantic.com/technology/archive/2017/12/agile-manifesto-a-history/547715/**.

Chapter 7 Leaders as Coaches and Designers

1 **http://www.gloriasteinem.com/news**.
2 Smith, Deborah. "Psychologist Wins Nobel Prize: Daniel Kahneman Is Honored for Bridging Economics and Psychology." *Monitor on Psychology*, 33, no. 11 (2002): 22. **https://www.apa.org/monitor/dec02/nobel.html**.
3 "Daniel Kahneman." Wikipedia, June 11, 2020. **https://en.wikipedia.org/wiki/Daniel_Kahneman**.
4 Guszcza, Jim, Jeff Schwartz, and Josh Bersin. "HR for Humans: How Behavioral Economics Can Reinvent HR." *Deloitte Insights*, January 25, 2016. **https://www2.deloitte.com/us/en/insights/deloitte-review/issue-18/behavioral-economics-evidence-based-hr-management.html**.
5 Holt, Jim. "Two Brains Running." *The New York Times*, November 25, 2011. **https://www.nytimes.com/2011/11/27/books/review/thinking-fast-and-slow-by-daniel-kahneman-book-review.html**.
6 Smith, "Psychologist Wins Nobel Prize."
7 Kahneman, Daniel. *Thinking, Fast and Slow*. Farrar, Straus and Giroux, 2013.
8 Fernando, Jason. "Daniel Kahneman." Investopedia, September 17, 2019. **https://www.investopedia.com/terms/d/daniel-kahneman.asp#:~:text= Despite%20having%20reportedly%20never%20taken**, human%20judgment% 20and%20decision%2Dmaking
9 Sims, Calvin. "Mobile Telephones For All Occasions." *The New York Times*, September 23, 1987. **https://www.nytimes.com/1987/09/23/business/mobile-telephones-for-all-occasions.html**.
10 Peng, Dennis. "Cell Phone Cost Comparison Timeline." Ooma, September 16, 2019. **https://www.ooma.com/home-phone/cell-phone-cost-comparison/**.
11 O'Dea, S. "Smartphone Users in the United States 2018–2024." Statista, April 21, 2020. **https://www.statista.com/statistics/201182/forecast-of-smartphone-users-in-the-us/**.

12 La, Lynne. "Best Phones under $300: Moto G Power, Galaxy A50, LG K40 and more for 2020." cnet, June 5, 2020. **https://www.cnet.com/news/best-phones-under-300-galaxy-a50-moto-g-power-lg-k40-and-more-for-2020/**.

13 Quigley, Robert. "The Cost of a Gigabyte Over the Years." *The Mary Sue*, March 8, 2011. **https://www.themarysue.com/gigabyte-cost-over-years/**.

14 Mims, Christoper. "Every Company Is Now a Tech Company." *The Wall Street Journal*, December 4, 2018. **https://www.wsj.com/articles/every-company-is-now-a-tech-company-1543901207**.

15 Andreessen, Marc. "Why software is eating the world." *The Wall Street Journal*, August 20, 2011. **https://www.wsj.com/articles/SB10001424053111903480904576512250915629460**.

16 Kane, Gerald, interview with Suzanne Riss and Jeff Schwartz, January 2020.

17 Ibid.

18 Buckingham, Marcus, and Ashley Goodall. "Reinventing Performance Management." *Harvard Business Review*, April, 2015. **https://hbr.org/2015/04/reinventing-performance-management**.

19 Ibid.

20 Ibid.

21 Chen, James. "Homo Economicus." Investopedia, September 12, 2019. **https://www.investopedia.com/terms/h/homoeconomicus.asp**.

22 Sunstein, Cass R. and Thaler, Richard. "The Two Friends Who Changed How We Think about How We Think." *The New Yorker*, December 7, 2016. **https://www.newyorker.com/books/page-turner/the-two-friends-who-changed-how-we-think-about-how-we-think**.

23 Ibid.

24 Harvard Business Review Staff. "How Companies Can Profit from a 'Growth Mindset.'" *Harvard Business Review*, November 2014. **https://hbr.org/2014/11/how-companies-can-profit-from-a-growth-mindset**.

25 Ibid.

26 Tett, Gillian. *The Silo Effect: The Perils of Expertise and the Promise of Breaking Down Barriers*. New York: Simon & Schuster, 2016.

27 Poole, Steven. "The Silo Effect by Gillian Tett Review—A Subversive Manifesto." *The Guardian*, October 17, 2015. **https://www.theguardian.com/books/2015/oct/17/the-silo-effect-why-putting-everything-in-its-place-isnt-such-a-bright-idea-gillian-tett-review**.

28 Hayes, Chris. "'The Silo Effect,' by Gillian Tett." *The New York Times*, September 2, 2015. **https://www.nytimes.com/2015/09/06/books/review/the-silo-effect-by-gillian-tett.html**.

29 Tett, Gillian, interview with Suzanne Riss and Jeff Schwartz, February 2020.

30 Ibid.

31 "Design Thinking." Wikipedia, June 11, 2020. **https://en.wikipedia.org/wiki/Design_thinking**.

32 ExperiencePoint. "How IBM's Innovation Lab Leverages Design Thinking." ExperiencePoint, June 26, 2019. **https://blog.experiencepoint.com/how-ibm-leverages-design-thinking#:~:text=Profiled%20recently%20on%20the%20Digital,**specifically%20for%20design%20thinking%20sessions.&text=IBM%20wants%20to%20help%20teams,real%20needs%20of%20their%20users.

33 Doblin, a Deloitte Business. "Innovation." Deloitte United States, n.d. **https:// www2.deloitte.com/us/en/pages/strategy/solutions/innovation-doblin-consulting-services.html**.

34 Himsworth, Jesse. "Why Design Thinking Should Also Serve as a Leadership Philosophy." *Forbes*, July 19, 2018. **https://www.forbes.com/sites/forbesa-gencycouncil/2018/07/19/why-design-thinking-should-also-serve-as-a-leadership-philosophy/#4e58b7585a90**.

35 Tischler, Linda. "Ideo's David Kelley on 'Design Thinking.'" *Fast Company*, January 2, 9AD. **https://www.fastcompany.com/1139331/ideos-david-kelley-design-thinking**.

36 Ibid.

37 Himsworth, "Why Design Thinking."

38 Bersin, Josh, Marc Solow, and Nicky Wakefield. "Design Thinking Crafting the Employee Experience." *Deloitte Insights*, February 29, 2016. **https://www2. deloitte.com/us/en/insights/focus/human-capital-trends/2016/employee-experience-management-design-thinking.html**.

39 Martin, Roger L. *The Design of Business: Why Design Thinking Is the Next Competitive Advantage*. Boston, MA: Harvard Business School Publishing, 2009.

40 Kurutz, Steven. "Want to Find Fulfillment at Last? Think Like a Designer." *The New York Times*, September 17, 2016. **https://www.nytimes.com/2016/09/18/ fashion/design-thinking-stanford-silicon-valley.html**.

41 Mabe, John. "Covid-19 and the Rapid Acceleration of Online Commerce." Tech Gistics, May 17, 2020. **https://www.techgistics.net/blog/2020/5/17/covid-19-and-the-rapid-acceleration-of-online-commerce-delivery-uber-grubhub-logistics**.

42 Ready, Douglas A., interview with Suzanne Riss and Jeff Schwartz, February 2020.

43 Ready, Douglas A, Carol Cohen, David Kiron, and Benjamin Pring. "The New Leadership Playbook for the Digital Age." *MIT Sloan Management Review*, January 21, 2020. **https://sloanreview.mit.edu/projects/the-new-leadership-playbook-for-the-digital-age/#chapter-8**.

44 Ibid.

45 Ibid.

46 Volini, Erica, Jeff Schwartz, and Indranil Roy. "Leadership for the 21st Century: The Intersection of the Traditional and the New." *Deloitte Insights*, April 11, 2019. **https://www2.deloitte.com/us/en/insights/focus/human-capital-trends/2019/21st-century-leadership-challenges-and-development.html**.

47 Agarwal, Dimple, Josh Bersin, and Gaurav Lahiri. "The Symphonic C-suite: Teams Leading Teams." *Deloitte Insights*, March 28, 2018. **https://www2.deloitte.com/ us/en/insights/focus/human-capital-trends/2018/senior-leadership-c-suite-collaboration.html**.

48 BrainyQuote,   n.d.   **https://www.brainyquote.com/quotes/f_scott_ fitzgerald_100572**.

49 Volini, Erica, Jeff Schwartz, and Brad Denny. "The Social Enterprise at Work: Paradox as a Path Forward." *Deloitte Insights*, May 15, 2020. **https://www2.deloitte. com/us/en/insights/focus/human-capital-trends/2020/technology-and-the-social-enterprise.html**.

50 Volini, Erica, Jeff Schwartz, Brad Denny, David Mallon, Yves Van Durme, Maren Hauptmann, Ramona Yan, and Shannon Poynton. "Returning to Work in the Future of Work Embracing Purpose, Potential, Perspective, and Possibility during

COVID-19." *Deloitte Insights*, May 15, 2020. **https://www2.deloitte.com/us/en/insights/focus/human-capital-trends/2020/covid-19-and-the-future-of-work.html**.

51 Ready, Douglas A. "4 Things Successful Change Leaders Do Well." *Harvard Business Review*, January 28, 2016. **https://hbr.org/2016/01/4-things-successful-change-leaders-do-well**.

52 "The Origins of VUCA." UNC Kenan-Flager Business School. UNC Executive Development Blog, March 10, 2017. **http://execdev.kenan-flagler.unc.edu/blog/the-origins-of-vuca**.

53 Ready, interview.

54 Ready et al., "The New Leadership Playbook."

55 Ready, interview.

Chapter 8 Carpe Diem

1 Darwin, Charles. *The Origin of Species*. New York: D. Appleton, 1900.

2 Durkin, Andrea. "Etsy's Growth Illustrates That Even Local Is Global." TradeVistas, February 23, 2018. **https://tradevistas.org/etsys-growth-illustrates-even-local-global/**.

3 Mazareanu, E. "Uber's Gender Distribution of Global Employees 2019." Statista, October 23, 2019. **https://www.statista.com/statistics/693807/uber-employee-gender-global/**.

4 "Why Etsy Loves Women and Women Love Etsy." *Yahoo! Finance*, November 23, 2018. **https://finance.yahoo.com/news/etsy-loves-women-women-love-etsy-163608149.html**.

5 Reader, Ruth. "A Brief History of Etsy, from 2005 Brooklyn Launch to 2015 IPO." *VentureBeat*, March 5, 2015. **https://venturebeat.com/2015/03/05/a-brief-history-of-etsy-from-2005-brooklyn-launch-to-2015-ipo/**.

6 Stinchcomb, Matt. "Etsy Crafts a Recession Success." eMarketer, May 1, 2009. **https://www.emarketer.com/Article/Etsy-Crafts-Recession-Success/1007066**.

7 Clifford, Tyler. "Etsy Shares Pop 14% on Strong Quarterly Report. CEO Says Company Feels 'Very Resilient' to Coronavirus Impact." CNBC, February 27, 2020. **https://www.cnbc.com/2020/02/27/etsy-stock-pops-14percent-ceo-says-it-feels-very-resilient-to-coronavirus.html**.

8 Ibid.

9 Dweck, Carol S. *Mindset: The New Psychology of Success*. New York: Ballantine Books, 2006.

10 "Erica Muhl." LinkedIn, n.d. **https://www.linkedin.com/in/erica-muhl-34300845/**.

11 "The Academy." USC Jimmy Iovine and Andre Young Academy for Arts, Technology and the Business of Innovation, n.d. **https://iovine-young.usc.edu/about/index.html**.

12 Young, Jeffrey R. "How Many Times Will People Change Jobs? The Myth of the Endlessly-Job-Hopping Millennial." EdSurge, February 19, 2019.

https://www.edsurge.com/news/2017-07-20-how-many-times-will-people-change-jobs-the-myth-of-the-endlessly-job-hopping-millennial.

13 Arena, Michael, interview with Suzanne Riss and Jeff Schwartz.

14 Ibid.

15 "What Makes Teams Smart." *MIT Sloan Management Review*, n.d. **https://sloanreview.mit.edu/article/what-makes-teams-smart/**

16 Hagel, John, interview with Suzanne Riss and Jeff Schwartz, June 2019.

17 Topol, Eric, interview with Suzanne Riss and Jeff Schwartz, July 2019.

18 Brown, John Seely, interview with Suzanne Riss and Jeff Schwartz, June 2019.

19 Schwartz, Jeff, Jennifer Radin, Steve Hatfield, and Colleen Bordeaux. "Closing the Employability Skills Gap." *Deloitte Insights*, January 28, 2020. **https://www2.deloitte.com/us/en/insights/focus/technology-and-the-future-of-work/closing-the-employability-skills-gap.html**.

20 Hagel, John, John Seely Brown, Maggie Wooll, Roy Matthew, and Wendy Tsu. "The Lifetime Learner." *Deloitte Insights*, October 27, 2014. **https://www2.deloitte.com/us/en/insights/industry/public-sector/future-of-online-learning.html**.

21 Hagel, John, and John Seely Brown. "Unlocking the Passion of the Explorer." *Deloitte Insights*, September 17, 2013. **https://www2.deloitte.com/us/en/insights/topics/talent/unlocking-the-passion-of-the-explorer.html**.

22 Hagel, interview.

23 Ibid.

24 Ibid.

25 Schwartz, Jeff, Kelly Monahan, Steven Hatfield, and Siri Anderson. "No Time to Retire." *Deloitte Insights*, n.d. **https://www2.deloitte.com/content/dam/Deloitte/at/Documents/human-capital/at-workforce-longevity.pdf**.

26 "Agency (Sociology)." Wikipedia. Wikimedia Foundation, June 5, 2020. **https://en.wikipedia.org/wiki/Agency_(sociology)**.

27 Bersin, Josh. "The Future of Work: It's Already Here—And Not as Scary as You Think." *Forbes*, September 27, 2016. **https://www.forbes.com/sites/joshbersin/2016/09/21/the-future-of-work-its-already-here-and-not-as-scary-as-you-think/**.

28 "Coursera." Wikipedia, June 8, 2020. **https://en.wikipedia.org/wiki/Coursera**.

29 Buchman, Mette, interview with Suzanne Riss and Jeff Schwartz, November 2019.

30 Ibid.

31 Ibid.

32 "About Us." Beats by Dre, n.d. **https://www.beatsbydre.com/company/aboutus**.

33 Whole. *The Defiant Ones*. HBO, 2017.

34 Ibid.

35 Ibid.

36 Ibid.

37 Lichfield, Gideon, and Charles Isbell. EmTech Next, MIT Media Lab, Cambridge, MA, 2019.

38 Ibid.

39 Schwartz et al., "No Time to Retire."

40 Dychtwald, Ken. *Age Wave*. New York: Bantam Books, 1990.

41 Gratton, Lynda, and Andrew Scott. *The 100-Year Life*. London: Bloomsbury Information, 2016.

42 Andrew, Scott J., and Lynda Gratton. *The New Long Life: a Framework for Flourishing in a Changing World*. London: Bloomsbury Publishing, 2020.

43 Freedman, Marc. *Encore: Finding Work That Matters in the Second Half of Life (Finding Work That Matters in the Second Half of Life)*. PublicAffairs, 2007.

44 Coughlin, Joseph F. *The Longevity Economy Unlocking the World's Fastest-Growing, Most Misunderstood Market*. New York, NY: PublicAffairs, 2017.

45 Kaufman, Micha, interview with Suzanne Riss and Jeff Schwartz, February 2020.

46 Malone, Thomas, interview with Suzanne Riss and Jeff Schwartz, July 2019.

47 Hyman, Louis, interview with Suzanne Riss and Jeff Schwartz, January 13, 2020.

48 Brynjolfsson, Erik, interview with Suzanne Riss and Jeff Schwartz, July 2019.

49 Brown, interview.

50 Arena, interview.

51 Carey, Kevin. *The End of College: Creating the Future of Learning and the University of Everywhere*. New York: Riverhead Books, 2016.

52 Winn, Zach, and MIT News Office. "Inclusive Innovation Challenge Recognizes Startups Improving the Future of Work." *MIT News*, November 22, 2019. **http://news.mit.edu/2019/inclusive-innovation-challenge-future-work-1122**.

53 Ibid.

Chapter 9 Create Opportunity

1 Hagel, John, John Seely Brown, and Maggie Wooll. "Can We Realize Untapped Opportunity by Redefining Work?" *Deloitte Insights*, October 24, 2018. **https://www2.deloitte.com/us/en/insights/focus/technology-and-the-future-of-work/redefining-work-organizational-transformation.html**

2 Huddleston, Tom, Jr. "Zoom's Founder Left a 6-figure Job Because He Wasn't Happy—and Following His Heart Made Him a Billionaire." *Make It*. August 21, 2019. **https://www.cnbc.com/2019/08/21/zoom-founder-left-job-because-he-wasnt-happy-became-billionaire.html**.

3 "Cisco Announces Agreement to Acquire WebEx." *The Network*. March 15, 2007. **https://newsroom.cisco.com/press-release-content?type=webcontent&articleId=3080774**.

4 Konrad, Alex. "Exclusive: Zoom CEO Eric Yuan Is Giving K-12 Schools His Video-conferencing Tools For Free." *Forbes*, March 13, 2020.

5 Brown, John Seely. Commencement Speech at Rochester Institute of Technology, Rochester, NY, May 10, 2019.

6 MIT Technology Review's EmTech Next 2020 Conference. MIT, Cambridge, June 10, 2020.

7 Hagel et al., "Can We Realize Untapped Opportunity by Redefining Work?"

8 Schwartz, Jeff, John Hagel, Kelly Monahan, and Maggie Wooll. "Reframing the Future of Work." *MIT Sloan Management Review*, February 20, 2019. **https://sloanreview.mit.edu/article/reframing-the-future-of-work/**.

9 Hagel, John, John Seely Brown, and Maggie Wooll. "Redefine Work: The Untapped Opportunity for Expanding Value." Report. Center for the Edge, Deloitte. **https://www2.deloitte.com/content/dam/insights/us/articles/4779_Redefine-work/DI_Redefine-work.pdf**.

10 Hunter, John. "Toyota's Management History." The W Edwards Deming Institute Blog, September 23, 2013. **https://blog.deming.org/2016/10/toyotas-management-history/**.

11 Hagel et al., "Redefine Work."

12 Schwartz, Jeff, Steve Hatfield, Robin Jones, and Siri Anderson. "What Is the Future of Work? Redefining Work, Workforces, and Workplaces." *Deloitte Insights*, April 01, 2019. **https://www2.deloitte.com/us/en/insights/focus/technology-and-the-future-of-work/redefining-work-workforces-workplaces.html**.

13 Ibid.

14 Schwartz, Jeff, Brad Denny, David Mallon, Yves Van Durme, Maren Hauptmann, Ramona Yan, and Shannon Poynton. "Belonging: From Comfort to Connection to Contribution," May 15, 2020. **https://www2.deloitte.com/us/en/insights/focus/human-capital-trends/2020/creating-a-culture-of-belonging.html#**.

15 Brynjolfsson, Erik, John J. Horton, Adam Ozimek, Daniel Rock, Garima Sharma, and Hong-Yi TuYe. "COVID-19 and Remote Work: An Early Look at US Data." NBER, June 11, 2020. **https://www.nber.org/papers/w27344**.

16 Lavelle, Justin. "Gartner CFO Survey Reveals 74% Intend to Shift Some Employees to Remote Work Permanently." Gartner, April 3, 2020. **https://www.gartner.com/en/newsroom/press-releases/2020-04-03-gartner-cfo-surey-reveals-74-percent-of-organizations-to-shift-some-employees-to-remote-work-permanently2**.

17 Volini, Erica, Jeff Schwartz, Indranil Roy, Maren Hauptmann, Yves Van Durme, Brady Denny, and Josh Bersin. "From Jobs to Superjobs: 2019 Global Human Capital Trends." *Deloitte Insights*, April 11, 2019. **https://www2.deloitte.com/us/en/insights/focus/human-capital-trends/2019/impact-of-ai-turning-jobs-into-superjobs.html**.

18 Acemoglu, Daron, and Pascual Restrepo. "The Wrong Kind of AI? Artificial Intelligence and the Future of Labor Demand." Report no. IZA DP No. 12292. IZA Institute of Labor Economics, April 2019.

19 Hagel et al., "Redefine Work."

20 Ibid.

21 Goodreads. **https://www.goodreads.com/author/quotes/16759765.Thomas_L_Friedman?page=2**.

22 Kleiner, Art. "Thomas Malone on Building Smarter Teams." *Thought Leaders*, May 12, 2014.

23 Agarwal, Dimple, Josh Bersin, Gaurav Lahiri, Jeff Schwartz, and Erica Volini. "The Symphonic C-Suite: Teams Leading Teams." *Deloitte Insights*, March 28, 2018. **https://www2.deloitte.com/us/en/insights/focus/human-capital-trends/2018/senior-leadership-c-suite-collaboration.html**.

24 Volini, Erica, Jeff Schwartz, Brad Denny, David Mallon, Yves Van Durme, Maren Hauptmann, Ramona Yan, and Shannon Poynton. "The Social Enterprise at Work: Paradox as a Path Forward 2020 Deloitte Global Human Capital Trends." *Deloitte Insights*, 2020. **https://documents.deloitte.com/insights/HumanCapital-Trends2020**.

25 Schrage, Michael, Jeff Schwartz, David Kiron, Robin Jones, and Natasha Buckley. "Opportunity Marketplaces: Aligning Workforce Investment and Value Creation in the Digital Enterprise." *MIT Sloan Management Review*, April 28, 2020. **https://sloanreview.mit.edu/projects/opportunity-marketplaces/.**

26 "Build Software Better, Together." GitHub. Accessed June 22, 2020. **https://github.com/.**

27 "Home." InnoCentive. June 18, 2020. Accessed June 22, 2020. **https://www.innocentive.com/.**

28 Hagel, John, interview with Suzanne Riss and Jeff Schwartz, June 2019.

29 Hsieh, Tony. *Delivering Happiness: A Path to Profits, Passion, and Purpose.* Grand Central Publishing, 2010.

30 "Learning and Strategy." Edge Perspectives with John Hagel, August 5, 2019. **https://edgeperspectives.typepad.com/edge_perspectives/2019/08/learning-and-strategy.html.**

31 Ibid.

32 Hagel, interview.

33 Brynjolfsson, Erik, John Horton, Adam Ozimek, Daniel Rock, Garima Sharma, and Hong Yi Tu Ye. "COVID-19 and Remote Work: An Early Look at US Data," April 8, 2020. **https://john-joseph-horton.com/papers/remote_work.pdf.**

34 Schatsky, David, and Jeff Schwartz. "Redesigning Work in an Era of Cognitive Technologies." *Deloitte Review* 17, 2015. **https://www2.deloitte.com/tr/en/pages/technology-media-and-telecommunications/articles/redesigning-work-cognitive-technologies.html**

35 Gratton, Lynda. Comment on "The Workplace Is Changing | in Conversation with Lynda Gratton and Andrew Scott." Audio blog. Accessed June 20, 2020. **https://soundcloud.com/londonbusinessschool/the-workplace-is-changing-in-conversation-with-lynda-gratton-andrew-scott**

36 Ibid.

37 Acemoglu and Restrepo, "The Wrong Kind of AI?"

38 Schwartz et al., "What Is the Future of Work?"

39 Ready, Douglas A., Carol Cohen, David Kiron, and Benjamin Pring. "The New Leadership Playbook for the Digital Age." *MIT Sloan Management Review*, January 21, 2020. **https://sloanreview.mit.edu/projects/the-new-leadership-playbook-for-the-digital-age/.**

40 Ibid.

41 Ready, Douglas A., interview with Suzanne Riss and Jeff Schwartz, February 2020.

42 Muhl, Erica, interview with Suzanne Riss and Jeff Schwartz, July 2019.

43 Tett, Gillian, interview with Suzanne Riss and Jeff Schwartz, February 2020.

44 Brynjolfsson, Erik, interview with Suzanne Riss and Jeff Schwartz, July 2019.

45 Schwartz et al., "What Is the Future of Work?"

46 **Goodreads.com.** 2020. *Tim Harford Quotes.* Available at: **https://www.goodreads.com/author/quotes/14442.Tim_Harford.** Accessed June 22, 2020.

47 Slack. "Stewart Butterfield: Leadership." Slack. Accessed June 22, 2020. **https://slack.com/intl/en-za/about/leadership/stewart-butterfield.**

48 Butterfield, Stewart. "Channels of Communication." Proceedings of MIT Technology Review EmTech Next 2020, Online Conference.

49 Ibid.

Chapter 10 Set New Agendas

1 Slaughter, Anne-Marie. "Forget the Trump Administration: America Will Save America." *The New York Times*, March 21, 2020.
2 Merit America, n.d. **https://www.meritamerica.org/**.
3 Burke, Lilah. "Google Releases New IT Certificate." *Inside Higher Ed*, January 17, 2020. **https://www.insidehighered.com/quicktakes/2020/01/17/google-releases-new-it-certificate**.
4 Fadulu, Lola. "Why Is the U.S. So Bad at Worker Retraining?" *The Atlantic*, February 27, 2019. **https://www.theatlantic.com/education/archive/2018/01/why-is-the-us-so-bad-at-protecting-workers-from-automation/549185/**.
5 Grose, Thomas K. "Sweden's Lesson on Worker Retraining—Before It's Too Late." *U.S. News & World Report*, February 6, 2018. **https://www.usnews.com/news/best-countries/articles/2018-02-06/what-sweden-can-teach-the-world-about-worker-retraining**.
6 Merit America, n.d. **https://www.meritamerica.org/ourimpact**.
7 Lohr, Steve. "Gaining Skills Virtually to Close the Inequality Gap." *The New York Times*, June 7, 2020. **https://www.nytimes.com/2020/06/07/technology/virtual-skills-inequality-gap-virus.html**.
8 Oxley, Dyer. "How Does a 32-Hour Workweek Even Work? Some Washington Lawmakers Want to Find Out." KUOW, February 4, 2020. **https://www.kuow.org/stories/32-hour-workweek-proposal**.
9 Wray, L. Randall, Flavia Dantas, Scott Fullwiler, Pavlina Tcherneva, and Stephanie A. Kelton. "Public Service Employment: A Path to Full Employment." Levy Institute, April 2018. **http://www.levyinstitute.org/pubs/rpr_4_18.pdf**.
10 Johnson, Eric. "Full Q&A: 'Temp' Author Louis Hyman on Recode Decode." *Vox*, August 29, 2018. **https://www.vox.com/2018/8/29/17793764/louis-hyman-temp-book-kara-swisher-rani-molla-podcast-transcript**.
11 Slaughter, Anne-Marie, interview with Suzanne Riss and Jeff Schwartz, May 2020.
12 Fitzpayne, Alastair, and Ethan Pollack. "Lifelong Learning and Training Accounts: Helping Workers Adapt and Succeed in a Changing Economy." The Aspen Institute, May 29, 2018. **https://www.aspeninstitute.org/publications/lifelong-learning-and-training-accounts-2018/**.
13 Deming, David, interview with Suzanne Riss and Jeff Schwartz, March 2020.
14 Hagel, John, interview with Suzanne Riss and Jeff Schwartz, June 2019.
15 Brown, John Seely interview with Suzanne Riss and Jeff Schwartz, June 2019.
16 Muhl, Erica, interview with Suzanne Riss and Jeff Schwartz, July 2019.
17 Slaughter, interview.
18 Hagerott, Mark. "Time for a Digital-Cyber Land Grant System." *Issues in Science and Technology*, January 15, 2020. **https://issues.org/time-for-a-digital-cyber-land-grant-system/**.
19 O'Connell, Sean. "Cornell's Land Grant Heritage: A Sinister Tradition?" *The Cornell Daily Sun*, April 24, 2020. **https://cornellsun.com/2020/04/24/cornells-land-grant-heritage-a-sinister-tradition/**.
20 Volini, Erica, Jeff Schwartz, Brad Denny, David Mallon, Yves van Durme, Ramona Yan, Maren Hauptmann, and Shannon Poynton. "Ethics and the Future of Work."

Deloitte Insights, May 15, 2020. **https://www2.deloitte.com/us/en/insights/ focus/human-capital-trends/2020/ethical-implications-of-ai.html**.

21 Edsall, Thomas. "Why Do We Pay So Many People So Little Money?" *The New York Times*, June 24, 2020. **https://www.nytimes.com/2020/06/24/opinion/wages- coronavirus.html**.

22 Fitzpayne and Pollack, "Lifelong Learning and Training Accounts."

23 Markell, Jack. "Note to Congress: Invest in Worker Training, Too." *U.S. News & World Report*, April 17, 2020. **https://www.usnews.com/news/elections/ articles/2020-04-17/trump-nancy-pelosi-should-focus-stimulus-on- worker-training**.

24 McQuarrie, Kylie. "The Average Salary of Essential Workers in 2020." **Business. org**, May 18, 2020. **https://www.business.org/finance/accounting/average- salary-of-essential-workers/**.

25 Edsall, "Why Do We Pay So Many People So Little Money?"

26 Deming, interview.

27 Friedman, Thomas L. *Thank You for Being Late an Optimist's Guide to Thriving in the Age of Accelerations*. Penguin Books, 2017.

28 Hyman, Louis, interview with Suzanne Riss and Jeff Schwartz, January 13, 2020.

29 "Rural Electrification Act." Wikipedia. Wikimedia Foundation, April 15, 2020. **https://en.wikipedia.org/wiki/Rural_Electrification_Act**.

30 Slaughter, interview.

31 Deming, interview.

32 Winterberg, Susan, interview with Suzanne Riss and Jeff Schwartz, February 2020.

33 Brynjolfsson, Erik, interview with Suzanne Riss and Jeff Schwartz, July 2019.

34 Edelman, Richard, Rick Levin, Helle Thorning-Schmidt, Mark Thompson, and Kishore Mahbubani. "20 Years of Trust." Edelman, 2020. **https://www.edelman. com/20yearsoftrust/**.

35 Agarwal, Dimple, Josh Bersin, Gaurav Lahiri, Jeff Schwartz, and Erica Volini. "The Rise of the Social Enterprise 2018 Deloitte Global Human Capital Trends." *Deloitte Insights*, 2018. **https://www2.deloitte.com/content/dam/insights/us/ articles/HCTrends2018/2018-HCtrends_Rise-of-the-social-enterprise.pdf**.

36 "Larry Fink's 2018 Letter to CEOs." BlackRock, n.d. **https://www.blackrock. com/corporate/investor-relations/2018-larry-fink-ceo-letter**.

37 Sorkin, Andrew Ross. "World's Biggest Investor Tells C.E.O.s Purpose Is the 'Animating Force' for Profits." *The New York Times*, January 17, 2019. **https:// www.nytimes.com/2019/01/17/business/dealbook/blackrock-larry-fink- letter.html**.

38 Ibid.

39 "About Unilever." Unilever global company website. Accessed June 27, 2020. **https://www.unilever.com/about/who-we-are/about-Unilever/**.

40 "IMPACT Thriving in an Upside-Down World." Event Marketing Platform. Accessed June 27, 2020. **https://ops.deloitteconference.com/impactthrivingi nanupsidedownwo**.

41 *The Unilever Story: Citizenship and Social Impact*. YouTube. *Deloitte Global Human Capital Trends*, May 28, 2018. **https://www.youtube.com/ watch?v=Z1wJQK-ESck**.

42 "The CEO Pay Ratio: Data and Perspectives from the 2018 Proxy Season." Harvard Law School Forum on Corporate Governance, October 14, 2018. **https://corpgov. law.harvard.edu/2018/10/14/the-ceo-pay-ratio-data-and-perspectives-from-the-2018-proxy-season/**.

43 Updated Statement Moves Away from Shareholder Primacy, Includes Commitment to All Stakeholders. "Business Roundtable Redefines the Purpose of a Corporation to Promote 'An Economy That Serves All Americans.'" *Business Roundtable*, August 19, 2019. **https://www.businessroundtable.org/business-roundtable-redefines-the-purpose-of-a-corporation-to-promote-an-economy-that-serves-all-americans**.

44 Taylor, Timothy. "States as the Laboratories of Democracy: An Historical Note." *Conversable Economist*, August 27, 2015. **https://conversableeconomist.blogspot.com/2015/08/states-as-laboratories-of-democracy.html**.

About the Authors

Jeff Schwartz is the founding partner of Deloitte Consulting's U.S. Future of Work practice, and the global editor since 2011 of its Global Human Capital Trends report. Jeff has led research on the evolution of work, workforces, and workplace practices and advised clients around the world on workforce transformation. A global consultant, Jeff has lived and worked in the United States, India, Russia, Belgium, Kenya, and Israel. In the past decade he has lived in India, leading the firm's global delivery capabilities for human capital and advised some of India's largest corporate domestic and multinational companies. Jeff has built practices for Deloitte in the United States, India, and Israel, including launching the firm's innovation tech terminal, Deloitte Catalyst, in Tel Aviv.

Jeff is the author of more than 30 articles on the future of work and talent strategies in publications including the *Deloitte Review*, *the MIT Sloan Management Review*, *The Rotman Review*, and *The Wall Street Journal*. He has traveled the world, starting his career as a U.S. Peace Corps volunteer in Nepal, and later served as one of the first Associate Directors of the Peace in the Russian Federation. A graduate of the Yale School of Management, MBA, and Princeton's School of Public and International Affairs, MPA, Jeff currently resides in New York City.

Suzanne Riss has been telling stories for more than 20 years, as a daily reporter, magazine editor, author, and, most recently, as a marketing strategist and integrated content creator. During her seven years as the editor-in-chief of *Working Mother*, the magazine received four Folio awards for excellence. Suzanne's expertise in work/life trends has been tapped for interviews with *The New York Times, The Wall Street Journal, USA Today*, NPR, *Good Morning America, The Today Show*, and CNN. She is the co-author of *The Working Mom Survival Guide* (Weldon Owen, 2011) and

The Optimist's Guide to Divorce (Workman Publishing, 2017). Suzanne has held senior marketing and communications roles at JPMorgan Chase and, currently, at Knopman Marks. She lives in Maplewood, New Jersey, with her son Jack and dog Messi.

About the Illustrator

Tom Fishburne started drawing cartoons on the backs of business cases as a Harvard Business School student. Tom's *Marketoonist* series has grown by word of mouth to reach a few hundred thousand marketers every week and his cartoons have been featured by *The Wall Street Journal, Fast Company,* and *The New York Times.* His cartoons have appeared on two billboard ads in Times Square and helped win a Guinness World Record. Tom is the founder of Marketoonist, a small communications agency focused on the unique medium of cartoons. Since 2010, the agency has developed marketing and internal communication campaigns for 150 businesses such as Google, IBM, LinkedIn, and Kronos. Tom draws (literally and figuratively) from 20 years in the marketing trenches, including roles at HotelTonight, Method, General Mills, and Nestlé. He started his marketing career selling advertising space for the first English-language magazine in Prague. He is the author of *Your Ad Ignored Here: Cartoons from 15 Years of Marketing, Business, and Doodling in Meetings* and gave a TED talk on The Power of Laughing at Ourselves. Tom lives and draws near San Francisco with his wife and two daughters.

Index